Croatia: through writers' eyes

Croatia: through writers' eyes

Edited by Peter Frankopan,
Francis Gooding &
Stephen Lavington

ELAND
LONDON

First published Eland Publishing Ltd
61 Exmouth Market, London EC1R 4QL in 2006

Historical Introduction and Afterword © Peter Frankopan 2006
All extracts © of the authors, as attributed in the text and acknowledgements
Chapter Introductions © Francis Gooding 2006

ISBN 0 907871 89 5

Cover design and typesetting by Katy Kedward
Cover image: Croatia/Rab Island © Corbis
Map © Reginald Piggott
Printed in Spain by GraphyCems, Navarra

Contents

Acknowledgements

T HE PUBLISHERS WOULD like to thank the following, and gratefully acknowledge permission to reprint copyright material as follows:

From Canongate for permission to reprint an extract from *Black Lamb & Grey Falcon* by Rebecca West; from Jan Morris for permission to reprint an extract from *Trieste and the Meaning of Nowhere* by Jan Morris; from Frank Joseph Campos for permission to reprint an extract from *Where the Turk Trod* by Anthony Rhodes; from Georgina Glover at David Higham Associates for permission to reprint an extract from *Noble Essences* by Sir Osbert Sitwell; from The Random House Group for permission to reprint an extract from *A Paper House* by Mark Thompson; from Orion for permission to reprint an extract from *Tito Speaks* by Vladimir Dedijer; from Hodder & Stoughton for permission to reprint an extract from *The Near East* by Robert Smythe Hichens; from Peters Fraser and Dunlop on behalf of the Estate of Ann Bridge for permission to reprint an extract from *Illyrian Spring* by Ann Bridge; from the University of Michigan Press for permission to reprint an extract from *The War Diaries of Vladimir Dedijer (1941-43)* by Vladimir Dedijer; from The Penguin Group for permission to reprint an extract from *Eastern Approaches* by Fitzroy Maclean; from Hodder & Stoughton for permission to reprint an extract from *The Island of Terrible Friends* by Bill Strutton; from Peters Fraser and Dunlop on behalf of the Evelyn Waugh Estate for permission to reprint an extract from *Sword of Honour* by Evelyn Waugh; from David R. Godine for permission to reprint an extract from *The Impossible Country* by Brian Hall; and from The Penguin Group for permission to reprint an extract from *The Fall of Yugoslavia* by Misha Glenny.

Every effort has been made to trace or contact copyright holders. The publishers would be pleased to rectify any omissions brought to their notice at the earliest opportunity.

All the extracts have been reprinted as they originally appeared in English, which accounts for any apparent discrepancies in spelling.

Notes

Pronunciation: Writing Serbo-Croat often requires authors to use accents which are unfamiliar to readers of English. The most commonly employed are given below.

ć – ch (hard), as in itch
č – ch (soft), as in chime
đ – dj, as in hedge
š – sh, as in shine
ž – zh, as in vision

Spelling: Croatia's complex history has meant that many places have had different names at different times. The map provided shows the current names of places which feature prominently in the text, and most of the alternative names which appear in the book are given below, with the old or differing name given first (eg Ragusa – Dubrovnik). We have tried to be as accurate and up to date as possible, but since there are various spellings our choices here are as provisional and subject to change as those of our authors. We have tried as far as possible to keep other spellings consistent, for example people's names, but there may still be some slight variations.

Brioni Islands – Brijuni Islands
Ragusa – Dubrovnik
Spalato – Split
Salona – Solin
Pola – Pula
Zara – Zadar
Fiume – Rijeka
Trau –Trogir
Abbazia – Opatija
Gulf of Quarnero – Gulf of Kvarner
Veliki Brion – Veli Brijun
Zagorje – Krapina-Zagorje

Historical Introduction:
A Brief History of Croatia
by Peter Frankopan

IF HISTORY REFLECTS the interests (and obsessions) of the historians who write it, then in the case of Croatia, there are two preoccupations which dominate the thoughts of modern commentators. Local historians devote their attentions almost exclusively to the question of where Croats come from – not only geographically, but also ethnically and linguistically. Outsiders, on the other hand, focus principally on the more recent past, on the emergence of a Croatian state from the dying embers of Yugoslavia at the start of the 1990s, and of course, the horrors which followed.

The result is a picture of the country and of its people which is confusing and skewed, one which is no more intelligible to the expert than to the novice. It is as though only two pieces of a much bigger puzzle have been taken at random from the play room, with no obvious connection, and offering no meaningful insight when taken together into the history and culture of the region.

One of the challenges of outlining the history of Croatia is defining exactly what 'Croatia' means. Does it refer to the physical boundaries of the modern state, or to a territory, which was larger and smaller at key points in the past; does it refer to Croatians, or to all inhabitants of this area – Illyrians, Greeks, Romans, Goths, Byzantines, Slavs of all kinds – who settled and were assimilated into society in one way or another? Does it refer equally to the three very distinct and very different parts of

11

Croatia – namely the littoral, the mountainous hinterland and the arable plains of Slavonia and Pannonia which lead into modern Hungary?

Perhaps the most practical and indeed productive way to address the question of what Croatia means is to see what this term has meant to visitors in the past. That is, to see what Croatia has been seen as, who the Croatians have been defined as being over the centuries. Croatia, and above all the coast, has a historical pedigree of the very highest order. It is a land which has been continuously settled since the Hellenistic period (Jason and the Argonauts passed by Pitheia, modern Hvar, in search of the Golden Fleece). It has extant Roman monuments, such as the magnificent amphitheatre in Pula, to rival similar sites in Italy and elsewhere. Diocletian's Palace in Split not only survives, but forms part of the beating heart of the city. The late antique and medieval heritage is no less impressive, with any number of towns along the coast, from Istria in the north, to Dalmatia and finally to Dubrovnik in the south, providing outstanding examples of architecture from the sixth century onwards for more than a thousand years.

The more recent past has not been kind to Croatia. With the extraordinary expansion of the Ottomans, first in Asia Minor and then in south-eastern Europe, Croatia found itself at the front-line of resistance against a Muslim Empire. With consolidation of empires elsewhere in Europe, Croatia's previous success in jostling for position between, and in playing off Venice and Hungary, eventually saw them overwhelmed by an Austria which was broadly uninterested in what happened in Croatia proper even before the Ottoman threat subsided, and likewise on the Dalmatian coast from the nineteenth century onwards. The formation of Yugoslavia in 1919 at first seemed to presage the space for Croatia and for Croatians to once again take control of their own identity and government, though this too went sour before the Second World War and again with the socialist dreamland which followed it. The decline, paralysis and death of

Yugoslavia ultimately laid the basis for Croatia to burst forth into an independent state in the early 1990s, though at a terrible cost in terms of human life and indeed international reputation.

The wider effect, then, has been that Croatia occupies a place in common awareness not at the forefront of the development of Europe from the Middle Ages onwards – as should be the case – but rather as a provincial and tribal backwater on the fringes of Europe, an impression entirely due to the pressures and strains of the immediate political circumstances of this region in the last three centuries or so. This collection of travel writing is a welcome corrective, for in the place of the expected Balkanised state is one of surprising sophistication, cultural significance and indeed political importance.

By the Hellenistic period, many points along the mainland coast of Croatia, and many of the thousand islands dotting the Adriatic Sea, formed communities which developed into trading towns, trading over both short and longer distances. For example, towns on the islands of Hvar and Vis were founded in 385/4BC by Ionian Greeks on the order of Dionysius the Elder, ruler of Sicily, to serve as a base for trade in and out of Syracuse. Other locations too were established around this time, and it was not long before a network of trade can be found criss-crossing the Adriatic.

By the second century BC, Rome was already casting its eye to the Adriatic's eastern seaboard, drawn by its wealth and by its natural resources in the form of timber, agriculture, cereals and ores. Local tribes such as the Illyrians and the Delmati were subjugated, and a full provincial administration set up, establishing the provinces of Illyria, Istria, Dalmatia and, further inland and in due course, Pannonia too. This region became a wealthy and important one, something which is evident from the monumental architecture which survives along the entire length of the coast, of which Pula and Salona are the two outstanding examples. The large number of shipwrecks and amphorae which have been recovered from this period likewise provide a compelling testimony to the flourishing towns along the coast and on the primary islands, such as Hvar and Vis in the south, and Krk and Cres in the north.

Indeed, so prosperous was the whole region, that when Diocletian took the unusual step of stepping down as Emperor at the start of the fourth century AD, it was to Dalmatia that he retired and built the home where he intended to perfect his skills at growing cabbages. The result, an enormous palace, which was fortified on three sides and apparently open to the sea on the other, was built in Split, just down the coast from the province's capital in Salona, the ruins of which are a primary archaeological site for the culture of Ancient Rome. The palace has been the subject of intensive study including an important publication by Robert Adam, who visited the palace with his draughtsmen in the 1750s and was evidently profoundly inspired by the classical extravagance and forms of the edifice, borrowing extensively from them in his own work.

The high-water mark in antiquity in Croatia was reached during the first centuries of the first millennium, particularly after the adoption of Christianity as the official religion of the Empire. A very large number of churches dating from the fourth and fifth centuries (and later) bear testimony to the widespread practice of Christianity and the rapid proliferation of the religion particularly along the coast, in and around the established towns. Again, the architectural heritage which survives is impressive and serves as an important source of evidence not only for the spread of Christianity in Croatia, but in the Mediterranean as a whole.

However, with the division of the Roman Empire into two halves and the foundation of Constantinople in the fourth century, Rome itself and the western provinces first failed and were then decisively shattered by the Goths and others. While Constantinople had not only survived but even flourished, particularly under the Emperor Justinian (himself of Illyrian origin), successive large-scale movements of aggressive, militarily ambitious peoples around the start of the seventh century – Avars, Slavs, Kutrigurs and not least Arabs – meant that the imperial government was forced onto a defensive which was to last until the reign of Constantine VII Porphyrogenitus (919-59). As a result, the eastern coast and the islands of the Adriatic, like the whole of the Mediterranean, experienced a rapid economic contraction, and seemingly a decline in population too, a clear reflection of local instability, the collapse of a regional bureaucratic infrastructure, and also of the reduction of trade networks.

In the period which followed, Constantinople periodically tried to maintain a degree of influence and even control over the larger towns along the coast. Essentially, however, the focus of the Byzantine Emperors was fixed closer to home, above all, set on consolidating their position in Asia Minor and in the eastern Mediterranean, and not in the Adriatic. The result was that by the time that conditions favourable to trade and prosperity returned – particularly following Basil I's strike against Arab pirates in southern Italy and his reimposition of imperial authority there in the later ninth century – Croatia had begun to form a sense of statehood and coherence. By the 880s, we start to find inscriptions referring to Branimir, Duke of the Croatians. A few decades later, more substantial evidence shows the trappings of what we would expect from an emerging, distinct state, with monumental complexes of churches and tombs being constructed in what might best be described as a royal capital, on the site of the old provincial Dalmatian capital, Salona.

The first kings of Croatia, in the sense of a royal title actually being used, appear in this period too, with this being confirmed formally to King Zvonimir by Pope Gregory VII in the 1070s, evidently as part of the Pope's efforts to extend his influence throughout the Christian world. By this time, the use of a script, known as Glagolitic, had become widespread both in the church and as an official script. It is widely held that the script was originally exported by the missions of Cyril and Methodius throughout the Balkans in the ninth century, as they sought to Christianise the Slavs well inland from the coast. Whether this is accurate or not, Glagolitic was to become specific to Croatia and served to establish and accentuate a distinct identity for the early Croatian kingdom. In due course, the Frankopan family sought to promote use of Glagolitic in the liturgy and in secular documents, above all on the island of Krk, precisely as a symbol which connected Croatia with its medieval past. It was only towards the end of the nineteenth century that the script and liturgy finally fell out of common usage with the ecclesiastical elite among whom it had survived for so long in the north of the country.

The centuries following the establishment of a Croatian kingdom marked the apogee of the wealth, influence and prominence of the littoral. Towns like Split, Trogir and Zadar experienced a prolonged period of sustained economic growth. Real wealth began to flow into these towns as a result of their position on the trade routes both from the Balkan interior out to the sea, but above all on the journey to and from Constantinople and eventually the Holy Land.

It is easy to look at Venice as the southernmost outpost of Europe, an exit route for people and goods heading south. In fact, it was quite the opposite: a staging post on the journey north. Indeed maps from the early medieval period, such as the famous Mappa Mundi held at Hereford Cathedral, present precisely the world as flowing south to north, rather than the more modern depiction which inverts this view. So while the growth of towns and islands on the Croatian coast was certainly intertwined with that of Venice, they were if anything at least initially greater beneficiaries of the trading boom than Venice itself, which after all had to put out a significant outlay to provide the ships, crews and resources required to make long distance journeys. The towns and islands in the Adriatic could therefore benefit not only from trade from afar, but also stood to benefit from supplying Venice and Venetian ships directly on their routes up and down the coast.

It is not a surprise, then, that Venice took every opportunity to extend its influence in this region: in a series of negotiations with Constantinople, which were spread over many decades, Venice succeeded in extracting nominal and titular authority over Croatia and Dalmatia. Indeed, at each turn, the Doge incorporated these areas into his official titles, leaving little doubt as to his intentions – even if in practice the towns on the coast stood outside his direct control, at least to start with. Such was Venice's keenness to assert itself over individual towns and indeed over the region as a whole, that the knights of the Fourth Crusade were persuaded to sack the town of Zadar in 1202 on their ill-fated and doomed attempt to reach the Holy Land. That an entire Crusade expedition was needed to breach the town walls, described by the Crusader and eye-witness Villehardouin as being of enormous size and quality, says a great deal about the prominence, affluence and success of the town at this time.

It was not just Venice which manoeuvred itself to try to close in on the ripe prizes on offer. Hungary to the north under King Coloman had turned its attention to expanding its influence on the coast from the start of the twelfth century, and like Venice, sought to achieve some degree of dominance over key areas. The principal theme of the history of Croatia and the coast in the middle ages then was that of the towns playing off Venice against Hungary, and trying to maximise breathing space to prevent interest and influence turning into direct political control.

One of the most striking features of the towns on the coast and on the primary islands was that they had largely retained their own identities from the Hellenistic period onwards. As in the Italian peninsula, each city-state was fiercely independent of the others, and notwithstanding occasional efforts by one to dominate a rival, each effectively functioned as a city-state, ruled by a council of nobles.

In this way, then, providing Venice and Hungary did not over-exert themselves, the towns themselves were generally happy to take a course of little resistance, accepting nominal over-lordship in return for being left to their own devices. Occasionally, the communities had to show their teeth in order to protect their own interests, and it is a mark of their genuine strength and power that they were able to do so efficiently and quickly. In 1222, for example, Andrew II of Hungary was forced to issue a Golden Bull agreeing to limits to his authority on the coast; likewise, twenty years later, his successor, Bela IV, was not only forced to concede significant guarantees to the municipal freedoms of these towns, but also to codify these legally to protect the concessions which had been extracted.

The heyday of the Croatian coast inevitably saw a programme of great cultural development. From the twelfth century onwards, the urban built environment began to reflect the affluence of the inhabitants, with grandiose secular architecture springing up. Municipal buildings, such as customs houses, administrative centres, and in Dubrovnik, the first quarantine in Europe, were also built. Fabulous Cathedrals were erected and consecrated, with those of the central Dalmatian coast, St Anastasia in Zadar and St Lawrence in Trogir, being particularly fine examples. The construction, masonry and artistry on these cathedrals – and on those in Sibenik and Split – represent craftsmanship of the very highest order and provide an unequivocal manifestation of the wealth, ambition and importance of these towns and of the coast as a whole.

Intellectually too, Croatia enjoyed a tremendous period of creativity in the period leading up to the renaissance. One scholar, Herman of Dalmatia, translated the works of Euclid and Ptolemy, and of the Arabic astronomers, as early as the twelfth century, putting these into circulation for the first time in much of Europe. Croatian scholars also played a prominent role in the Humanist movement of the Renaissance. Marco Marulic in particular became widely known for his texts on Christian morality which were published both in Latin and in translation, with the same author producing the first secular poetry in the Croatian language (rather than in Latin) in the early fifteenth century.

The best mark of the importance and profile of Croatia in a context wider than the Adriatic and even the Mediterranean, comes from the fact that as late as the seventeenth century, Illyric, or Croatian, was designated as a set language to be studied at all church universities in Europe. At the universities of Bologna, Padua, Cologne, Paris and Salamanca, Croatian was studied alongside Latin, Greek, Hebrew, Arabic and Chaldaean (Aramaic) for a minimum of two years, following formal prescription by Pope Urban VIII in 1623.

Part of the reason for this was that by the end of the fifteenth century, Croatian merchants were dealing far from home. Shakespeare for example makes numerous references to Ragusan sailors, that is from Dubrovnik, in his plays, indeed using the adjective Argosy (or Ragusan) as a generic name for a competent merchant or military fleet. While the playwright was obviously not familiar with this region personally, he may have been familiar with inhabitants from this part of Europe, at least to judge from his depictions in Twelfth Night (which is set in Illyria). In this play, Shakespeare refers to the coast, to its strong maritime tradition and to the height of the Illyrian people – and also to the robustness of its wines, all elements which have a resonance to this day.

We know that there was a guild of Croatian seamen in Venice by 1451, when the School of the Dalmatians, which is also known as the School of the Slavs, was established. A similar guild was founded in England forty years later, as testified by an inscription found in Southampton dating from 1491. Croatian sailors can be found further afield still, with individuals from the islands of Rab and Hvar, and also from Dubrovnik, accompanying the Cabots' expeditions to the New World. Indeed, the earliest maps from the sixteenth century record a Capo de Arause (Ragusa) between New York and Cape Cod. Just as Croatian sailors manned the earliest crossings to America, so they also played a significant role in manning the galleys of the Spanish Armada which came to grief in 1588 off the coast of England.

The breakpoint for Croatia came with the rapid expansion of Ottoman power into Europe. Although the Turks had expanded deep into south-eastern Europe before finally taking Constantinople in 1453, it was only after this date that their ambitions and success began to impact on the coast. The effects, at least initially, were not immediate. But by the start of the sixteenth century, Croatia – both the hinterland and the coastal region – began to come under sustained pressure. The northern part of Croatia looked to Austria, in 1527 fatefully inviting Ferdinand to become King. The coast, on the other hand, was by now under the control of Venice and did what it could to minimise the impact of Ottoman pressure.

Dubrovnik, for example, was quick to deal with the Ottomans in a typically practical way, gaining concessions from them and making the most of the fact that it was both the first point of entry from Muslim to Christian Europe – at least in the Adriatic – and also the last point of exit for the reverse. As such, there was little negative to be had from the emergence of the Turks; if anything the town boomed even more. As early as the twelfth century, the Arab geographer al-Idrisi commented on the industriousness of the inhabitants of Dubrovnik. And this town, of all those along the coast, continued to flourish well into the early modern period, until a catastrophic earthquake in 1667 destroyed a substantial part of the town and killed a very large proportion of the population.

Elsewhere, things became bleak following Ferdinand's assumption of the throne. His accession led to a massive decline in the fortunes, literal and otherwise, of the Croatian hinterland, and the effect soon began to be felt on the coast too. Little money was spent on defence or on construction, let alone on maintaining an effective military border – something which was left instead to local aristocratic families. In the circumstances, large scale loss of land to the Ottomans was inevitable, and it was not long before Croatia began to call itself 'the remains of the remains of the formerly glorious kingdom.' There were occasional heroic defences against the Turks, such as that of Nikola Subic Zrinski at Sziget in 1566, where a small garrison held out for long enough to hold up a force of one hundred thousand men under the personal command of Sultan Sulayman the Magnificent, and thwart what had threatened to be a massive strike deep into central Europe. But these were small and rare successes which ultimately did little to stem the tide – even if Subic Zrinski's heroism became fabled throughout Europe and earned him a place in folklore, epic poetry and opera.

Venice too began to suffer, partly as a result of the Ottoman gains and the obvious effects this had on stability and trade, but also because of the emergence of new markets and new resources in the Americas which the Venetians were poorly placed and ill-equipped to exploit. This provided an opportunity for free-booters, known as Uskoks, to take easy pickings from merchant shipping in the Adriatic, particularly in the north around the town of Senj, which served as a pirate nest for the best part of half a century.

To an extent, therefore, Croatia – hinterland and coast – paid the price for the arrival of the Ottomans, the weakening of Venice, the Reformation and the subsequent consolidation of empires in Europe, for this region began to be used as a bargaining chip by the neighbouring powers, each of whom was prepared to trade position, land and responsibilities in search of wider settlements. In the 1660s, Petar Zrinski, the Ban or effective viceroy of Croatia proper, took matters into his own hands, delivering a series of stunning victories against the Turks, and penetrating deep into Ottoman territory – feats for which Louis XIV made him a French peer. His gains were shamefully given away by the Austrians in 1664 at the treaty of Vasvar, where a return to the status quo prior to Zrinski's successes was agreed.

By the late 1660s, disaffection with Austria reached a peak. Petar Zrinksi and his cousin, Fran Krsto Frankopan, members of two of the most powerful families in Croatia whose ancestors had governed as Ban, were implicated in a plot against Leopold of

Austria. Rather than wait for discontent to break out openly, a deliberate and concerted smear campaign was made against both men, who were then brought to Wiener Neustadt having been given assurances and guarantees for their safety by the Emperor. These were not kept, and after being tortured and abused, both men were executed, their lands and possessions looted and confiscated.

The dealings with Zrinski and Frankopan were truly shocking and provoked uproar in Croatia and beyond. Moreover, the vicious propaganda disseminated by Austrian agents both at the time and indeed later, was a mark of the way in which Croatia was perceived and dealt with by Vienna. Not surprisingly, the manner in which this had been carried out, and the fact that instead of the independence for Croatia and the crown he had sought for himself, Zrinski was rewarded with a sword dripping in blood, meant that this signal event became a powerful touchstone and was remembered right up until independence in the 1990s. The two men were held up as the last attempt made by Croatia to govern itself, and the treachery with which they were dealt as an indicator of the frustrations which the country felt right up until its secession from Yugoslavia. The remains of Frankopan and Zrinski are buried in the Cathedral in Zagreb, and their memory is still revered and their cult deliberately maintained.

The centuries which followed represented a substantial if gradual decline from the glories of the previous seven centuries. Certain individuals, of course, made their mark internationally in their respective fields. Roger Boskovic, an outstanding scientist, developed atomic theory and the theory of forces and enjoyed high positions in Paris, London and St Petersburg in the eighteenth century, communing with Samuel Johnson, Edward Burke and Benjamin Franklin. He was an exception rather than the norm, as Croatia receded into the outer extremities of political and cultural significance.

By the start of the nineteenth century, the flurry of Napoleonic conquest through Europe saw a renewed focus on the region again. Following Bonaparte's occupation of Venice and of the eastern seaboard of the Adriatic, all the Croatian lands along the coast including Istria, Dalmatia, and Dubrovnik came under French rule briefly before passing to Austria. This period of flux had been closely monitored by the British navy. Indeed, a detachment of British ships were garrisoned on the island of Vis during the Napoleonic wars in order to keep an eye on naval traffic in the Adriatic and Ionian Seas, eventually taking on and defeating a much larger French fleet off the island in 1811. A fort dedicated to St George was constructed by the British forces, and it seems, the game of cricket introduced to bemused locals. In any event, cricket has taken off with the formation of a thriving club which has provided several players for the a national team which plays regularly and with some success against other cricket playing nations in Europe. The club team on Vis took the name of Sir William Hoste, the commander of the British warships from the early nineteenth century, as a nod to the first importers of the game to Croatia.

The second half of the nineteenth century saw Croatia continue to struggle to assert its own identity, albeit in a different way and considerably less successfully than in the Middle Ages. Croatian intellectuals became convinced that the way to detach from Austria, and from the increasingly clumsy and heavy-handed interference of Hungary, was to express solidarity with other specifically Slavic peoples, countries and agendas. This had much more to do with political circumstance, and with the reality of the situation in which Croatia and Croatians had an all but inaudible voice, than it did with any deep-rooted conviction about the unity of the South Slavs, about Illyria as a geographic or ethnic concept, or about Yugoslavism. It was thought, rightly or wrongly, that full independence for Croatia was too difficult or improbable a goal to aim for. Individuals such as Kvaternik who did articulate a vision of Croatian independence were unable to translate this into significant support, and as a result, a pan-Slavic political philosophy emerged with an increasingly

23

strident momentum, provoked of course by the envious glances which were cast towards Belgrade and the Serbs, who had gained self-determination and burgeoning ambition following the end of Ottoman rule.

The desire to escape from Austria-Hungary continued until the end of the First World War. While this period saw a degree of economic improvement as well as investment in some parts of the country and a series of important building projects, it also saw harsh oppression of anyone or anything deemed to be specifically Croatian, from political activists to the use of the language in official documentation. Publications such as those of Matica Hrvatksa, a Zagreb publishing house, were banned; protestors against rule from Budapest were mercilessly put down, incarcerated and if they were lucky, beaten; civic order was maintained through force as much as through law. Visitors to the region, such as Arthur Evans, the celebrated archaeologist of Crete, found himself hugely sympathetic to the conditions under which the local population were living, and as he travelled, his support for the nationalist south Slav cause grew, identifying this – as increasing numbers of locals did – as the means of escaping from imperialist tyranny.

By the time of the First World War, tensions were simmering, not least since the annexation of Bosnia by the Austro-Hungarians led to renewed interest in the surrounding area and a reason to meddle further still in Croatia's affairs. After war broke out, it did not take long for discussions to turn to the future shape of the region. To start with, Italy was promised a large part of the eastern Adriatic in return for their support against the Axis powers under the terms of the Treaty of London in 1915. After the war, though, the concept of a country of Southern Slavs, taking the name of the Kingdom of Slovenes, Croats and Serbs, began to find favour internationally and also locally. In spite of a brief attempt by the Italian Gabriele d'Annunzio to annex Rijeka and Istria, Croatia finally slipped the shackles of Austrian rule to cast its lot with its neighbours to the south.

It did not take long for the experiment to sour. Over-valuation of the currency, economic instability and agrarian reform did not help. Nor did immediate animosity between the peoples of the new state. Repression and brute force became widespread and common, with physical violence and police brutality standard. Again, expressions of Croatian-ness were clamped down on in the attempt to forcibly fuse a national identity which sought to obviate regional differences but which in practice simply replaced the interests of one of the constituent peoples of Yugoslavia (the Croats) with those of another (the Serbs).

Matters reached a head with the assassination of the prominent Croatian politician, Stjepan Radić, in parliament while in session in 1928, and the failure of the authorities to arrest the assassin, whose identity was well-known. Radić had been vocal in his demands for recognition of the Croatian identity and had complained stringently about an overwhelming imbalance within the new state which left Croatia and Croatians at a severe disadvantage. In the wake of his murder, King Alexander abolished the constitution, a move which only served to inflame passions, while singularly failing to take any measure which might address the roots of the problems.

By 1930, even British scholars like Robert Seton-Watson, an expert on the region who had played an important role in the congresses which followed the war, concluded that the balance within the new state was not working and what he called the Croatian problem – that is to say its persistent demotion within the new state – did not look likely to be solved. Through the 1930s, the situation deteriorated further still. International outcry followed the murder of the scientist Milan Sufflay in broad daylight in Zagreb, and the resultant failure of the authorities to condemn the actions of the killer, let alone to bring him to justice. So great was the sense of oppression by the authorities in Belgrade that Albert Einstein and Heinrich Mann wrote to the *New York Times* pleading for the international community to act to protect human rights in Croatia specifically, and condemning the behaviour of the national government.

The effects of the disillusionment were not hard to predict, and extremist causes grew rapidly to counter what was perceived as outright oppression in Croatia. Croatian nationalists assassinated King Alexander I in Marseilles in 1934; a political movement known as the Ustasha, whose hour would come in 1941, began to win increasing levels of popular support; so too did the communist parties, whose time was destined for shortly after that of its right-wing extremist peers. Support for both of these groups was conditioned in the first instance by profound disappointment at what Yugoslavia (as it had by now been renamed) stood for, by the frustration of ambitions and by the failure of the dream of self-determination.

Yugoslavia declared its neutrality at the outset of the Second World War. When the Germans and Italians invaded in 1941, the former in particular were quick to exploit the discontent within Croatia by establishing an independent state under Ante Pavelić. Like many countries in continental Europe, this period was a shameful one, for it saw the persecution, internment and mass murder of Serbs as well as of other minority groups, and it has tarnished Croatia's reputation ever since.

The aftermath of the war saw the creation of a different Yugoslvia to the one which had preceded it. Like in many countries which fell behind the iron curtain, the victors – in this case the partisans, who had been supported strongly by the British in the closing stages of the war – devoted much energy in peace time to blackening the reputation of their enemies within the state, in this case carefully crafting an image which allied Croatia with fascism, a tag which has proved hard to remove. The purpose of this was of course to weaken the sense of national identities in Tito's Yugoslavia in the aim and hope of strengthening that of the federal state which naturally needed its own mythology in order to survive and breathe.

The Western powers too, after their support for Tito during the war (notably through the missions of Fitzroy MacLean), had a vested interest in promoting the concept of Yugoslavia as a sympathetic, idyllic state where national identities were subsumed by a greater good of Yugoslavism and a special form of socialism. In fact, Tito worked hard to promote the soft face of socialism, a welcome change from the hard-headed, charmless apparatchiks of much of Communist Europe, inviting heads of state on bear hunts and entertaining them in style in the Brijuni islands. As the acceptable face of socialist government in Europe – enshrined in Tito's creation of the Non-Aligned Movement of states – the projection of Yugoslavia was as a state where identities, language, symbols and the past were meaningless, where only the present and the future were of any significance. This was a vision which was both sympathetic and widely believed inside and outside the country, even if the reality was rather different, for this idyll came at an increasingly expensive price.

Things came to a head twice. First in the early 1970s, when the Croatian Writers' Union made a seemingly innocuous complaint about the standardisation of Serbo-Croat and the suffocation of the Croatian language, which provoked large-scale protests and mass strikes, before being effectively suppressed through the imprisonment and harassment of leading figures in the movement. And then, more seriously, at the end of the 1980s, when following increasingly vocal opposition to Belgrade from all corners of Yugoslavia, from Kosovo, Slovenia and eventually from Croatia too, one of those figures who had been involved with the Writers Union, Franjo Tudman, was elected President of the Socialist Republic of Croatia within Yugoslavia.

Long books (and good ones) have been written about the break-up of Yugoslavia. At the time, though, many *canards* were stressed through the media regarding ethnicity, religion or ancient tribal hatreds. In fact, the Croats and the Serbs had almost never had a military dispute of any kind before the disintegration of Yugoslavia; likewise, to find armed conflict between Orthodox and Catholics, we need to go back a long way, most plausibly to 1204. The more productive way to understand the break-up was that it involved power and specifically the reluctance of the federal government in Belgrade to relinquish this in an appropriate way. I dare say that had the ties within Yugoslavia been loosened sufficiently, there might have been no parting of the ways at all, or at least that the different nations would in due course have parted more slowly and less bloodily than they did – as happened in the Soviet Union and in Czechoslovakia.

As it is, the fact that Croatia did eventually reach independence, albeit through such a tragic and traumatic path, does represent a conclusion of sorts to the problems, aspirations and ambitions which Croatia as a region, and which the Croatians as a people, have held for many centuries. The ability to self-determine certainly marks a new dawn, in that it places the country today as master of its own destiny, at least in so far as international law allows it to be.

Ironically, there have been some positive results of Croatia's bloody secession from Yugoslavia, for the country has had to examine itself carefully to try to understand why it really is distinct from its neighbours; to assess what the connection is historically and politically between its own constituent regions; to consider how it positions itself in the international arena, whether through the UN, through its close ties with and likely membership of NATO and through the seemingly imminent accession to the European Union. In all these cases, work is very much still in progress, and barely a decade on from the Dayton accords which brought an end to military conflict in Croatia and Bosnia, the concepts of what Croatia is and who the Croatians are remain disconnected – which at least partly explains the almost schizophrenic insecurity where Croatia in turn depicts itself as a small country for a big holiday (for a long time the official motto of the Croatian tourist board), or as a uniquely important state with an outstandingly important and significant historical pedigree, second to none in the medieval Mediterranean.

As readers of this book will be able to see from the accounts of visitors to Croatia in the past, and perhaps will see for themselves during their own travels to this region, the two images of Croatia coexist side by side. Providing the country's cultural heritage is preserved diligently, it is only a matter of time before the true nature of the mainland and of the peppering of islands which scatter the coast, which caused the Romans to name spotted hunting dogs Dalmatians, emerges. This will finally allow modern visitors a clearer and fresher insight into the history of this region than they have been able to enjoy since it disappeared into the abyss of its more dominant neighbours.

I: Travel

FOR A VERY LONG TIME, Croatia was an unknown quantity to travellers from Western Europe. Pressed between the Austro-Hungarian empire to the north, and the Turks to the south, its interior was hardly known to explorers at all; following the Second World War, its half-century in the orbit of the USSR did not make it an obvious choice for travellers from the other side of the Iron Curtain. The marvellous, urbane cities of the coast were known, but even these were poorly visited by English-speaking travellers until the early twentieth century, and journeys to any part of Croatia were a rarity.

Rebecca West (1892–1983) is one of the most distinguished women writers of the twentieth century. Her work, though regarded highly, is now unjustly neglected. Born in London as Cicily Isabel Fairfield, West was educated in Edinburgh, and then trained as an actress. Her time on the stage was brief and unsuccessful, and in 1911 she began a writing career, contributing varied articles to the left-wing and feminist press under the name by which she is now known (her *nom de plume* is taken from a character in Ibsen's *Rosmersholm*). She swiftly became a leading writer at a number of journals and newspapers, going on to write criticism and essays on various subjects for publications including *The New Yorker* and *The Times*. Her affair with H G Wells (by whom she had a son) is well documented, and she mixed in the highest literary company, her circle including George Bernard Shaw, Ford Madox Ford and Wyndham Lewis.

Justice cannot here be done to a varied and prolific career which spanned seven decades, during which she published numerous books including accounts of the Nuremberg Trials (*A Train of Powder*) and the trial of William 'Lord Haw-Haw' Joyce (*The Meaning of Treason*); several critical works (*Henry James; The Strange Necessity*); a biography of St Augustine and many short stories, essays and travel writings, not to mention her many novels (including *Harriet Hume; The Thinking Reed* and *The Judge*). The celebrated *Black Lamb and Grey Falcon: A Journey through Yugoslavia* was written after a trip to the country in 1937, with the shadow of war lowering over Europe. Not merely one of the finest books ever written about the Balkans, the magisterial *Black Lamb* is a literary masterpiece in its own right.

The unknown English author – identified only as 'Snaffle' – of *Camp Life and Sport in Dalmatia and the Herzegovina* (originally published in 1897 as *In the Land of the Bora*) was, in travelling to some of the wilder parts of Dalmatia at the close of the nineteenth century, visiting a part of Europe that few British travellers had seen. This was part of its attraction for him, as he notes in the introduction: 'When your neighbour at every dinner-party is equally familiar with Cairo and Calcutta, Boston and Bendigo, Reykjavik and Rio, it really is an achievement to discover a country with which the British tourist has not yet familiarized himself.' Dalmatia was, as he puts it, *terra incognita*; even a letter to the famous tour operator Thomas Cook (eponymous founder of the travel agency) furnished him only with knowledge of the fare to Split, since Cook himself had never been beyond Trieste. Indeed, it seems that the parts of Croatia that the small hunting group explore in the extract presented here are not only unknown to visitors, but are semi-abandoned altogether (though of course this may be exaggerated for effect – for no doubt every hunter, like every explorer, wants to break the newest of ground). The author, though naturally preoccupied with the successes and failures of his hunting, does not neglect to give some historical background and, as so often in this part of the world, it is the actions of foreign powers which explain the parlous state of the once populous towns. In this case, 'Snaffle' identifies the cavalier attitude of the previously ruling Turks as being responsible for the ruination of Vrana, since in letting the swamp drainage system fall into disrepair they had allowed malaria to return, and the inhabitants (by this time under Austrian influence) are only just beginning to rebuild it. The author has a good eye for detail, a readable style, and a dry wit, and the book is a testament to the remarkable remoteness of Dalmatia from western European travel and trade, despite its proximity to very well-known parts of Europe and its long history in the Mediterranean.

The third extract in this chapter is from the renowned archaeologist Sir Arthur John Evans (1851-1941), chiefly associated with the discovery and excavation of Bronze Age Minoan sites on the island of Crete. His excavations at Knossos, considered the centre of Minoan civilization, led to his identification of two distinct written languages in use there, languages which are now known as Linear A and Linear B. Evans was educated at Oxford, and was curator of the Ashmolean Museum from 1884 to 1908. His period in the Balkans began in 1874, when he visited Bosnia with his brother, and was there to witness a peasant rebellion against Ottoman rule. It is this journey which is recorded in *Through Bosnia and the Herzegovina on Foot During the Insurrection of the Summer of 1875*. He later worked from Ragusa (now Dubrovnik) as a correspondent for the *Manchester Evening News*, but he aroused the suspicions of the Austro-Hungarian government, and was expelled in 1882 after being tried for treason. His excavations at Knossos remain his crowning achievement, and the discoveries there are chronicled in his classic work of archaeology, the four volumes of *The Palace of Minos at Knossos*.

Jan Morris, who was born in 1926, was described by Alistair Cooke as the 'Flaubert of the jet age'. 'The Biplane and the Steamer' is extracted from her 2001 book *Trieste and the Meaning of Nowhere*. As its name suggests, the book is not about Croatia, but is rather a meditation on the Italian city, which she first visited as a young soldier (then James Morris) at the end of the Second World War, and which, she writes, 'curiously haunted me ever since'. The city's intimate and vital connection with what is now the Croatian province of Istra has largely been lost, and this loss is eloquently explored by Morris. She also takes the reader deep into the Croatian heart of Istria (as it was then known), crucible and keeping house of Glagolitic, the now extinct medieval Croatian script devised in the ninth century by St Cyril and St Methodius in order to translate the Bible into local languages. This script now lends its name to the architecture and art of the period. The document to which she refers is an old parish record in Glagolitic, kept in the church vestry at San Dorligo, a village some few miles from Trieste – a testament to the tenacity with which the language held on in this part of the Balkans. *Hiraeth* is a Welsh word which may be loosely translated as homesickness or longing. Jan Morris's many books include *Venice, Pax Brittanica* and *Sultan in Oman* as well as several collections of travel writing.

Rebecca West
From *Black Lamb and Grey Falcon: The record of a journey through Yugoslavia in 1937*

'Let us wire to Constantine and ask him to meet us earlier in Sarajevo,' I said, lying on the bed in our hotel room, 'I can't bear Dubrovnik.'

'Perhaps you would have liked it better if we had been able to get into one of those hotels nearer the town,' said my husband.

'Indeed I would not,' I said. 'I stayed in one of those hotels for a night last year. They are filled with people who either are on their honeymoon or never had one. And at dinner I looked about me at the tables and saw everywhere half-empty bottles of wine with room numbers scrawled on the labels, which I think one of the dreariest sights in the world.'

'Yes indeed,' said my husband, 'it seems to me always when I see them that there has been disobedience of Gottfried Keller's injunction "*Lass die Augen fassen, was die wimper halt von dem goldnen Ueberfluss der Welt*" [Let the eyes hold what the eyelids can contain from the golden overflow of the world]. But you might have liked it better if we were nearer the town.'

'No,' I said, 'nothing could be lovelier than this.'

We were staying in a hotel down by the harbour of Gruzh, which is two or three miles out of Dubrovnik or Ragusa, as it used to be called until it became part of Yugoslavia. The name was changed although it is pure Illyrian, because it sounded Italian: not, perhaps, a very good reason. Under the windows were the rigging and funnels of the harbour, and beyond the crowded waters was a hillside covered with villas, which lie there among their gardens with an effect of richness not quite explicable by their architecture. The landscape is in fact a palimpsest. This was a suburb of Dubrovnik where the nobles had their summer palaces, buildings in the Venetian Gothic style furnished with treasures from the west and the east, surrounded by terraced flower-gardens and groves and orchards, as lovely as Fieole or Vallombrosa, for here the Dalmatian coast utterly loses the barrenness which the traveller from the north might have thought its essential quality. These palaces were destroyed in the Napoleonic wars, looted and then burned; and on their foundations, in the nineteenth and twentieth centuries, have been built agreeable but undistinguished villas. But that is not the only confusion left by history on the view. The rounded slope immediately above the harbour is covered by an immense honey-coloured villa, with arcades and terraces and balconies hung with wisteria, and tier upon tier of orange trees and cypresses and chestnuts and olives and palms rising to the crest. It makes the claim of solidity that all Austrian architecture made, but it should have been put up in stucco, like our follies at Bath and

Twickenham; for it was built for the Empress Elizabeth, who of course, in her restlessness and Habsburg terror of the Slavs, went there only once or twice for a few days.

'I like this,' I said, 'as well as anything in Dubrovnik.'

'That can't be true,' said my husband, 'for Dubrovnik is exquisite, perhaps the most exquisite town I have ever seen.'

'Yes,' I said, 'but all the same I don't like it, I find it a unique experiment on the part of the Slav, unique in its nature and unique in its success, and I do not like it. It reminds me of the worst of England.'

'Yes,' said my husband, 'I see that, when one thinks of its history. But let us give it credit for what it looks like, and that too is unique.' He was right indeed, for it is as precious as Venice, and deserves comparison with the Venice of Carpaccio and Bellini, though not of Titian and Tintoretto. It should be visited for the first time when the twilight is about to fall, when it is already dusk under the tall trees that make an avenue to the city walls, though the day is only blanched in the open spaces, on the bridge that runs across the moat to the gate. There, on the threshold, one is arrested by another example of the complexity of history. Over the gate is a bas-relief by Mestrovitch, a figure of a king on a horse, which is a memorial to and a stylised representation of King Peter of Serbia, the father of the assassinated King Alexander, he who succeeded to the throne after the assassination of Draga and her husband. It is an admirable piece of work. It would surprise those who know Mestrovitch's work only from international exhibitions to see how good it can be when it is produced under nationalist inspiration for a local setting. This relief expresses to perfection the ideal ruler of a peasant state. Its stylisation makes, indeed, some reference to the legendary King Marko, who is the hero of all Serbian peasants. This king could groom the horse he rides on, and had bought it for himself at a fair, making no bad bargain; yet he is a true king, for no man would daunt him from doing his duty to his people, either by strength or by riches. It is enormously ironic that this should be set on the walls of a city that was the antithesis of the peasant state, that maintained for centuries the most rigid system of aristocracy and the most narrowly bourgeois ethos imaginable. The incongruity will account for a certain coldness shown towards the Yugoslavian ideal in Dubrovnik; which itself appears ironical when it is considered that after Dubrovnik was destroyed by the great powers, no force on earth could have come to its rescue except the peasant state of Serbia.

For an ideal first visit the traveller should go into the city and find the light just faintly blue with dusk in the open space that lies inside the gate, and has for its centre the famous fountain by the fifteenth-century Neapolitan architect Onofrio de la Cava. This is a masterpiece, the size of a small chapel, a domed piece of masonry with fourteen jets of water each leaping from a sculpted plaque set in the middle of a panel divided by two slender pilasters, into a continuous trough that runs all around the fountain: as useful as any horse-trough and as lovely and elevating as an altar. On the two steps that raise it from the pavement there always lie some carpets with their sellers gossiping beside them. At this hour all cats are grey and all carpets are beautiful; the colours, fused by the evening, acquire richness. On one side of this square is another of the bland little churches which Dalmatians built so often and so well, a town sister of that we had seen in the village where the retired sea-captains lived. At this hour its golden stone gives it an air of enjoying its own private sunset, prolonged after the common one. It has a pretty and secular rose-window which might be the brooch for a bride's bosom. Beside it is a Franciscan convent, with a most definite and sensible *Pietà* over a late Gothic portal. The Madonna looks as if, had it been in her hands, she would have stopped the whole affair; she is in no degree gloating over the spectacular fate of her son. She is not peasant, she is noble; it is hardly possible to consider her as seducible by the most exalted destiny. Facing these across the square is the old arsenal, its façade pierced by an arch; people walk through it to a garden beyond, where lamps shine among trees, and there is a sound of music. For background there are the huge city walls, good as strength, good as honesty.

Ahead runs the main street of the town, a paved fairway, forbidden to wheeled traffic, lined with comely seventeenth-century houses that have shops on their ground floor. At this time it is the scene of the *corso*, an institution which is the heart of social life in every Yugoslavian town, and indeed of nearly all towns and villages in the Balkans. All the population who have clothing up to the general standard – I have never seen a person in rags and patches join a *corso* in a town where good homespun or manufactured textiles are the usual wear, though in poverty-stricken districts I have seen an entire *corso* bearing itself up with dignity in tatters – join in a procession which walks up and down the main street for an hour or so at about sunset. At one moment there is nobody there, just a few people going about the shops or sitting outside cafés; and the next the street is full of all the human beings in the town that feel able to take part in the life of their kind, each one holding up the head and bearing the body so that it may be seen, each one chattering and being a little gayer than in private, each one attempting to establish its individuality. Yet the attempt defeats itself, for this mass of people, moving up and down the length of the street and slowly becoming more and more like each other because of the settling darkness, makes a human being seem no more than drop of water in a stream. In a stream, moreover, that does not run for ever. The *corso* ends as suddenly as it begins. At one instant the vital essence of the town chokes the street with its coursing; the next, the empty pavement is left to the night.

But while it lasts the *corso* is life, for what that is worth in this particular corner of the earth; and here, in Dubrovnik, life still has something of the value it must have had in Venice when she was young. A city that had made good bread had learned to make good cake also. A city that had built itself up by good sense and industry had formed a powerful secondary intention of elegance. It is a hundred and thirty years ago that Dubrovnik ceased to exist as a republic, but its buildings are the unaltered cast of its magnificence, its people have still the vivacity of those who possess and can enjoy. Here the urbanity of the Dalmatian cities becomes metropolitan. Follow the *corso* and you will find yourself in the same dream that is dreamed by London and Paris and New York; the dream that there is no limit to the distance which man can travel from his base, the cabbage-patch, that there is no pleasure too delicate to be bought by all of us, if the world will but go on getting richer. This is not a dream to be despised; it comes from man's more amiable parts, it is untainted by cruelty, it springs simply from man's desire to escape from the horror that is indeed implicit in all man's simpler relationships with the earth. It cannot be realised in a city so great as London or Paris or New York, or even the larger Venice; it was perhaps possible to realise it in a city no larger than Dubrovnik, which indeed neither was nor is very far from the cabbage-patches. For on any fine night there are some peasants from the countryside outside the walls who have come to walk in the *corso*.

To taste the flavour of this *corso* and this city, it is good to turn for a minute from the main narrow street into one of the side streets. They mount steep and narrow to the walls which outline the squarish peninsula on which the city stands; close-pressed lines of houses which are left at this hour to sleeping children, the old, and servant-maids, rich in carved portals and balconies, and perfumed with the spring. For it took the industrial revolution to make man conceive the obscene idea of a town as nothing but houses. These carved portals and balconies are twined with flowers that are black because of the evening, but would be scarlet by day, and behind high walls, countless little people from these houses and gardens sweep down towards their piazza, past a certain statue which you may have seen in other towns, perhaps in front of the Rathaus at Bremen. Such statues are said to represent the hero Orlando or Roland who defeated the Saracens: they are the sign that a city is part of liberal and lawful Christendom. To the left of the crowd is the Custom House and

Mint, in which the history of their forebears for three centuries is written in three storeys. In the fourteenth century the citizens of the Republic built themselves a Custom House, just somewhere to take in the parcels; in that age the hand of man worked right, and the courtyard is perfection. A hundred years later so many parcels had come in that the citizens were refined folk and could build a second storey for literary gatherings and social assemblies, as lovely as Venetian Gothic could make it. Prosperity became complicated and lush, the next hundred years brought the necessity of establishing a handsome Mint on the top floor, in the Renaissance style; and for sheer lavishness they faced the Custom House with a loggia. Because the people who did this were of the same blood, working in a civilisation that their blood and none other had made, these different styles are made one by an inner coherence. The building has a light, fresh, simple charm.

They mill there darkly, the people of Dubrovnik, the buildings running up above them into that whiteness which hangs above the earth the instant before the fall of night, which is disturbed and dispersed by the coarser whiteness of the electric standards. The Custom House is faced by the Church of St Blaise, a great baroque mess standing on a balustraded platform, like a captive balloon filled with infinity. In front is an old tower with a huge toy clock: at the hour two giant bronze figures of men come out and beat a bell. The crowd will lift their heads to see them, as their fathers have done for some hundreds of years. Next to that is the town café, a noble building, where one eats well, looking on to the harbour; for we have reached the other side of the peninsula now, the wind that blows in through the archways is salt. Then to the right is the Rector's Palace, that incomparable building, the special glory of Dubrovnik, and even of Dalmatia, the work of Michelozzo Michelozzi the Florentine and George the Dalmatian, known as Orsini. Simply it consists of a two-storeyed building, the ground floor shielded by a logia of six arches, the upper floor showing eight Gothic windows. It is imperfect: it once had a tower at each end, and these have gone. Nevertheless, its effect is complete and delightful, and, like all masterpieces of architecture, it expresses an opinion about the activities which are going to be carried on under its roof. Chartres is a speculation concerning the nature of God and of holiness. The Belvedere in Vienna is a speculation concerning political power. By the balanced treatment of masses and proliferating capitals, the Rector's Palace puts forward an ideal of an ordered and creative society. It is the most explicit building in an amazingly explicit town, that has also an explicit history, with a beginning and an end. It is another example of the visibility of life which is the special character of Yugoslavia, at least so far as those territories which have not been affected by the Teutonic confusion are concerned.

The *corso* says, 'This is the city our fathers made'. The city says, 'These are the men and women we have made'. If you should turn aside here and go into the café to eat an evening meal, which here should be preferably the *Englische Platte*, an anthology of cold meats chosen by a real scholar of the subject, the implications of this display will keep you busy for the night. There is, of course, the obvious meaning of Dubrovnik. It was quite truly a republic: not a protectorate, but an independent power, the only patch of territory on the whole Dalmatian coast, save for a few unimportant acres near Split, that never fell under the rule of either Hungary or Venice. It was a republic that was a miracle: on this tiny peninsula, which is perhaps half a mile across, was based a great economic empire. From Dubrovnik the caravans started for the overland journey to Constantinople. This was the gateway to the East; and it exploited its position with such commercial and financial and naval genius that its ships were familiar all over the known world, while it owned factories and warehouses in every considerable port of southern Europe and in some ports of the north, and held huge investments such as mines and quarries in the Balkans. Its history is illuminated by our word 'argosy', which means nothing more than a vessel from Ragusa. It is as extraordinary as if the city of London were to have carried out the major part of the commercial achievements of the British Empire and had created Threadneedle Street, with no more territory than itself and about three or four hundred square miles in the home counties which it had gradually acquired by conquest and purchase. That is the primary miracle of Dubrovnik; that and its resistance to Turkey, which for century after century coveted the port as the key to the Adriatic and the invasion of Italy, yet could never dare to seize it because of the diplomatic genius of its defenders.

Anonymous
From *Camp Life and Sport in Dalmatia and the Herzegovina (1897)*

Pakostane is utterly unprovided with the necessaries of life. Even water is not to be had, and we were beholden to the priest for a supply from his tank of rainwater. Not being able to get any supplies locally, I had to go to Zaravecchia the morning after our arrival, to lay in stores – bread, meat, and other necessaries. Fortunately for me, the priest was driving to San Filippo, which lies beyond, so I got a lift there. As, however, he was to be away all day, I had to walk back, and six miles in that heat – it was past noon when I returned – I found quite enough, especially with a heavy load in my rucksack. Zaravecchia, though a place of great antiquity – it is the Biograd of the Croatian kings, and was destroyed by the Venetians in the year 1127 – is entirely without interest, and is nowadays only a large village with some coasting trade.

In the afternoon the priest sent us his boat, and after a bathe off it I felt fit enough. We then sailed to a neighbouring rocky islet, where there were some rabbits, which, however, did not condescend to give us a shot, though the dogs found and hunted several.

Next day was to be devoted to an excursion to Vrana. The priest had kindly introduced us to a local landed proprietor, Pelicaric by name. He promised to drive us out there at daylight.

Vrana is some five miles from Pakostane. The road to it passes round the northern end of the largest Dalmatian lake – also called Vrana – and runs along a beautifully shaded causeway between the water and the marshes. These latter extend many miles to the northward, and account for the fever which plays such havoc with the population. The lake itself is about nine miles long, and the whole district provides the best shooting in northern Dalmatia. Even at this time it was literally covered with duck, but in winter there are immense quantities of woodcock and snipe, besides other migrants rare to us in England, such as wild geese and swans. I was also told wild boar come down every winter, but I have some doubts as to the accuracy of this statement.

Seen across the lake Vrana appears a place of some size, but when approached nearer turns out to be principally ruins – a few scattered huts containing a population of some three hundred souls, all lantern-jawed and yellow with fever. The principal ruin is that of a large castle, built by the Templars, but soon afterwards taken by the Turks. It was in such a state of decay that I wondered how anyone could identify the various portions Pelicaric pointed out, such as the chapel. I myself should be sorry to swear to anything more than the well, now dry. Our host's house is an old Turkish bey's palace, also extensive, but mostly in ruins. In it stands a shooting-box of the Counts of Vrana.

The story of Vrana is simple. Originally a flourishing Venetian colony – indeed, it is said to have had as many as thirty thousand inhabitants – it fell into Turkish hands. These latter neglected – as they always do everything – the canals which then drained the marshes, and they fell into disrepair; then came the fever, and for centuries the place has been what it is now. It is said that the Austrian Government intends to redrain the marshes shortly – an immense reform, however prejudicial to the sportsman. It would present no great difficulties, there being a fall of something like forty feet from the upper end of the marshes to the lake.

We let E to rest for a while, and went out into Pelicaric's vineyards to look for quail. He bagged some half-dozen, and I missed about as many, greatly to my surprise. No explanation was forthcoming till next day, when I opened some of my cartridges, and found that, instead of being, as I supposed, small shot, they were number fours – useless of course for quail, especially in a small-bore gun such as I was using. The dogs worked capitally, the red dog twice retrieving wounded birds.

After a couple of hours of this sport we returned, and walked with E to see the old castle, and thence on to the celebrated Grotto of Vrana. From a wall of rock a stream of water flows, but it is possible to pass behind the wall and enter a sort of cavern, or rather cleft in the rock, for it is open to the sky. In this there are two streams of water. By wading waist-deep up the first, a series of caverns, all full of water, can be entered. The cleft itself is a pretty spot, the rocks being covered with maidenhair fern and other damp-loving plants. Unfortunately, they are also disfigured by hundreds of names being scrawled upon them, among which I was surprised to see several times that of the noble family who own the place, and who might have been expected to know better.

From the grotto we returned to Pelicaric's house to lunch. In the afternoon we shot again, and returned to Pakostane in the cool of the evening.

We had decided that our present camp was too dirty to be endured, for everybody – including the dogs – who came into the tent brought in a plentiful supply of earth, and the possibility of rain was awful to contemplate. Accordingly on August 23rd we moved to a green *scoglia*, or, as we should say, holm, a couple of hundred yards out to sea. This is called the Island of St Justina, and on the land side still exists her tiny chapel. At the time of our stay it had been recently re-roofed, but not yet re-consecrated. This islet served as a refuge to the inhabitants of Pakostane when the Turks came down; and one can readily imagine the Slavs cursing in impotent wrath as they watched the smoke going up from burning houses and crops, the Moslems, for their part, riding along the beach and shaking their long spears in idle threat. A few ruined walls still mark what no doubt have been buildings of refuge, but probably no one has slept on the islet for centuries.

The islet is of course waterless, but this is a remark that applies to almost all Dalmatian camps. It is about a hundred and fifty yards in length, and little more than half that width. Where not rocky it is covered with coarse grass, and we soon found a clear and green spot, somewhat to seaward of the centre, on which to camp. Whilst we were pitching our tent, I heard squeals, and, going to the spot, found Rex with a full-grown hare, which he had caught in its form. Some days after, some men came to look after 'five hares which the schoolmaster had turned down there.' I told them I presumed four had died a natural death, but that I knew one had died a violent one, and very poor eating he was. When camp was pitched, a small water-barrel was placed in the chapel, and our Crusoe-like existence commenced. It had many advantages, first and foremost being the privacy. Then the bathing was much better, the water near our last camp having been both shallow and rocky. There was still, however, more sea-urchins than might have been wished. The sea-water, as it is everywhere in Dalmatia, was clear and delicious, and as it is particularly rich in iodine, the bathing is most beneficial.

The first day, as usual, was consumed in little else than arranging our new camp; but on the following one I went off to the mainland by the milk-boat, and walked over to the lake. I did not, however, succeed in getting a shot; and it was rather tantalizing, after wading up to my thighs for half an hour in the vain hope of getting a chance from behind some clumps of reeds at a duck, to be met by a Morlak with five nice widgeon for sale, shot, he said, on the marshes at daybreak or at dusk – a process for which I had not time, and, moreover, one not unlikely, in summer, to result in an attack of fever. Now, I am like the Frenchman, who, when asked to go out hunting, replied, 'I've been.' I have had fever and ague, of which it took me a good five years to get rid, and I don't want to try it again.

The next evening, however, I walked down to the marshes – nearly an hour's walk – getting there at about five o'clock. I had not gone through much of them before, to my delight, a snipe got up, and although they were rather wild, I managed to get a nice little bag of longbills before dusk. I then sat down for a bit, but though I saw plenty of duck, I soon found out that I was not in the right spot to get a shot, as they all passed too high up and too far to the eastward.

As I was stumbling home in the dark, a wagon full of Morlaks overtook me, and one of them who spoke a little Italian offered me a lift, which I was not sorry to accept, but I think I never had such a rough drive. The roads in this district are made by the simple process of removing all the larger loose stones and piling them into dikes. The smaller loose, and larger fixed, stones remain and form the roadway. I had already been fairly well bumped in Pelicaric's 'shay,' but that was quite a joke to this, for the ponies rattled along at a good pace, and springs there were none. I can conceive no finer exercise for the liver. The very flesh on my cheeks shook; and had not our Jehu come slowly off the top of the hill into Pakostane village, I feel convinced we should all have been shot out by the mere bumping.

The following evening I returned to the marshes, but met with the worst of bad luck, for the first cartridge with which I dropped a bird jammed hopelessly, and I had to turn homewards. I was well out towards the middle of the fen, and as I was floundering back a skein of widgeon swept over me. Although they were rather high up, I gave them the left barrel, and the one I had picked out, after staggering about a bit, fell a long way on. Of course I turned back to get him, but to my regret the bog got so deep that that and the rapidly setting sun warned me to give it up, and I turned regretfully away, only reaching *terra firma* just before dark. As I have before said, these marshes are many miles in length, and here, near the lake, they must be a couple of miles wide. I cannot conceive any more fascinating spot for winter shooting, or, rather I could not then, but perhaps the Narenta marshes in South Dalmatia should be awarded the palm.

This was the last day of our Crusoe-dom, and much we regretted to leave our pleasant islet. The priest, who is an enthusiastic sea-fisherman, had placed his boat at our disposal for our move, which we fixed for August 28th.

Sir Arthur John Evans
From *Through Bosnia and the Herzegovina on Foot During the Insurrection of the Summer of 1875*

August 31st – Next morning, after considerable bargaining, we engaged a flat, beetle-like craft to convey ourselves and our fortunes to Stagno, *via* the left arm of the Narenta. The landscape now afforded most startling contrasts of fertility and barrenness. The heights that overhung the Narenta, or stretched away to environ its broad alluvial plains, were mere rock heaps, of that lunar desolation already described; so bare that the mountain goat can scarce glean a pittance on their bony terraces. But the broad delta below, formed by the double-armed Narenta, is the richest land in all Dalmatia; the maize by the river-side attains a gigantic stature; on other places the soil is covered by a luxuriant network of vines, which, without any training or apparent cultivation, yield grapes as fine as those of Mostar; and there are mulberry trees at Fort Opus fifteen feet in circumference. But how little of this marvellous rich soil is even culturable nowadays!! To the right of us, what was once a blooming champaign, covered with tilled fields, and dowering a city wealthy and refined, is now a stretch of fever-breeding marshes which it would cost millions to drain. The wretched inhabitants of the few villages that now remain, are, during the summer months, never free from intermittent fever, and the stranger who values his life must not tarry at this season, even to explore the interesting relics of antiquity that we are now passing on our right.

Among the swamps that lie two or three miles to the north of Metcovic are still to be seen the foundations of many of the houses of the Illyrian Narbonne, further remains of which, including many inscriptions, are scattered on the hill above, which takes its name from the modern village of Viddo. Here stood the old Narbona, or as it was called in the later days of Rome, Narona; a city so ancient that it was already of renown five centuries before our era, and which lost none of its eminence when, in 168BC, Lucius Annius added it to the possessions of Rome. At Narbona, now known as Narona, the Romans planted a colony, and among the many inscriptions that have been discovered, we find ample witness to its municipal liberties; while from others we learn that temples of Jove, Diana of the woods and Father Liber once graced this spot. Another inscription on the tomb of a Naronian *lapidary*, to which I shall have occasion to refer, may, perhaps, bear witness to an art which attained considerable perfection in the cities of Roman Illyria, and of which many traces, in the shape of beautifully engraved gems, are still discovered on this site.

Yet it was not under the Romans that Narona and the rich alluvial plains of the Narenta, amidst which our boat is meandering, attained that importance which makes the name of the Narentines familiar to the student of European history.

In the year 639AD Narona, which till then had remained a flourishing Roman city, was reduced to ashes by a mingled horde of Avars and Slavs, and a few years later the Serbian Slavs called in by the Emperor Heraclius took possession of the vacant sites of the lower Narenta. Out of the ruins of the Roman Narona they built a new town, and here, on the site of classic temples, reared a fane to a Slavonic god, whose name, Viddo, is still perpetuated in that of the modern village. The site of this Illyrian Narbonne thus became a stronghold of heathendom in these parts, just as with the Slavonians of the Baltic shores paganism found its last defenders among those staunch Rügen islanders who guarded the precincts of the sacred city of Arkona. It was not till the year 873 that Nicetas, the Admiral of the Byzantine Emperor Basis, prevailed on the Narentines to accept baptism; the temple of their country's god underwent a strange conversion and Viddo lived again in a Christian guise as St Vitus!

In the next century the country of the Narentines is still known as *Pagania*, the land of the Pagans, by which name Constantine Porphyrogenitus mentions it in his account of the Serbians; and it was during the ninth and tenth centuries that these barbarous Slavs, yet untamed by a civilized religion, issued forth from the swamps and inlets of the Narenta to ravage the coasts of the Adriatic, and to rival their heathen counterparts and contemporaries, the sea-kings of the north. As early as 827 their 'Archons,' as the Byzantine Emperor calls the Starosts of their republic, refused to pay the customary tribute to eastern Rome; and soon after this date we find them in possession of Curzola, Lagosta, Meleda, Lesina, Brazza and other islands of the Adriatic. But it is their rivalry with Venice which exalts the history of the Narentines into world importance. The rising city of the lagoons saw her commerce cut off by these hardy corsairs, and was at last actually forced to pay them an ignominious tribute. It was not till 997 that the Doge Pietro Orseolo II succeeded in throwing off the yoke and attacking the pirates in their Narentan fastnesses. After three centuries of piratic domination, the Narentines saw all their island empire taken from them, and themselves not only forced to disgorge their plunder, but to swear allegiance to their rival. The power of the pirate state was broken for ever; but the fate of Venice had trembled in the balance, and for a moment the whole current of European civilization seemed destined to be perverted from its channel by the inhabitants of the now obscure valley through which we are passing. It were perhaps as idle to speculate what might have been the history of Europe, had the Queen of the Adriatic been smothered in her cradle, as to discuss the fates of Lerna or Nemea, had infant Hercules perished in the coils of the serpent which he strangled; but the most casual student of Venetian annals must perceive that the final triumph of Venice over the Narentines is the great climacteric in the history of her rise.

We thought we detected something of the old piratic genius of the race in the way in which our boatmen plundered the maize and vine fields as we passed; but there was nothing of pagan savagery in their demeanour and conversation, which on the contrary formed a marked contrast to the rudeness and asperity of the ordinary Bosnian or Herzegovinian. They spoke indeed a dialect closely akin to the Illyrian of the interior, but they spoke it with energy, vivacity, elegance; with a softness of cadence so thoroughly Italian, that when, as all of them did at times, they changed to that language to address the *signori*, we hardly detected the change. Their very form is lither, suppler; of lesser mould, but a striking contrast to the overgrown, ungraceful Bosnian. The eyebrows of these Narentines are not so arched, the hair is darker; they seemed to be many of them Slavonized Italians, descendents perhaps of the Roman colonists of Narbona. One of our boatmen was a very interesting type of man. He spoke Dalmatian like the rest but his face – which like that of many other Dalmatian faces that I recall, beamed with all the openness of a sea-faring people – was typically Scotch; and, oddly enough, he wore what looked like a Scotch cap, minus the tails. His hair was of a lighter and more reddish hue than the others. One almost fancied that we had here before us a waif of that early Celtic population of Illyria already invoked as nomenclators of the Illyrian Narbonne whose ruins we are passing to our right.

Meanwhile we have been making very slow progress, since a fierce *sirocco* has set dead in the teeth of our small craft; and as we arrive at Fort Opus, an old Venetian station at the apex of the Narentan delta, our boatmen inform us that our two-master is too lubberly for them to hope to take us to Stagno in it while the *sirocco* continues to blow, in which case the voyage might take two or three days. They professed their willingness to find a smaller vessel which should be able to cope with the elements and to resign half the wages, which we had agreed upon, to the new boatmen. 'You see, Sirs, it is not for want of will – but we cannot struggle against God!'

At Fort Opus, accordingly, we shifted into another smaller craft, pointed at both stern and stem, and beetle-like as the other, and were soon on our way again along a part of the Narenta's course which might well be the source of weirdest myth and legend. Just beyond Fort Opus, the hills on the left – bonier skeletons, if possible, than before – draw nearer to the river, till they frown over its depths. It is at this point that ever and anon mysterious boomings and bellowings are heard to proceed as from the inmost recesses of the mountain. It is, say those who have heard it, as the bellowing of a bull, sometimes here, sometimes there, and sometimes everywhere at once. At other times it seems to issue forth from the darkest pools of the Narenta itself. I cannot say that we ourselves heard the 'hideous hum,' but these noises cannot be set down as the creatures of superstitious imagination; for a competent observer, Signor Lanza, who was physician in this district, and to whom is due a scientific account of this part of the Narenta valley, has himself borne ample witness of the existence of this phenomenon; nor does it stand alone, for there are equally authentic accounts of similar subterranean murmurs and explosions having been heard in Meleda and other islands of the Dalmatian littoral. The explanation given by some is that the detonations are due to the pressure of the tide on the air pent up in the subterranean caverns which honeycomb the limestone Karst-formation of these Illyrian coastlands; but Dr Lanza – who notices that the phenomenon generally takes place either at sunrise or sunset – confesses that 'a veil of mystery hangs over the whole.' Meanwhile, nothing but the portent is certain; and fearful as I am of giving publicity to ill-omened words, I cannot refrain from breathing a suspicion that this unhallowed bellowing may proceed from some hideous minotaur, caverned in his labyrinthine den.

This neighbourhood is also much subject to earthquakes, which generally occur during winter months; and as our boat toiled heavily past a succession of rocky headlands, we ourselves experienced a natural phenomenon scarcely less awful than these subterranean bellowings and convulsions. The wind rose higher and higher, whistling among the limestone 'ruins of the older world' that frowned above us. Our two boatmen knit their brows and muttered '*la Fortuna!*' Dame Fortune, the old goddess of the way by sea and land, still retains some of her old attributes of wheel and rudder among these Romanized Dalmatian Slavs; her name is still used on these coastlands as equivalent to a tempest; and even in the interior of Bosnia the Slavs have so far adopted the idea that a snowstorm – the kind of snow dreaded most in the Bosnian mountains – is known to the peasants as '*Fortunja.*'

At last, on steering between the two rocky hills, whose barren masses rise on either side at the mouth of this arm of the Narenta like twin pillars of Hercules, a tremendous scene burst upon us. Just opposite to where the river widened into the sea, towered before us – its limestone crags and boulders up-piled and jumbled in cataclysmic confusion – a small desolate island, a fit abode for nothing unless it were departed spirits of the evil. The rays of a pale ominous sunset fell upon these cadaverous rocks and flooded them with a spectral light. On either side of the island the sea shone with abnormal emerald lustre; but what made the brilliance of the foreground so unearthly, was the unutterable darkness of all behind. The rocky island rose like a phantom against a sky as black as night.

The question for us was whether there would be time to round the nose of rock on the left side of the Narenta mouth, and cross a narrow arm of green sea to a promontory where we might obtain shelter, before the impending hurricane came down to us.

The sailors thought it possible and with set teeth laboured at the oars as for grim life. But the black pall of clouds that darkened the western hemisphere drew nearer and nearer; the white sea mews swept wildly and more wildly hither and thither against the face of coming night, shrieking weirdly like the banshees of coming doom. The wind and thunder roared louder in our ears, and a thin snowy line of surf stretching across the emerald horizon swept like a charge of cavalry across the intervening fields of sea – but now, so treacherously smooth! – and dashed down upon our little craft. The night was already upon us; the brilliant beams of sunset were suddenly transformed, first into darkness, and then into the lurid twilight of an eclipse which lit up our men's faces with a pale ashy grey, ghastly to look upon. These hardy descendants of corsairs seemed really cowed, and shouted to us 'Pray to God, *signori*! Pray to God! *La Fortuna è rota!*'

The storm had burst with a vengeance. The wind rose to a hurricane. The surf and tempest struck our boat and beat her head round. It was in vain that the men struggled at the oars; we were borne back, and swept along helpless as a log in a torrent. We were driven towards the mouth of the Narenta which we had left, and I thought every moment we should have been dashed against the rocks; but Dame Fortune was merciful to us, and notwithstanding that the men lost all command of the vessel, we rounded the rocky headland, and found ourselves in comparatively sheltered waters where oars were again available, so that we were presently anchored near another small Narentan vessel in smoother waters – though even the river was one sheet of foam. It now began to rain in torrents beyond all our experience; so we covered ourselves with our macintoshes, and lay down in the bottom of our boat, resolved not to emerge till the hurricane should have abated somewhat of its fury. But hardly were we settled, when a tremendous clap of thunder rent the air, followed by a series of sharp blows which made us start to our feet, when we found that hailstones varying in sizes from a bullet to a walnut, and in shape like tangerine oranges, were rattling about our heads, With our helmet hats on, and under cover of our macintoshes, we avoided being actually bruised, but the thunder and lightning that accompanied the hail were still more terrific. The forked lightning literally played around our craft, and it seemed that it must be struck; the thunder was such as we had neither of us heard the like of before. For a quarter of an hour we endured the full brunt of this celestial cannonade, and then the storm passed away as suddenly as it had come, and rolled on among the more inland ranges of the vivid and unexpected reliefs behind us; while in front and overhead, sky and rocks and sea were illumined with the renewed splendour of sunset, and the surface of the troubled Narenta calmed down into its wonted serenity.

But it was a storm such as one does not meet with twice in a lifetime; it was a fit initiation into this iron-bound coastland, with it earthquakes and subterranean thunders – the cavernous home of winds and tempests – the last refuge of pirate races.

We now renewed our voyage, and crossing a narrow arm of sea, landed in a sheltered cove, where we took refuge in a spacious stone house, the abode of a Dalmatian family-community, hoping for the *sirocco* to subside, in order to be able to pursue our course up the Stagno. We were shown into the common eating and cooking room, a spacious chamber on the ground-floor, where the family gathered round us; and the men, when they had heard that we were English, at once claimed us as brothers, and entered into a most friendly conversation. 'We like the English,' said one; 'we know your greatness on the sea, and we too are a nation of seamen; England and Dalmatia – there are no sailors but in your country and ours!' Another of the men had been to London and Plymouth, and he and the others aired a string of English phrases with a decidedly nautical flavour, amongst which we detected 'Or' right,' 'cup o' tea,' 'grog,' 'haul up,' 'ease her;' and other expressions proving their *entente cordiale* with 'Jack.' About nine in the evening the woman-kind, the children, and some of the men, betook themselves to sleeping chambers above, and we were shown a bed in the spacious hall below, on whose floor slept our seamen and some of the inmates. But the stuffiness was so suffocating within, that I preferred the gnats and night air without; and finding a convenient rock on which to pillow my head, imitated the example of Jacob.

About midnight the adverse wind fell and I, being by now sufficiently disillusioned of patriarchal repose, hastened to rouse L and our men, and we were again on our way before 1am, the wind shifting enough to enable us every now and then to use our sail. We steered along the Canale di Stagno Piccolo, passing in the dark the inlet in which the Turkish harbour of Klek is situated. About 8am we landed at Luka, on the peninsula of Sabbioncello, and making our way on foot across the isthmus, entered the old town of Stagno by a gateway through its high machicolated Venetian walls. It was a small friendly place with clean narrow streets, and many old stone palaces of the citizen nobility with stone escutcheons over their doors, quaint rope mouldings and carved corbels under the windows, some of which were of Venetian-Gothic style. Other houses, whose owners probably could lay no claim to coats of arms, displayed over their doorways medallions on which IHS was engraved in a variety of ornamental forms. In the Piazza just inside the gate by which we entered lay an old font with many noble shields upon it, and in the city wall opposite was a Renaissance fountain with a sixteenth-century date upon it. Stagno was once a port of the Bosnian kings, till sold by one of them to Ragusa at the end of the fourteenth century.

The peasants in the Piazza were highly picturesque; the men, like the inhabitants of the lower Narenta, strongly resembling the Turks in their attire, except for a yellow sash around their waist, a Dalmatian peaked fez on their head, and an earring – a plain golden circle – in one ear. The women, with their kerchiefs crossed about their bosom, showed more slavonic characteristics in their dress, but their straw hats with long streamers gave them a certain Swiss air.

While sketching the little group above, in the Piazza, I was somewhat surprised to hear the inspiriting tune of *Men of Harlech* proceeding from a neighbouring house; but the mystery was cleared up by our shortly receiving a message to the effect that 'the daughter of the Judge of Stagno' wished to secure an interview with the Englishmen; and then it was that we found that this amiable young lady, having lived some years in Wales, and looking back with a tender regret to her sojourn in our island, had resorted to the innocent device of playing the national melodies of the Principality in order to attract our attention... But alas! the boat is starting for Ragusa – the parting has taken place, – we have left our romantic damsel to sigh once more for English society, and stagnate at Stagno.

Our boat – a *Trabaccolo*, I believe it is called – is equipped with an expansive lateen sail, and as a propitious breeze, the *maestro*, has sprung up, we soon left Stagno, its olives and oleanders and pretty flowering shrubs, its siren music and bright eyes, far in our wake and scud along between rocky islands to our right, and the bare Karst mountains of the mainland to our left. The desolate, monotonous hills, perpetually repeating themselves, were hardly relieved by a stunted tree – it was the same scenery so well described by Ovid in his Pontic exile:

Rara, nec haec felix, in apertis eminet arvis
Arbor, et in terra est altera forma maris!

At one point, indeed, the village of Canosa, there was an oasis of green in the desert landscape; this was the gigantic group of plane trees, which are said to rank among the finest in the world. But we are nearing Ragusa, and after passing a line of jagged *scoglie* which start up from the deep like the teeth of a gigantic antediluvian, the sea, hitherto hardly recovered from its frenzy of yestereen, becomes tranquil once more, and we glide into the harbour of Gravosa, the port of modern Ragusa, for depth and capacity reckoned the finest in Dalmatia.

Jan Morris
From *Trieste and the Meaning of Nowhere (2001)*

The Biplane and the Steamer

In Istria the Glagolithic alphabet long ago became a symbol of Slavness, a defiant declaration, defying both political and ecclesiastical disapproval through conquest and conflict, assimilation and oppression. It was still alive at the start of the twentieth century. The peninsula was Triestine territory until the Second World War, and just as that one strange document is stored in the parish vestry at San Dorligo, so Istria is always in the city's consciousness, still there in sight as in mind. The hundreds of refugee Italian families who came to the city when the Communist Yugoslavs took over Istria still form a tightly organized and influential community, resentful of the past and often fervently anti-Slav, and perhaps it is the loss of Istria, almost as much as the loss of purpose, that has given Trieste its sense of deprivation – a country so close, so familiar, yet now foreign territory!

I spent my childhood in Somerset, on the English side of the Bristol channel, and Wales was my Istria. I could always see its mountains, so close across the water and yet apparently so unattainable. I knew it was my dead father's country, and so properly mine too. A lumbering old De Havilland biplane used to fly heavily over each morning on its way from Bristol to Cardiff, and its slow passing gave me my very first intimations of *hiraeth*.

Istria is now almost entirely within Croatia, only a thin corridor running across it, just outside Trieste, to provide Slovenia with its outlet to the sea at Koper. It is a triangular wedge of land, about fifty miles long north to south, never more than thirty miles wide, and its history has been labyrinthine. Its original inhabitants were apparently Illyrians. Its indigenous people now are all Croats or

Slovenes, but it has been ruled in its time, in one part or another, by Romans, Byzantines, Franks, Venetians and Austrians. Bavarian Counts and Aquilean Patriarchs have lorded it there. Napoleon annexed it for his Illyrian Province. German armies occupied it. Yugoslav partisans fought all over it. It has been threatened in its time by Ostrogoths, Lombards, Genoese, impious Turks and sinister Uskoks from Senj. The Venetians built lovely towns all around its coast, to sustain their command of the Adriatic, and one of them, Muggia, is now part of Trieste itself. Tito's Yugoslavia made most of the other islands into a People's Paradise, lapped by myriad hotels and camping sites. The eastern flank of the peninsula, the Čičen, was described by Baedeker in 1905 as 'a bleak plain inhabited by poor charcoal burners,' and is now inhabited mostly by Romanians.

In Austro-Hungarian times, when the peninsula was under Trieste's jurisdiction, there were close sea-connections between the city and the former Venetian towns on the coast. Capodistria, Pirano, Cittanova, Parenzo, Rovigno, all had, besides their familiar Italian *campaniles*, an Italian-speaking citizenry which thought of itself as part of a wider Trieste. Its business people came to Trieste to make deals or insurance arrangements, its ladies came to shop or go to the opera – imagine the demand for tickets, and the happy shipboard parties, when Smareglia's *Nozze Istriane* had its first performance at the Trieste Municipal Opera on March 28th 1895! Even in my own early days in Trieste, when the empire had long gone and a hostile communist army occupied those ports, a small black steamboat belching smoke pushed off for Istria every morning. It reminded me of that old DH Rapide on its way to Glamorgan.

The Austrians themselves created two Istrian coastal cities in their own kind, and both were familiar to Triestini. When rich and loyal entrepreneurs of the Chamber of Commerce wanted a fashionable holiday, they took their families down to the peninsula to the resort of Abbazia, which was a favourite of the Viennese aristocracy. It stood in the most beautiful situation imaginable, looking across the gulf of Quarnero to the celestial isles and coasts of Dalmatia, and like Trieste itself it was more or less an invented town. In the 1840s it had been discovered as a winter health resort, and swiftly developed with hotels, gardens and villas. The most expensive Viennese doctors recommended it; the lordliest Austrian valetudinarians, the swankiest Hungarian socialites, the wealthiest Triestini speculators took their advice; in its late nineteenth-century prime Abbazia was almost as smart as Nice or Monte Carlo.

It is still delightfully evocative of *K u K* [*Kaiserlich und Königlich* – Imperial and Royal]. Some of the old hotels still thrive, curled and preposterously grand beside the sea, and on the hills behind, many a comfortable villas writhes with putti and dolphins, among gardens sentimentally fragrant with jasmine and magnolia. Franz Joseph himself often came here, and put up his mistress in neighbouring accommodation; a promenade along the seafront is named for him, and she is not forgotten either, for all the guide books mention her. Abbazia is much modernized now, with the usual noise and concrete, but still Austrians come here by the thousand, together with a few Triestini, and it is easy to imagine the flowered hats and epaulettes strolling the Promenade Franz Joseph in the evenings. (Did Franz Lehár conduct for them here, too? Perhaps, because for a time he directed a naval band in Istria, and in 1908 he published a piano arrangement of *Nozze Istriane*...) Just occasionally to this day one still meets aged relics of the old regime, last representatives of the Habsburg patriciate, who incline their heads graciously when one meets them in the Botanical Garden, or bow in courtly manner from the waist.

The other Austrian city of Istria was Pola, at the southern tip of the peninsula. This was very old, had been a Roman naval base, and was celebrated for its splendidly preserved Roman amphitheatre above the sea. It had a fine protected harbour, and when in 1856 the Austrian naval command decided that Trieste was unsuitable as a war-base, the fleet moved its headquarters here. The developers fell upon the town at once, to make of it a smaller more martial replica of Trieste itself. Franz Joseph journeyed down to lay the foundation stone of its Arsenal, and all around it rose the familiar streets and buildings of an imperial town. There were the barracks, there the shipyards, the grand hotel for important visitors, the naval church, the offices of the bureaucracy, the club, the railway station for the track to Trieste. It gives me an odd sensation even now, for it is still like a miniature, shabbier version of that greater seaport up the line.

Where the citadel is in Trieste, so the citadel is in Pola. Where the offices of the Maritime Government used to be in Trieste, the Admiralty building still stands in Pola. The Riviera Hotel in Pola is like a poor relative of the Albergo Savoia Excelsior in Trieste, and there is a *Caffè degli Spechhi* here too. And the lingering melancholy of Trieste is more potent still in Pola. The railway station down on the waterfront no longer sends its steam trains up to Trieste, only diesel railcars to Buzet, forty miles up the peninsula, and it is a bleak, forlorn cluster of buildings beside the tracks. Joyce, who lived here for a few weeks, likened Pola to Siberia, but this sad station, on waste ground beside the sea, suggests to me a final depot on some remote South American coast, where the trains make their last stop before returning with relief to civilization. Like as they were to each other, the two ports had diametrically opposite purposes. Trieste was a great trading port, dependent upon peace for its prosperity. Pola was dedicated to war. The most pompous buildings of the one were banks and insurance offices; the palaces of the other were structures of militarism. Comfortable passenger liners dominated the Trieste quaysides; grim warships were lined up, stern-to-shore, in the harbour of Pola. Trieste had an opera house. Pola had a Navy Band, with one hundred and eighty musicians.

Still, their fortunes were always linked, to the very end of the Austro-Hungarian Empire. In Trieste the end was to be remembered always by the arrival of the *Audace* at the waterfront. It was marked in Pola, in the last week of the First World War, by the exploits of two Italian frogmen who penetrated the harbour's powerful defences and sank the battleship *Viribus Unitis*. She was the ship that had brought the Archduke Ferdinand's body home from Sarajevo to Trieste, and she had been built there six years before.

Istria's heartland, though, high in its karstic hills, remains to this day a purely Croatian territory of recondite fascination. It is the only place in the world where I have seen lightning go up from the ground.

This is what you must do when you arrive at the minute village of Draguć, far from the sea in the limestone uplands. Leave your car at the entrance to the village, which only has one narrow street, and walk between its old terraced houses to the small piazza beyond. The whole village is likely to seem utterly deserted, with not a sign of life, but if you cry a shout for assistance into the silence, four or five doors will open and four or five old ladies will simultaneously tell you where to find the key to the church of San Rocco (since they are all old enough to have been educated under an Italian educational system, they will tell you in Italian). 'Number twenty-four,' they will say, and sure enough there at its door you will find a sixth old lady already holding out a venerable iron key to you. Up to the very end of the village you must go then, and where it peters out into muddy, rutted farm tracks, there all alone is the little church. A bit of a struggle with its antique lock, a loud creak as the door opens, and before you is a glorious Istrian surprise. About twenty feet long and empty of pews, the church is covered all over, ceiling and all, with wonderfully lively frescoes. They are naive representations of the Christian story, a bible in bright colour, and they were painted by an Istrian master some time in the sixteenth century. They are a masterpiece of Glagoliticism.

For here, although we are never more than a morning's drive from Trieste, we are in the heartland of esoteric abstraction. It is a hard country, like the Karst, and its villages are mostly built on ridges or hilltops, and surrounded by walls to keep out the Turks or the Uskoks – even little Draguć stands there *cap-à-pie*. They are scattered and often deserted, sometimes abandoned altogether. They feel closely knit, though, perhaps because you can frequently see one from another, on a neighbouring high ridge across a valley, even when no road connects them; or perhaps because from their small taverns, as a mealtime approaches, an identical smell of stew follows the traveller from Roć to Vhr, from Cerovlje to Sovinsko Polja and down to Hum. Among them all, too, is a shared sense of inherited defiance, and this is because they were for so many centuries the inner keep of the Croatian culture, and of its ancient script. One can sense the presence of Glagoliticism always in these hills, a wistful, waif-like substance still drifting across the stony landscape.

The most celebrated of all the villages is a very depository of the tradition. You are led to it by a series of modern monuments, all in honour of Glagoliticism, its values and its heroes, forming an esoteric sacred avenue through the fields: a half-circle of stone chairs beneath an oak tree, to remember the teachings of Liment – a stone circle commemorating the Book of Istrian Law – a column in the shape of the Glagolitic letter Slovo – a stone block in the memory of Bishop Grgur – the pillar of the Čavac Parliament – the resting place of Žakan Juraj – until, dazed or inspired by these queer monuments, you arrive before the gates of Hum, where a Glagolitic inscription offers you a welcome if you are friendly, a severe injunction if you are not.

Once a complete and prosperous medieval municipality, Hum is now a mostly empty tumble of grey stone houses, many of them derelict, within the minuscule circle of its walls. It proclaims itself the 'Smallest Town in the World', and it is the true capital of Glagoliticism. In the tavern near its gate you may buy a postcard of the script, in one of the better-preserved houses there is a museum of it, and in the cemetery chapel outside the walls you may see graffito written in it: a priest scrawled this in the twelfth century, it seems, as a reminder that Martin the Blacksmith was entitled to have thirty masses said for the salvation of his soul, and still had one to come.

When I wandered through Hum one dark and blustery morning I met nobody at all. Not a soul was around. A cock repeatedly crowed, a dog barked somewhere out of sight. But every house seemed locked and empty, and the wind blew cruelly through the delapidations. Faintly, from some inmost hovel of the little place, I heard a telephone ringing. It rang and rang and rang, while the wind blew and the dog barked, but nobody answered it, and by tea-time I was back in Trieste.

In the summer season a hydrofoil goes down the Istrian coast from Trieste, but it is no longer an organic connection. It is just for tourists. Today the peninsula looks more often eastwards towards Zagreb, capital of Croatia, or south to its companion holiday coast of Dalmatia. Few ladies of Parenzo come to the opera in the city nowadays, and only in the minds of those ageing refugees, forever brooding over their lost patrimony, is Istria still part of Greater Trieste. Even the names of the peninsula have foresworn all Trieste affinities. Today Abbazzia is Opatija, Pola is Pula, Pirano is Piran, Rovingo is Rovinj, Parenzo is Poreč, Cittanuova is Novigrad, Capodistra is Koper, the Gulf of Quarnero is Kvarner Bay. Istria itself is now officially Istra, and that little black steamer never sails away, trailing its black smoke, from the Molo Bersaglieri towards the blue-green shore in the south.

II: People

VERY COUNTRY produces remarkable figures, and for better or worse every country also attracts them. Having been struggled over by the Venetians, Ottomans and Habsburgs, invaded by the Germans and Italians, and subsumed in socialist Yugoslavia before finally achieving its modern independence, Croatia has had no shortage of dealings with larger powers. It has thus no shortage of experience with the extraordinary personalities which so often appear in times of political and social tension. This section introduces Gabriele D'Annunzio and Josip Broz Tito, two of the more striking characters from Croatia's past, but also makes room for the ordinary people of the country, who have had to live with upheaval, war and external interference ever since antiquity.

Abbé Alberto Fortis (1741-1803) travelled to Dalmatia at the suggestion of the Earl of Bute, in order to 'enquire into the Truth of the prevailing Report concerning the extensive Strata of Fossil Bones in the Islands of Liburnia'. His account of his journeys, in the form of letters to various important personages, was presented, translated from the Italian, to the Earl in 1778 as *Travels in Dalmatia; Containing General Observations on the Natural History of That Country and the Neighbouring Islands, the Natural Productions, Arts, Manners and Customs of the Inhabitants*; an Italian edition had been published a few years earlier. Fortis, of Padua, was a natural historian by vocation, rather than an explorer, but as the full title suggests his *Travels* detail all aspects of the land he was visiting. Appearing in English, German and French, as well as in Fortis's native Italian, it was the first authoritative book on Dalmatia, and was referred to by Gibbon and Goethe amongst others. The following edited extract concerns the Morlacchi, a people of the Dalmatian mountains who are frequently met with in travel accounts of the area. The Abbé Fortis paints a detailed and sympathetic picture of an agreeable rustic people, strongly at odds with their fearsome reputation as bandits and brigands, and the portrait is as precisely observed as one would expect from a scholar of natural history. His letters were addressed to the great and good of England and Italy, and it is to his great credit that he does not produce a sensational picture of a notorious barbarian nation, a picture which one imagines would have found a ready audience. Instead he reports with an unprejudiced eye of his stay amongst an orderly and punctilious people, and tells of their honest concern for him in such a way as to gently but firmly underscore the humanity he holds in common with them.

The Coward by Dinko Simunović can be found in the excellent volume *Yugoslav Short Stories*, a wide variety of tales translated and edited by Svetozar Koljević, which was first published in 1966 by Oxford University. Koljević's selection naturally includes tales from all over the Balkans; the author of *The Coward*, Dinko Simunović (1873-1933), was born in Knin, and made a living as a teacher first in the mountains of Dalmatia, then in Split. The story related in *The Coward* is surely set in the evening of the Ottoman Empire's dominion over the Balkans, when the imperial system had become so corrupt that the pashas and janissaries, nominally the loyal backbone of the empire, had become a self-interested strata of feudal lords actually hostile to the Sultan. Deeply opposed to any meddling from the centre and dedicated to enriching themselves, their subjects were little more than indentured serfs. Told to a novice by an aged monk (the coward of the title), it is a bleak tale of brutality, feuding, and honour, and is made all the more unredeemed by the refusal of the monk to consider any other way than the vengeful mentality of his fathers. An eye for an eye, a tooth for a tooth – in the end this credo is his true cowardice, a passionate devotion to the very brutality which had humiliated him from childhood.

The extract which follows is from the collection *Yugoslav Folk Tales*, retold by Nadia Ćurčija-Prodanović. Though the exact location of the village is unspecified, *How the Peasants Bought Wisdom* takes place by the sea, and the peasants of the title visit Venice in their attempt to obtain wisdom, so it is fair to assume we are on the Dalmatian coast. The tale is rather like a very gentle *Jack and the Bean-Stalk* – instead of Jack's magic bean, which leads him to the Giant's great wealth, the peasants obtain merely the means to a much more modest kind of richness. Even that is to be got in a very oblique fashion, since the actual object which they pay for is immediately lost, before they even reach the shores of home. The tale seems to express something of the exasperation and resignation felt by those living in the shadow of a great power, and speaks also of the pragmatism of those who are perpetually disappointed by the people who represent them and wield power over them – the peasants give up their earnings and time to dubious business dealings in Venice and, getting nothing in return due to the bungling of those entrusted with the mission, end up relying on their own inventiveness. It is interesting to note in passing that the swindle perpetrated by the canny Venetian at the expense of the gullible peasants bears out the Abbé Fortis's remark about the 'want of probity' that the Dalmatian Morlacchi frequently experienced in business deals with Italians.

Anthony Rhodes (1916-2004) wrote *Where the Turk Trod: A Journey to Sarajevo with a Slavonic Musselman* after a six-week-long visit to Yugoslavia with his brother in the early 1950s; the trip also gave him the material for another book on Yugoslavia, *The Dalmatian Coast*. Educated at Cambridge, the outbreak of war took him to France as a sapper with the 3rd Division of the British Expeditionary Force. His experiences form the basis of one of the classic wartime accounts, *Sword of Bone*, which became a bestseller after its publication in 1942. Taking up a literary career after the war, Rhodes published widely as a novelist, travel writer and historian. As a journalist he covered the Hungarian crisis for the *Telegraph*, and filed reports from all over eastern Europe. Other books include his defence of the conduct of Pope Pius XII during the the Second World War, *The Vatican in the Age of the Dictators*; a biography of Gabriele D'Annunzio, *The Poet as Superman*; and his travel account of Italy, *A Sabine Journey*. He also authored an art historical study entitled *Art Treasures of Eastern Europe*, which treats of the artistic heritage of the Yugoslav Balkans, much of which has since been lost during wartime.

Sir Osbert Sitwell (1892-1969) was the middle sibling of the well-known literary family (his older sister Dame Edith and younger brother Sir Sacheverell have reputations of their own, and together the siblings are generally known as 'the Sitwells' for their numerous collaborative projects). Born Francis Osbert Sacheverell Sitwell, he was educated at Eton and then, having failed the entrance exams for Oxford, joined the army and was stationed in London as a Grenadier Guard. Part of a highly cultured social scene while in the capital, he was separated from it in 1914, when he was sent to the trenches of the First World War. On his return to England, he became directly involved in the literary world, publishing poetry and satires in newspapers and periodicals, and collaborating with his siblings on various projects including exhibitions of modern art and ballet productions. He began to travel widely during the 1920s, visiting the United States, the Orient, as well as Europe, and his first collection of travel writing, *Discursions on Travel, Art and Life*, was published in 1925. He continued to publish fiction, journalism and travel writings until the early 1960s, dying in 1969. The extract included in this chapter is taken from his book of portraits entitled *Noble Essences* (1955), and concerns his encounter with the notorious Italian warrior-poet Gabriele D'Annunzio (1863-1928) during one of the most extraordinary incidents in post-First-World-War Europe, the occupation of the city of Fiume (now Rijeka). Sitwell, enthusiastic about what he had heard of the poet's personal realm, was anxious to visit the city, and traveled there to meet D'Annunzio as a reporter for the liberal weekly *Nation and Athenaeum*.

The situation in Fiume was roughly thus: employing an irregular army, Gabriele D'Annunzio – already famous as poet, First World War hero and daredevil – had taken control of the city, ostensibly for Italy, but had subsequently declared it an independent city-state. Applauded by the anti-art Dadaists and fascist-leaning Italian Futurists, and evidently a magnet for idealists, eccentrics, nationalists, criminals, army deserters and various other cadres of the dissatisfied, D'Annunzio announced himself 'commandant' of the 'Italian Regency of Carnaro'. His administration was initially quite precise and foreshadowed the organization of Mussolini's fascist state (on which it was influential), but the constitution was eccentric and poetic in places, and the city became famously licentious and chaotic during the period of the experiment. D'Annunzio's dream came to a close, after sixteen heady months, in the winter of 1920; after a diplomatic stand-off, the Italian gunboats which had been blockading the city shelled the Municipal Palace on the instruction of the Italian premier Giovanni Giolitti. D'Annunzio, who narrowly escaped death during the shelling, capitulated; he withdrew his militias and swiftly left the city. On his return to Italy he retired to Lake Garda. Fiume was then returned to Yugoslavia, but it was eventually to be handed back to Mussolini's Italy in 1924.

The last two extracts in this chapter on Croatian characters both concern Josip Broz, more commonly known as Tito. Mark Thompson spent the years 1987-91 in the former Yugoslavia; *A Paper House: The Ending of Yugoslavia* presents a historical and social view of the country refracted through the lens of his journeys. In the following extract, Thompson visits the island of Brioni, a once forbidden place which was Tito's private retreat and playground, and finds it transformed into an ambiguous monument to Yugoslavia's political history. Mark Thompson worked as a policy analyst for the United Nations in the Balkans during the 1990s, has written policy briefs on the area for the International Institute for Democratic and Electoral Assistance (IDEA), and until 2002 was Balkans Programme Director for the International Crisis Group in Brussels. His other books include *Forging War: The Media in Serbia, Croatia, Bosnia and Herzegovina* and *Forging Peace: Intervention, Human Rights and the Management of Media Space.*

The other extract is by Vladimir Dedijer (1914-90), who was in Tito's partisan unit, and *Tito Speaks: his self portrait and struggle with Stalin*, was the result of interviews between the two men, which Dedijer rendered into a first person narrative. A close comrade, Dedijer had clearly been entrusted with the task of presenting the life and times of the Communist leader in a period which had recently seen the Communist Party of Yugoslavia (the CPY) thrown out of the nascent official eastern bloc, the Cominform (the 'Information Bureau of Communist and Workers' Parties'). Stalin had become weary of Tito's activities in the south Balkans (principally Albania and Greece), and in 1948 he had unsuccessfully attempted to purge the CPY leadership. This is the 'struggle with Stalin' of the book's title. Tito thwarted his former ally, and maintained control of the Yugoslav state apparatus; Stalin rejected the military option and instead denounced Tito, imposed sanctions and expelled Yugoslavia from the Cominform. *Tito Speaks*, then, was published at a time when Tito was attempting to reposition Yugoslavia within the international system, and to move towards the West; by 1953 (the year of Stalin's death, and of the book's publication in England), Yugoslavia had entered into a pact with Turkey and Greece which included informal relations with NATO. The death of Stalin, however, led to a measure of reconciliation with the USSR under Khruschev, and Tito's decision to maintain Yugoslavia as a one-party state rather than follow a democratic model was the cause of his 1954 split with another former partisan, Milovan Djilas, and also with Vladimir Dedijer himself (the episode is known as 'the Djilas affair'). Relations with the Soviet Union remained cool however, and the citizens of Yugoslavia enjoyed far greater social freedoms than their counterparts within the eastern bloc proper.

Yet Yugoslavia was not integrated into the West; as always, the Yugoslav Balkans were caught between greater powers, and from this situation Tito, with typical astuteness, initiated talks towards the creation of a bloc of 'non-aligned' states which was to include other countries whose leaders had similar concerns. This would result in the formation of the Non-Aligned Movement, whose inaugural meeting took place in Belgrade in 1961, with Nehru, Nasser and Sukarno among prominent contributors to its development.

Tito (1892-1980) had come to power in Yugoslavia after the Second World War, when his Allied-backed partisans had formed the major military resistance to Axis power and Ustasha terror in Yugoslavia (see the extracts from Bill Strutton and Fitzroy Maclean in Chapter IV). His political life began after the end of his locksmith's apprenticeship in 1910, when he joined the Social Democratic Party. He worked at his trade during the years leading up to the First World War, at which point he was drafted into the Austro-Hungarian army. After serving in Serbia, he was transferred to the Russian front where he was injured, captured and interned by the Russians. It was here that he became acquainted with Bolshevism, and after his release he became steadily more politically committed, serving as a Red Guard in the Russian Civil War. Returning to Croatia in 1920, he joined the Communist Party of Yugoslavia (CPY), which was banned later that same year. He continued to be active in the trade unions, and made contacts in the underground communist networks, later acting as a party official. In 1928 he was arrested for his political activities and jailed for five years – the police found him to be in possession of explosives. On his release he was accepted into the CPY inner circle based in Vienna. He was instrumental as an organizer of clandestine CPY activities within Yugoslavia, and with the coming of the Second World War to the Balkans, Tito took the opportunity to launch a Communist insurgency aimed at both defeating the Nazis and their collaborators, and at seizing control of the Yugoslav state.

The extract at the end of this chapter, from the beginning of Dedijer's book, deals not with war and the intrigues of the great powers and their clients, but with the childhood and adolescence of a poor peasant boy. Tito (or perhaps it is Dedijer) is skilled in the art of mythologising the past, and wastes no opportunity to impress on the reader the universal features and political credentials of his personal history, from the ancient roots of peasant rebellion in his home province, to the fate of his father at the hands of greedy debtors. But the tales have something of the charismatic Tito's famous charm about them, and even if the life of an ordinary peasant is transformed into a parable about the conditions of the proletariat and the emancipation of the poor, the message carried by the myth contains a truth – for why indeed should a hungry child see the family's precious food given away to a priest, in the name of an archaic tradition?

Abbé Alberto Fortis
From *Travels in Dalmatia (1778)*

To his excellency J Morosini, Noble Venetian,

You have, no doubt, often heard the Morlacchi described as a race of men, fierce, unreasonable, void of humanity, and capable of any crime. The inhabitants of the sea coast of Dalmatia tell many frightful stories about the cruelty of those people, that, induced by the avidity of plunder, they often proceed to the most atrocious excesses of violence, by fire and sword. But these facts are either of ancient date, or if some have happened in later times, they ought rather, from the characters they bear, to be ascribed to the corruption of a few individuals, than to the bad disposition of the nation in general. It is but too true, that, after the late wars with the Turks, the Morlacchi, habituated to murder and plunder with impunity, gave some examples of cruelty and rapine: but what instance can be given of troops just returned from war, and dismissed from the exercise of arms, against the enemy of their sovereign, that have not peopled the woods and highways with thieves and assassins? I think it, however, a duty incumbent on me, to write what I personally saw relative to their customs, and inclinations, and thereby to form some apology for that nation, by which I was so well received, and treated with so much humanity. It is usual for travellers to magnify the dangers to which they have been exposed, and the hardships they have suffered in remote countries; but I am far from that kind of affectation, and you will see by the detail that I am going to give you, of the manners and customs of the Morlacchi, with how great security and ease I travelled amongst them.

Origins of the Morlacchi

The origin of the Morlacchi, who inhabit the pleasant valleys of Kotar, along the rivers Kerka, Cettina, Narenta and among the mountains of inland Dalmatia, is involved in the darkness of barbarous ages, together with that of many other nations, resembling them so much in customs and language, that they may be taken to be one people, dispersed in the vast tracts from the coasts of our sea to the frozen ocean. The emigrations of the various tribes of Slavi, who, under the names of Scythians, Geti, Gaths, Huns, Slavini, Croats, Avari and Vandals, inundated the Roman provinces, and particularly the Ilyrian, during the decline of the empire, must have strangely perplexed the genealogies of the nations which inhabited it, and which, perhaps, removed thither in the same manner at more remote periods of time.

The Morlacchi generally call themselves, in their own idiom, *Vlassi*, a national term, of which, as far as I have been hitherto able to discover, no vestige is found in the records of Dalmatia before the thirteenth century: it signifies men of authority, or powerful. The denomination of *Moro-Vlassi*, and corruptly Morlacchi, as the inhabitants of the towns call them, might perhaps point out their original to us; that by great journeys, they came from the coasts of the Black Sea to invade these distant kingdoms. I think it not unlikely (although I undertake not strenuously to defend my conjecture) that the denomination of *Moro-Vlassi* signified, at first, the powerful, or conquerors that came from the sea, which is called *Moor* in all dialects of the Slavonian language.

The inhabitants of the maritime towns, true descendants of the Roman Colonies, are no friends to the Morlacchi, who, in return, look upon them, as well as inhabitants of the islands, with the greatest contempt: which reciprocal dislike, no doubt, proceeds, in part, from ancient discord between the two races. A Morlack bows indeed, before a gentleman of the city, or an advocate, of whom he stands in need, but loves them not; and treats all others, of whom he is independent, with the name of *Bodolo*, which, according to his meaning, is an injurious term. This puts me in mind of the Morlack soldier, who is still remembered in the hospital of Padua where he died. The priest appointed to assist him in his last moments, not knowing the force of the word, begun his exhortation, with 'Courage, Signor *Bodolo*!' 'Friar', interrupted the dying man, 'do not call me *Bodolo*, or you will make me damn myself'.

The great difference in dialect, dress, disposition, and customs, between the maritime and transalpine inhabitants of Dalmatia, seems clearly to prove, that they sprung not from the same origin. There is also a remarkable diversity amongst the Morlacchi themselves, in several districts; derived, perhaps, from the different countries from whence they came. For the inhabitants of Kotar are generally fair, with blue eyes, a broad face and flat nose and those of the plains of Seign and Knin, resemble them much;

but those of Duare, and Vergoraz, have dark coloured hair, a long face, tawny colour, and tall stature. The qualities of their mind are also as different as those of the body; for the Morlacchi of Kotar are generally mild, respectful and tractable; while those of Vergoraz are surly, proud, bold, and enterprising. They also have a very strong inclination to theft; owing, in part, to their situation among inaccessible and barren mountains, where they are often exposed to want, but are sure of impunity; and, perhaps, the ancient blood of the Varali, Ardiei, and Autariati, who were confined to those mountains by the Romans, still runs in their veins. For the most part their robberies fall on the Turks; though, in cases of necessity, they are said to use the same freedom with the Christians. Among the artful and bold strokes of knavery, which they tell of one of these Vergorazani, the following is characteristic. The rogue was at a fair, and a countryman having bought a copper kettle, laid it down, together with his bundle, just by his side; the Vergorazan, who stood hard by, took up the kettle, while the peasant was talking to an acquaintance, and set it on his head, without stirring from his place; the other, having finished his conference, turned about to take up his things, but the kettle was gone, asking him, who had it on his head, if he had not seen somebody carry it off, he was answered; 'Truly, Friend, I was not minding these things, but if you had put your kettle on your head, as you see I did, you would not have lost it'.

On the moral and domestick Virtues of the Morlacchi

The morals of the Morlack are generally very different from ours. The sincerity, truth, and honesty, of these poor people, not only in contracts, but in all the ordinary actions of their life, would be called simplicity and weakness among us. It is true that the Italians, who trade in Dalmatia, and the littoral inhabitants themselves, have but too often taken advantage of this integrity; and hence the Morlacchi are become much more diffident, than they were in former times; insomuch, that the want of probity, which they have so often experienced, dealing with Italians, is passed into a proverb among them, and the words *passia-viro*, and *Lanzmanzka-viro*, that is, the faith of a dog, and the faith of an Italian, are used to express the same reproachful meaning. The prepossession against us might prove incommodious to an unknown traveller, and yet it seldom happens. For the Morlack, naturally hospitable and generous, opens his poor cottage to the stranger, and serves him to the utmost of his power, without demanding, nay, often obstinately refusing, the least recompense; and I have more than once got a dinner from one of those men, who knew nothing about me, had never seen me, and could not expect to see me again.

I shall never forget the cordial reception and treatment given me by Pervan Vajvod, of Coccorich; to whom I had nothing else to recommend me but my being in friendship with a family who were also his friends. He lent his horses, and an escort to meet me on the road; and, during the few days which I spent in that neighbourhood, loaded me with all the luxury of national hospitality. He sent his own son, and several of his people, to escort me as far as the plains of Narenta, a good day's journey from his house, and furnished me with provisions in abundance; and all this was done without my being allowed to spend a single penny. On my departure from that hospitable mansion, he and all his family came out and followed me with their eyes, till I was out of sight; which affectionate manner of taking leave raised a kind of agitation in my mind, which I have never felt before, and can scarcely hope to feel again.

The Morlacchi are extremely sensible of mild treatment, and, when they meet with it, are ready to perform every possible service, and to become cordial friends. Their hospitality is equally conspicuous among the poor as among the more opulent. The rich prepares a roasted lamb, or sheep; and the poor, with equal cordiality, gives his turkey, milk, honey, or whatever else he has. Nor is their generosity confined to strangers, but generally extends itself to all who are in want.

When a Morlack is on a journey, and comes to lodge at a friend's house, the eldest daughter of the family, or the new married bride, if there happens to be one, receives, and kisses him when he alights from his horse, or at the door of the house. But a foreigner is rarely favoured with these female civilities; on the contrary, the women, if they are young, hide themselves, and keep out of his way. Perhaps more than one violation of the laws of hospitality has made them thus reserved to strangers; or perhaps the jealous customs of the neighbouring Turks have spread among the Morlacchi.

While there is anything to eat in the houses of those villagers, the poor of the neighbourhood are welcome to partake of it; and hence it is, that no Morlack ever humbles himself to ask alms of a passenger; at least, I never met one example of it. I indeed, have often been forced to ask something from poor shepherds, but I always found them liberal; and many times, in travelling through the fields in the heat of summer, I have met poor reapers, who, of their own accord, presented me with their flasks to drink, and offered me a part of their rustick provisions, with an affecting cordiality.

The Morlacchi, in general, have little notion of domestick economy, and readily consume in a week, as much as would be sufficient for several months, whenever any occasion of merriment presents itself. A marriage, a holiday of the Saint, protector of the family, the arrival of relations or friends, or any other joyful incident, consumes, of course, all that there is to eat and to drink in the house. Yet the Morlack is a great economist in the use of his wearing apparel; for, rather than spoil his new cape, he takes it off, let it rain ever so hard, and goes bareheaded in the storm. In the same manner he treats his shoes, if the road is dirty, and they are not very old. Nothing but an absolute impossibility hinders a Morlack from being punctual; and if he cannot repay the money he borrowed, at the appointed time, he carries a small present to his creditor, and requests a longer term. Thus it happens sometimes, that, from term to term, and present to present, he pays double what he owed, without reflecting on it.

Dinko Simunovic
From *Yugoslav Short Stories (1966)*

The Coward

So beautiful is this shade and so rich the scent of walnut leaves that I've almost fallen asleep. But as you've asked me, I'll tell you the whole story of my strange coming to this ancient monastery. Look at the bridge, with the water rustling below – but I cannot see it glittering in the sun: it was over this bridge that Abbot Tanasije brought me in his lap, and ever since I've served my people to the glory of God.

I'll relate to you everything I can call to mind of how I came here, so that you will not believe young monks when they make conjectures about me and tell lies. The other day that old peacock and wiseacre Tanasije told you that they called me 'the Coward' but he did not say why.

Where I come from every child, before it can walk, gets a nickname: chance gives a nice one to some, an ugly one to others, as it did to me. It is true that I was a timid boy, but I'll tell you what happened so that you will know what life was like in the old days. But I do not mean to justify myself or boast of courage and knowledge – let them call me what they like. I do not know how to write, and there is no reason why I should, but the late Abbot Tanasije, now blessed in God's peace, taught me to repeat the church book and the liturgy, and the Metropolitan received my vows as he did theirs.

I was only a miller's son, my father a Turkish serf, but I want the newly-fledged Solomons to know that I have also seen and heard something in my long lifetime. They don't believe anything which is not written down in that schoolboy history of theirs, and they laugh even at the old exploits because they've never seen what I have.

I may be over ninety, and I've been blind for more than ten years now, but my mind is clear and I do not want to blemish my soul by lying on the eve of my death. I only fear I won't be able to relate everything minutely and clearly as it happened, but I hope for help from Christ who can bring light even into the darkness of my childhood.

I've told this to them as well, these young monks of ours, but they don't believe it, saying this is just how the story has it, and that this has happened to me only in my imagination! But is it possible that those events have wormed their way into my memory just by themselves, considering I remember many things as if they happened last year, though some others seem like dreams? This is not surprising, I was so small then, and now I am over ninety, and it is ten years that I have seen neither God's sun nor human face.

I was not like my father or my elder brother Spasoje, for they were never afraid of anything, whereas I suffered great fear even when sleeping. As soon as I dropped off, terrible snakes, dragons and vampires used to appear before my eyes, ready to devour me!

So I turned timid in my earliest childhood, when I was two and a half or three years old. I don't remember clearly but I've been told how I disappeared in a strange way. I only remember making a house of flat stones and splinters in the meadow, when all at once I felt a violent wind and a roaring noise. Something hit my eyes, gripped me by the back, and lifted me up in the air. I don't know what followed, but they told me that shepherds found me on the same day far away, high up, in the old castle, half alive. Look here and you'll still see scars and pits on my arms and face!

I cannot say what it was – for some said that I had come among the fairies dancing in a ring and that the fairies lifted me up in the air, and others claimed that it was an imperial eagle, for there were many of them around the castle. I only know that from the day when I disappeared my mother fell seriously ill. Whether it was from grief and fear, or because my father beat her violently for not having taken better care of me, I cannot, in all honesty, say. Be that as it may, she fell ill and a year later she died.

On another occasion (I was a little bigger then) I was sent to the wood to find the goat which had been left behind. When I came there – what should I see: the goat had climbed up a steep, high crag, shaped like someone's hip. I tried to tempt her down again and again, but she wouldn't come, so somehow I clambered up to her. The goat escaped down a steep precipice, and as I could not follow her, I was left on the crag.

After struggling for a long time, when it began to grow dark I noticed a small, round cave and decided to creep in there. I clambered into it with great difficulty, and the cave was wider inside. Yes – but what should I find in it?

As soon as I began to wriggle, I heard a humming and buzzing, and then it seemed that living fire was burning my face, my hands, and all of my body. However, I managed to pull myself out, and I moaned and howled in front of the cave all night long. At dawn my father came up and on a twisted rope I climbed down to the wood.

In fact, there was a swarm of wild bees in the cave, but as I did not know this, I thought I had to do with the Devil's charms again.

So, from the day when something carried me up to the castle, I became a timid boy.

I was afraid even of my dead mother, and all the time while she lay stiff in the mill, I howled like a wolf, not with grief but with fear, and so terribly that my father thrashed me with a whip until I stopped.

At that time people already called me Coward; my father and Spasoje first, and then everybody else. I was afraid because I was weak, but this ugly name has remained with me to the present day.

It is not surprising, my son, that fear had crept into my bones, for our master, Mehmed-Bey, was a huge man. He had enormous moustaches, a dishevelled beard, bristling eyebrows, the look of a lynx in his eyes. When he suddenly appeared and shouted: 'Where's your father, little one?', the whole mill would shake. We were his serfs, and my elder brother Spasoje was his shepherd.

I usually began to howl as soon as he opened his mouth, and he would throw me a honey cake, adding in a lower voice:

'Here's something for you, Coward, just stop that braying!'
And again I tell you it was my fault, because my father and Spasoje
bowed to the master, but they were not afraid of him. They spoke
sharply as he spoke to them, all the time looking straight into his
eyes. Whereas I wrapped my head up into whatever was at hand,
just so as not to look at him, and my heart pounded in my breast.

In the long nights wolves used to howl round the mill and more
than once they pawed in front of the door while the mountains
were breaking up in the storm. Father was glad when Spasoje
drove the wolves away with a flaming brand from the fire or with
the shots of his rifle, and they mocked me for being afraid even of
wolves. Could I help it? I thought then that they were going to tear
us to pieces.

About this time the outlaws appeared. There are no more of
them now, and Father Tanasije thinks that there never were any, as
there are no wolves now.

In those days the outlaws often fought the Turks not far away
from our mill, and then rifles thundered and echoed at the bottom
of the gorge; I could clearly hear moans and curses even with the
tarpaulin coat wrapped around my head.

Just above the troughs running to the mill, there was a lake, and
huge rocks overhung the lake on all sides – we could not see the
end of it, so that terrible echoes were heard in the mill. Every shot
sounded as if a hundred shots were fired in close succession, and a
moan of a wounded outlaw or Turk, as if ten angry throats were
snarling.

Numb with fear, afraid even of silence, I used to prick up my
ears, trembling and waiting for what would follow that wily peace.

So we lived now in unrest, now in peace, and days flowed by
one another like the water: from below the rock into the lake, from
the lake down the cascades to our mill, and then below the bridge
– and where it flowed after that I myself could not tell. Imperial
eagles soared above the lake and disappeared towards the Castle,
while rock doves, rooks and other birds fluttered their wings and
hid in the chinks of the rock, from day to day always the same.

But one evening a storm broke out, so thick it seemed that we were floating in a cloud of snow.

My father sat by the fire in gloom. From time to time he went out to listen, coming back quickly and shaking the snow off his tarpaulin overcoat. A little further away Spasoje was turning a ram on the spit, and above the fire a kettle was boiling, full of dried meat. They were not saying anything to each other, let alone saying anything to me, so that I had a vague sense that something was going to happen. I was frightened of the heavy waiting and silence, but I did not dare ask them anything.

We sat like that for a long time, and I had almost dozed off, when there was a sly whistling from far away, and my father grasped the flaming brand and waved it in front of the door of the mill. I huddled up, beginning to expect something.

Water was thundering under me, and through the open door the snow was blowing in as far as the fireplace. I was almost frozen stiff, but I did not want to wrap myself up, so that I could see and hear better what was going on.

In that moment I heard heavy steps in front of the mill, and someone laughed so terribly that I felt the bed shake under me. I jumped and began to shriek, but Spasoje flared up and struck me with the brand on my bare foot, and the fear disappeared at once.

'That's a colt snorting, Coward!' he told me, and I stared at the open door in order to see the colt. I waited and waited, but in vain – because it was led past the door into the stable: I could just see the dim outlines of something black against the snow. Someone was fidgeting and fumbling on the doorstep, and then they entered and laid something down by the fireside – a stretcher!

A large, bloody man lay on it, bespattered with snow and greenish with pain and ice. The stretcher was followed by my father and some other men – judging by their figures, clothes, and arms, I thought they were outlaws.

They sat up the man who was lying on the stretcher, and undressed him down to the waist, and I noticed a terrible wound on his lean ribs. They bandaged it quickly with what they had at hand, and then the oldest of them laughed and said:

'Do you call that a wound – it won't hold even a pound of gunpowder!'

The others laughed, even the wounded man himself, and they started to drink, but I began to cry bitterly, and could not be stopped until they poured some plum-brandy down my throat. I was pacified then and dozed off without waiting for dinner.

However, I could hear their conversation from time to time. They talked about a Turk they had killed and dragged to the border in order to cover up their tracks. They counted the money, and then I heard one of them say to my father:

'The colt, the flintlock, and the dagger are yours!'

'But what will the Bey say when he sees them?' said my father.

'Why should he see them? Hide the flintlock and the dagger, and if he happens to see the colt, tell him you found it by the Crazy Brook: and if the owner turns up, you'll give it back. As to the rest we are leaving with you, take good care of it and hold your tongue!'

Then they were silent and I listened to the crunching of meat under their sharp teeth and to the gurgling sound as they drank from their flat bottles.

I was hungry and I began to wriggle and cough, until my father guessed my meaning and flung me a large slice of meat and a lump of unleavened bread. By that time I was not afraid of anything anymore and, quietly chewing, I listened to their conversation.

One of the outlaws, having gnawed the meat off a blade, began to stare into the fire through the bone and then, having carefully examined it, he leaned towards the flame and said:

'Brothers, this is not a good sign: here's a "man's grave" on the blade!'

'And whose ram was this?' asked another outlaw.

'I don't know,' replied my father, 'but Micun brought it yesterday.'

'They looked towards where Micun was lying by the stretcher, and the oldest of them leaned towards him: he raised his head and his arms in turn, and then, in the total silence, he said:

'Brothers, Micun has died!'

They all crossed themselves without saying a word, bowed, and began in turn to kiss the dead.

'What now? Now the Turks will easily find out everything!' My father was the first to remember this.

'What about tying a stone round his neck and throwing him into the lake?' asked the youngest.

'God strike you dumb!' cried the chief. 'If we all perish, we must take him back this night to his people. We must not betray him – living or dead. We are sworn to that!'

I went numb and did not utter a sound, but when they began to tie the dead man to the stretcher again, and when his head, with its bloody mouth, rolled over to my side, I began to wail with fear.

'What's the matter with the little one... is there something ailing him?' shouted one of them, and my brother, ashamed, struck me and again poured plum-brandy down my throat.

Meanwhile they took the dead man out and I fell asleep, and on the next day I did not dare to mention that anything had happened.

A day later Spasoje took me to see the colt. Spasoje himself was a handsome, sturdy lad, but the colt was even more handsome: shining and supple, and as fast as a swallow. My brother wanted to take him for a ride, but father said that it should not be taken out but kept inside, so it had to be as father said.

But one day, when father was not in the mill, Spasoje took the flintlock, put the dagger at his waist and mounted the colt!

Spasoje rode away with his eyes merry and shining, and he came back on foot, his eyes dim and bloody! Our Bey had met him and:

'This is not for a giaour!' he shouted. 'Sell me the colt and the arms!'

My brother would not hear of it, so the Bey grasped him by the neck! He took both the horse and the arms and then said:

'The mill is yours now. I will give you a mill for a horse!'

He liked the black horse so much! But Spasoje also liked the horse better than the mill and he began to think up a revenge.

So time went by till spring, when he began to tend the Bey's sheep again. Before he left the mill, he held counsel with father, but I could not make out anything except that he was going to avenge himself.

As I said, there was a huge, high rock around the lake, with a fathomless cave below it, a cave fiercely boiling with water which filled the lake. A path was cut in the stone leading to this spring of underground water and, once every five or six days, about sunset, my father went along the path to the spring. He used to take me with him, and the first time I was very much surprised.

We sit and sit for a long time by the water, and father stares at it unblinkingly. I am afraid that something may be wrong with him, so I ask:

'It will be dark soon, what are we waiting here for?'

But this annoys him:

'God tie your tongue!' he shouts. 'We shall go on waiting and you'll see something, but what you see – you haven't seen, or I'll twist your neck like a sparrow's.'

We wait, wait, all the time looking at the spring boiling from the cave. All at once – something white begins to whirl in it, and father takes it with both his hands and pulls it out on to the path.

It was a large, slaughtered, second-year ram: although it had been rolling about in the water for a long time, there were spots of blood on its neck and elsewhere on the fleece. Father ordered me to take the ram by the front legs, while he took the hind ones, and so we started carrying it. But after a few paces the ram became so heavy that I dropped it and its head struck against the path. My hands were weak then, but in spite of that my father was angry. He did not strike me, but he said that I was good for nothing, in every way a coward. He flung the ram on his back, and raced, with me behind him, all the way to the mill.

So it went on – every few days the spring used to turn out a fat ram, on one occasion there were even two, so that meat was plentiful both in our house and in the houses of our cousins in the village.

You may be surprised at this, but I was also surprised then: I thought that the spring was charmed and was bearing rams! Later on, to my great grief, I came to know how it happened.

Far away over the high hill with the castle on it there is a field through which a big brook flows and then disappears into an abyss. This water comes out again below the mountain and it springs out at the bottom of the gorge where my father and I used to wait.

The whole plateau was called the Bey's field, and it was there that Spasoje tended rams and ewes, and there were as many of them as there are stars in heaven. His job was not difficult, because there was no fear of the sheep straying on to someone else's land.

To take vengeance on the Bey and to help father, Spasoje would kill one of the best rams and put it down the abyss at the bottom of the field, so that water rolled the ram down to the spring, throwing it out on the appointed day. This is how it was!

Sometimes my brother came to the mill, and father used to reproach him, not because he was sending rams by the underground brook but for another reason.

Our Bey had a daughter called Ajka, beautiful as the sun, hardly much more than a child: her face, people said, still uncovered. Probably there was no need to cover it because their tower rose far and high in the mountain where nobody came except a woman, a serf, or an occasional bey or aga on urgent business.

Well, Spasoje began to take milk and cream to the tower at the times when the Bey was absent and he also fidgeted around by night. Whether it was because he fell in love with Ajka, or to take vengeance on the Bey – I have not been able to tell to this day.

This is why father was angry with Spasoje, telling him that he would lose his head foolishly, but it did not help. Perhaps he was also glad of it in secret, but he only wanted Spasoje to take better care of himself.

I was already in my seventh year and father began to take me to church, far away: all the way east through the valley, then over a hill, it was a good two hours' walk.

Even such occasions never went by without people being injured and killed, and I always wondered in the foolishness of my mind: why do they fight, why do they hate and kill each other? I did not understand; but I soon began to understand, on the feast-days of great patron saints of a village or family, when we used to gather under the elms behind the church.

Sentries were set to watch lest a stranger should come and hear our old men taking counsel and reminding the people of old native tsars and heroes. I thought the Turks hated us because of our faith, but faith, my son, did not have much to do with it.

At the other end, at the bottom of the hill, there was a Catholic, Roman church, but the Turks did not send their spies in that direction and did not interfere with those going to church there. They knew that their priest did not talk to people of valour and freedom, but of the Holy Trinity and of some saints with strange names, and neither the Turks nor the Latins in the littoral minded that. He taught, further, that every government was of God and that they should be as meek as lambs, and both the Turks and the Latins appreciated this instruction.

Whereas our monk and our aged men were always saying to us: if revenge does not wipe out your taint, you'll never become a saint! This was what my brother kept telling me every day, ever since the Bey took his black horse, although he had given him a mill just for the horse.

Well, it was because of this that there were wounds and bleeding heads, not because of matters of faith, so that we Serbians were persecuted both by the Turks and by the Latins more fiercely than anybody else. They wanted to uproot us, because they knew they could not make either Turks or Latins of us, for our churches and our monasteries belonged not only to God but also to the people.

But I could not do anything else at the time: I was afraid both of the Turks and of the outlaws, and therefore my father kept telling me that I was not his son, but that a cuckoo had laid me in the Serbian nest.

It is easy now, but in those days our Turks were not what they are today. There is no wounding or slaughtering now, but we still have our misfortune with us. Father Tanasije is also our misfortune – he mocks our ancient heritage!

...All sorts of things were happening then, my son, many strange things, some of which I've never come to understand.

One morning, in the spring, at the break of day, father ordered me to go to the field where Spasoje tended the sheep, and to tell him:

'On Holy Sunday two!'

To tell him that and to come back at once.

I had already been there twice (Spasoje took me with him) so I followed a short cut, meaning to climb the gorge into the mountain. The gorge was near the Bey's tower, but I knew that I was so small that neither the Turks nor the outlaws would do me any harm, so I went along singing merrily.

I was going up the mountain, up and up, but when I had climbed high, fog began to press down so that you could not see clearly three paces in front of you. This was not enough to make me give up, so I went on, climbing, trusting to my luck.

In the fog the field looked like a lake, bushes like haystacks, what was near seemed distant, what was distant seemed near... I walked for a long time off the track, but I knew that all I had to do was to keep right at the forked beech and I couldn't miss my way.

As I climbed higher the fog thinned out and then there was no more of it. But over there round the castle, at the bottom of the Old Woman's Hip, above the Black Spring, some white monsters were bending, slowly waving – now their arms, now their legs, now covering the lonely tops of the mountain with their white hair. And they were changing – you couldn't see how or when.

Fog it was not, for the fog was left behind me, and fog is never so white. Nor was it a cloud, for the sky was blue and the sun was shining.

My mouth opened in wonder and I was afraid that I had come to a different world where there were no living creatures: the silence was so deep that there was not a rustle of a bird or a lizard moving. There was a small rise in front of me, and when I climbed it I could see a small valley below, drowned in more fog. I began to descend the slope, going into the gloom, when all at once – I heard muffled laughter and I was frightened as I had never been in my lifetime.

I stared into the fog – what should I see – would you believe me? My brother Spasoje and a fairy snowballing each other.

'Where was the snow from?' thought I. There hadn't been any that winter, and now Spasoje was standing on one snowdrift and the fairy on another, they were snowballing each other through the fog and laughing. The fairy was a beauty – as fairies are: tall, slim, and from top to toe she was wrapped in a veil whiter than the snow under her feet, so that I could swear that she had grown out of the snow. I could not see her properly, for she was in fog and bending down every now and then and yet I saw her hair was golden, her teeth like pearls, and her laughter tinkled like silver.

But when she noticed me, she disappeared into the fog – without a trace or a sound; I called Spasoje, but, taking long strides, he was also lost in the fog.

What was I to do, where to go by God! I followed them and took the path leading by the Bey's tower; then along the ravine between the heads I came to the bare slope descending into the field. It was only with great difficulty that I reached my destination about midday and found Spasoje with the sheep: sitting quietly by the brook and piping.

'Was that you?' I asked him.

'Where? What?' he was bewildered.

'You've been snowballing with the fairy in the mountain: I saw you.'

And he swore that he had been there from the early morning without moving an inch since he drove the sheep out of their pens.

I shut up – what could I say to him? Probably he was afraid because of the fairy – she would shoot him with an arrow if he were to tell. But so far as he was concerned there was not to be a happy ending anyway, as you'll soon hear.

'Father sends you a message – so and so,' I said to him.

'I see: on Holy Sunday two!' he repeated.

He saw me off a little of the way, gave me a cheese, and went back to his sheep again.

That was on Friday and when evening approached on Sunday father called me to come with him to the spring. I remembered what the message was: 'On Holy Sunday two!' We were expecting our relatives from the village, so father had sent a message to Spasoje about rams.

We sat by the spring staring into the water. It was fairly early still, but I did not see well because clouds were gathering from the west: it was thundering at first and then it began to drizzle.

It thunders and pours, it pours and it thunders; it is getting darker and darker and we are staring more and more intently into the underground spring, but there is nothing to be seen. Rock doves and rooks flutter above our heads trying to find shelter in the chinks of the cracked rock, but they are afraid and continue fluttering above us. Farther away and higher up imperial eagles are cruising, but we do not hear the beat of their wings, because the noise of roaring and boiling water under our feet is louder.

After a while the rain and wind stopped, but night had also set in so that the spring had become black and everything else gloomy. Before long we could not see anything and father decided to go to the mill to fetch a light.

But he waited a little, spat into the water, and began to reproach Spasoje wrathfully, saying that he was a coward like myself, and then he went to fetch kindling.

I had to stay to keep an eye on the spring, although I was afraid – alone in such darkness and desolation.

Before he went, father put a stake into the mouth of the spring so that the rams should be caught and not go down into the lake. But as soon as he left, it became a little lighter and I noticed that the stake had disappeared. Therefore I pricked up my ears and opened my eyes wide, so that the water would not carry the rams into the lake and I prepared to get hold of them and so please father.

He must have been long about it, looking for kindling wood in the mill, when suddenly there was a splash, and the mouth of the spring began to gurgle in a different, hoarse pitch – as if it were being drowned. I looked and looked to see if the white rams would appear, but instead of a whiteness I noticed something black. I thought they were black rams and grasped hard so that the strong current would not take them into the lake. I held fast, but the water spurted fiercely, as cold as frost, so that my little hands went numb. I would not have dared let go, even if both my arms had broken, for I well knew what I would be in for.

Meanwhile father turned up with kindling wood, but still we could not see what the black thing was, because the water was rolling it this way and that and the kindling wood was only hissing and smoking, giving very little flame. Father passed it to me, and he himself got hold of the black thing rolling by the underground stream into the spring. It was big and heavy, and it was only when he exerted all his strength for the third time that he pulled it out on to the path.

I put the kindling wood to it... and what should I see... Christ, my God!... my brother Spasoje without his head! We recognized him by his clothes and a big scar above the fist. This was where a wolf had bitten him when he was taking it out of a trap alive.

It was terrible to see the deflated, bleeding neck without the young, dark head of Spasoje! But the neck was not torn, the head must have been cut off, not by a dagger, but by a real Damascus sword, and the Bey's hand must have been like thunder!

You think I was afraid? A man, and even a child, is afraid of small misfortunes, but in the great ones he only goes numb.

And father only waved his hands twice above him, and then leaned down, flung the headless Spasoje over his shoulder, and took him to the mill.

As soon as he had laid him down on the bed and covered him with a cloth, he became thoughtful and wanted to cross the arms. But he seemed to remember that the body had no head, so he did not cross them, but he bit his own arm so strongly that blood ran from under his own sleeve. And he left the mill without looking at me, without telling me where or why.

I remained sitting by the headless Spasoje that night and all the next day waiting for father, but father never came back.

It was only on the second day, when night was approaching, that our cousins and aunts came and wanted to take me with them. But I did not go; I sat on, thinking, by the fire until they were ready with Spasoje and carried him away.

Late in the evening Aunt Vasilija and Aunt Stana came again and began to tell me what had happened, what I was vaguely guessing myself.

The Bey came to know that Spasoje was making approaches to Ajka, went to look for him in the field, and found him at the moment when he had just killed the rams and was preparing to send them by the underground water down to the mill. He flared up, cut off his head with his sword, and threw the trunk into the abyss so that it should come to us in the evening instead of the rams.

But they also told me what I did not know.

My father, wishing to take vengeance for Spasoje, set off for the Bey's tower and the Bey, having spotted father in the distance carrying arms, guessed why he was coming and shot him with his flintlock.

I didn't say a word, I only lay down by the fireside and pretended to sleep. My aunts said something else in muffled voices and keened, and I was quiet until they were asleep. At dawn they were still sleeping and I began to make noiseless preparations for what I had worked out in my mind during the night.

And what could I work out, a foolish child, what else but what I saw my father had done? I took an old, short, embellished gun, flung it over my shoulder, and quietly sneaked out of the mill. I wanted to shoot the Bey or Ajka or any other of their people from an ambush, to avenge Spasoje and father.

I walked on and on, along the same way I took on the day when the fairy and Spasoje were snowballing each other, and suddenly met Abbot Tanasije riding on horseback. He was surprised and cried out from far away:

'Where are you heading for, brave knight, with that gun – bigger than yourself? Where are you going my foolish child?'

I told him that I'd decided to kill the Bey or one of his people, and he laughed and took away my beautiful gun, which was muddy as I was dragging it behind me.

He blew into the barrel, and then grinned sadly and said:

'Your gun is empty, my Coward! You leave vengeance to others and come with me,'

I drooped with shame, and he took me with one arm and raised me up to his saddle, tossing my beautiful, empty gun across his shoulder.

I felt so fine in his lap that I wept quietly and stroked his bony hand as I sobbed. And he pressed me to himself with that hand, saying:

'Don't cry, my child, I will bring you up and you'll be a monk in our ancient monastery.'

After the long night's watching, lulled by his stroking, I fell asleep and woke up only when something thundered under the horse's hoofs. This was the bridge which you can see down there, and I cannot.

Well, thank God, I've seen much in my lifetime. Not only am I blind now, I should like to go deaf as well, just not to hear what some people say nowadays.

However, the old days were better than these: we crushed force by force, and all you can do now is to hold your tongue and suffer, even if they spit into your grey beard!

I know how to hold my tongue and bear it when they call me a coward, but whenever I administer confession to one of my Christian brothers, I remind him handsomely of his need to love his other brothers in Christ, but I end by telling him not to forget the old saying of our grandfathers which saved and kept us to the present day: 'if revenge does not wipe out your taint, you'll never become a saint,' they said!

Go on my son, and if the young monks ask you what I've been talking about for so long, tell them that the new wisdom cannot match the old.

Do not listen to the lies of their schoolboy histories, but listen and ponder what our gusle* is saying.

I hear the walnut leaves rustling and smelling always the same forever and ever. Can they rustle or smell differently?

So it is with the people.

Amen, my son, go in God's peace, but don't allow every rascal to have his way with you!

Nadia Curija-Prodanovic
From *Yugoslav Folk-Tales (1957)*

How the Peasants Bought Wisdom

The peasants in a certain little village by the sea found life rather hard, and tried to discover why it should be so. The head of the village and the elder men sat talking about it one day, and one of them said: 'The reason for this state of things must be in our lack

---

* A musical instrument played in the Balkans, having a round concave body, parchment soundboard, and one or two horsehair strings. The instrument was usually played by blind men at fairs and church gatherings and the playing was accompanied by a recital of an epic poem glorifying an event from national history. So the playing of the instrument has come to stand for a sense of deep attachment to the cause of national tradition: primarily courage in fighting the invader.

of wise men. Look, in all the other villages there is at least one wise man among the peasants, but we haven't a single one.'

They all agreed that this might be the reason for their wretchedness, and started thinking what to do about it. At last the man who was considered to have the best brains among them spoke: 'I think I know what we should do, brothers. Let's collect fifty ducats among us, and send three of our men to Venice to buy wisdom; for I've always heard that Venetians are the wisest people in the world and that they so brim over with wisdom that they have a surplus to sell to other people. Of course this rare commodity will be very dear.'

All the peasants thought this a very good plan and acted accordingly; and within three days the golden ducats were collected and the three men dispatched to Venice to bring wisdom to their little village.

The three arrived in Venice safely, and started at once to look for wisdom and to inquire about its price. They soon came across a cunning man who thought this too good a chance to be missed.

'I can't sell you a stone of wisdom for the amount of money you've brought,' he said, 'but I'll let you have a quarter.'

The peasants agreed to the bargain, happy to have found the right man so soon. The Venetian, however, caught a mouse, shut it in a little box, wrapped the box tightly, and said to his customers:

'Here is wisdom for you. You'd better hurry home with it, but don't open the box before you reach your village.'

The happy villagers returned on board their boat and started on their way home. As they drew near, one of them said: 'Listen, brothers; I don't think it right to share this wisdom in equal parts with the whole village. We've taken more trouble over it than all the others together, and I believe we're entitled to have one half of it among the three of us. Let the village have the other half.'

His two friends nodded approvingly, and he took the box and unwrapped it. The moment he opened it the mouse escaped – as any mouse would do. It hid somewhere in the hull, and the three peasants were left to moan and lament the loss of their dearly purchased wisdom. However, when their hunt proved unsuccessful and when their lamenting came to an end, one of them was struck by a bright idea.

'Listen, brothers! There's really nothing to worry about, for our wisdom is still on board this ship – it hasn't run away.'

Soon afterwards they reached their own shore. The whole village was at the little harbour to welcome them, waving bright handkerchiefs and cheering. But when the elder peasants wanted to look at wisdom, the three men confessed, though somewhat reluctantly, to having let it go loose. Their friends on the shore were grieved for a while, but, as they all agreed that wisdom must still be hiding in the boat, they decided to pull the boat ashore and keep watch over it day and night. So everyday from that time on a man would stand sentinel by the boat; and the peasants, whenever there was a serious matter to be solved, or a wise letter to be written, would come into the boat, sit there for a while to absorb as much wisdom as possible, then do their task with confidence.

Anthony Rhodes
From *Where the Turk Trod: A Journey to Sarajevo with a Slavonic Mussulman (1956)*

In Homer no one thought it impolite to be asked whether he were a pirate or not. *The Odyssey* is full of 'good' pirates, the Robin Hoods of the seas. And so it was in the town of Sinj, my first port of call, where I had the letter of introduction. Sinj is the most perfect town for pirates in the whole history of buccaneering. Here, the Uskoki pirates preyed on the Turks in the sixteenth century, countenanced and protected by the local population who, it was whispered, frequently shared in their spoils. (For the Yugoslav, owing to his endless series of foreign overlords, has often expressed his genius best, today as yesterday, in activities outside the law). 'It was a frequent sight,' said an inhabitant proudly, when I asked about these pirate ancestors, 'to see a hundred Uskoki attacking a thousand Turks. And putting them all to flight.'

Operating from behind the labyrinth of complicated channels which protect the town, the Uskoki caused havoc not only to the Turks, their theoretical enemy, but also to the Venetians, their theoretical ally. Tradition says they even became adept at raising the *Bora* wind at will, that by simply lighting a fire in a certain cavern, they could raise an off-shore gale in which no vessel could live. So destructive did they quickly become, to friend and foe alike, that friend and foe, Venetian and Turk, at last came together and by a most unnatural crusade, obliterated them entirely. But it took nearly a hundred years to do so, and by then the Uskoki had enriched themselves with most of the argosies of the Adriatic. The attraction of Sinj to pirates is immediately apparent as the ship threads the thirty miles of intricate channels which protect it. It consists today of no more than a few hundred houses nestling around a little wooded hill, on top of which stands a church, whose bright green cupolas and gilded pinnacles were resplendent in the sunshine.

My letter of introduction from *Putnik* [the Yugoslav travel agency] was addressed to the Archimandrite Iraeneus Shengli, a pro-vicar of the Bishop in Sinj, who had written the book about the outgoing Turks. He was also, I had discovered, a descendant of the famous Uskoki pirate, Shengli, 'the Hammer of the Turk,' a legendary figure, half-warrior, half-ascetic, who finally laid down his life in some bloody battle or other against the Turks in the sixteenth century. What, I thought, could be a finer start to my quest for the Turkish past?

Some sheep were grazing inside the walls of this ancient place; and one or two urchins squatting in the main street directed me to the house of the Archimandrite, where I entered a courtyard with a flight of marble steps leading high to the pillared gallery of a small *palazzo* in the Venetian style. Climbing vine cascaded about its decaying stone, and an ancient coat-of-arms hung over the door. I was admitted by a manservant, and taken into the presence of the Archimandrite, who was working in his library.

Archimandrite Shengli was a middle-sized man with a dark beard; he was dressed entirely in black. The custom too, of wearing their hair long, like a woman, adds much to the picturesque appearance of these Greek 'papas' (for the word Archimandrite simply means 'father' or leader of the flock). He spoke correct if somewhat old-fashioned English – corroborated by a number of English books, including several volumes of Chambers' *Universal Encyclopaedia* bound in apricot linen, which lined the shelves behind his desk. The luminous eyes, the nervous, delicately formed hands proclaimed the visionary; and he seemed a trifle disconcerted when I said I was interested in piracy, in particular his famous ancestor and his exploits against the Turks.

'But you are an Oxford man?' he said, tapping my letter of introduction.

I admitted I had been at a university, but added that piracy had, since my childhood, always exercised a spell over me.

'How old are you?'

'Thirty-seven.'

He nodded his head sadly. Feeling I had embarrassed him, I changed the conversation for the moment, and asked about the classical researches, Turkish and Grecian, I knew he was engaged upon. Whereupon, he took me to his desk and showed me a monograph he was writing on the Bogomil tomb inscriptions in Mostar, a town of which he had been civic curator for many years. There was something of the Victorian humanist in this man, I thought. And when I admired his antique researches, he replied, referring obliquely to my taste for piracy, 'Yes, it is only by the use of the classics that we can distinguish what is essential from what is showy and exciting. They act as a proper compass in the cross-currents of fashion.'

His old-fashioned English made me feel suddenly as if an essay by Matthew Arnold, or an excursus by Walter Pater, had marvellously sprung to life on these Illyrian shores. After this, we talked amiably of Turkish matters, of the tomb of Ackbar the Great in Scutari, of the advance and recession of Islam, of Issa Baïgambar (that is, in Turkish, Jesus the Prophet); and he seemed to approve of me more when he heard that I had a letter to the Head of the Moslem Church, the Reis-ul-Ulema in Sarajevo. But before leaving, I could not resist leading the conversation back to piracy again. Seizing a favourable opportunity when there was silence, I asked him point-blank what, in his opinion, constituted piracy.

He thought for a moment, spoke not a word, but turned and went to the shelf, where he took down one of the volumes of Chambers' *Universal Encyclopaedia*; he searched in it, and then pointed to a definition, which I read:

> *Piracy*: Taking a ship on the High Seas from the possession of those who are lawfully entitled to it, and carrying away goods, tackle or furniture under circumstances which would, on land, amount to robbery.

I thanked him for his information, and for the two books, one, his *Outgoing Turk*, and the other on his archaeological discoveries in Mostar, both of which he inscribed for me. I made no further assaults on his hospitality, apart from asking what chance I had in the neighbourhood of finding a Slavonic Mussulman, to accompany me on my journey inland to Sarajevo. In spite of his general surprise at my request, he kindly gave me the name of a man who lived some way up the coast, who kept horses, and had once worked for him.

Although I am not a violent man, it disappointed me somehow as I left, I cannot explain why, to think that this bearer of the mighty name of Shengli (a name to stand in history beside Robin Hood's), should only be interested today in unearthing in a rubbish-heap in Zara, a fragment of Menander – or learning, as

97

he stated in the preface of his Turkish book, that a fisherman looking for sponges off Cape Matapan had found entangled in his nets the turban of a Moslem sarcophagus.

The ancestors of this erudite Archimandrite must have been one of the fiercest races imaginable, a veritable 'Hammer of the Turk'. Their name Uskoki means 'fugitive' in one dialect of Croatian, and 'galloping' in another. Both meanings are appropriate, for they were fugitives from the Turks – and made fruitful forays by horse into Turkish territory in Bosnia and Herzegovina, at that fateful moment in the sixteenth century when the Osmans found the road to the Occident open again. They started as land-robbers, but on their main fortress, Kliss, falling to the Turks, they practised their craft, with even greater success, on the high seas. As my second morning in Sinj dawned fine and cloudless, I decided to walk up the coast to the village the Archimandrite had spoken of, to find my Slavonic Mussulman. He had said that this man, whose name was Riza Ibramović, lived near the ancient castle of Nechaj, a name which I discovered in my guidebook, means 'without care' in Serbo-Croat, an allusion apparently to its supposed impregnability. Certainly, if the landscape I crossed that morning had any part in its baptism, no name could have been more appropriate. Spare shrubs and wiry wind-bent trees struggled for a foothold on the barren slopes of the Karst country – a wilderness of rocks pasturing some scraggy goats, and one or two sheep whose fleece seemed to be of hair rather than wool. As in so many parts of this coast, these animals roaming unchecked inland, eat every seedling tree before it has time to grow. 'The green Illyrian hills' of the poet's fancy must be on some other part of the coast, for they are not here.

But one of the oddities of the Karst country, responsible for sudden occasional fits of vegetation, is the 'rock-born' river, which springs from the face of a cliff, to disappear for a mile or so underground again, and then re-emerge still further on. For the short period while it is in the open, the valley is rich with vegetation. Fertile fields flourish side by side with fig-trees and vines, and the red bloom of the pomegranate waves to and fro in the breeze. Then abruptly, the earth swallows the river up, and a waste of rock lies before one's eyes again. Here, not even a goat can find a living.

The castle of Nechaj stands in one of these fertile patches near a stream – a building of the rudest construction, possessing neither doors nor windows, and which one enters by a ladder through a sort of square opening in the floor. For many centuries it has been uninhabited and is now simply a rugged ruin, not even under the care of the Yugoslav National Trust. Impregnable indeed! The stream has in many places undermined and hollowed out the walls, and grass and moss grow inside in the crevices of what must once have been the dining-hall. Only at one point, in the corner, was there evidence of life. Rings in the walls, with rusty chains hanging from them, told of the time when it had been used as a prison – transporting one back suddenly to those heroic days when Begs, Kapetans, Waywodes, Serdars and Glavares fought one another without let or hindrance on this violent coast; when the Uskoki pirates nailed the turbans of Turkish prisoners to their heads, and the Turks, in return, tied the Uskoki naked to a tree, covered him with sticky sweetmeats, and left him to the insect world.

A footpath strewn with stones so hard and angular that the stoutest shoes were poor protection led to it, past a small cottage with smoke coming through a hole in the roof, surrounded by two cultivated fields taking advantage of the nearby stream. I asked a man working in the fields if he could tell me where Riza Ibramović lived. He turned on me the round features of the Slav, benevolent and yet somehow expressionless, and asked me politely to take a seat in front of the cottage while he fetched him.

I sat wondering what sort of man I should find, whether the Archimandrite's name would carry much weight with a Mussulman. At last, the blank-faced Slav returned, leading a man of indeterminate age, whose swarthy features and hooked nose certainly spoke of oriental origin, but who was dressed in depressingly Western costume. A fez or turban sits with dignity on a dusky brow, but a cloth cap looks ridiculous; and instead of the long plush coat or brilliantly embroidered waistcoat and baggy trousers of his race, he had an old tweed jacket and a frayed tie of some tartan design. A Slavonic Scot is a horrible thought!

'You are Riza Ibramović? I asked hesitantly, presenting the letter and speaking German – for the Archimandrite had told me that Ibramović had spent some years of captivity in Germany during the war. And my Serbo-Croat was poor.

He replied in a kind of dog-German interlarded with Serbo-Croat which I found barely comprehensible; and he almost shrieked the word, 'Englishman!' when he read the letter. 'Yes, I have some horses,' he said. 'I am about to sell them in Macarsca at a high price.'

I said that it would be a shame to do this. Would he not prefer to accompany me to Sarajevo, earning money on the way, and sell them there? He said if I would care to take a glass of wine with him at this table outside the cottage, he would explain exactly why Macarsca was so much better as a horse-market than Sarajevo, and we could go into the matter in detail. We accordingly sat down and, over a glass of red wine, entered into discussion.

Now as everyone knows, the Mussulman views financial transactions from a different standpoint than the Christian one. An old religious law forbids him from bargaining. But cunning, calculation, subtlety in commerce, there is nothing to stop this. For it is important to remember that Trade is recommended by the Prophet, who says that he who has money shall buy from him who has not. Your act is, in this sense, a form of benevolence. In all commercial dealings with Mussulmans, therefore, there is this religious basis which we can hardly recognize in our more abstract Christian faith. Commercial dealings we would consider reprehensible in moral or legal terms, become perfectly honest when considered in the light of Fortune's injustice, the blindness of Chance, the Fate of the poor and needy. So it is not surprising that the price varies according to the individual purchaser, the seller's feeling about him, and the way the negotiation runs. I mention this to explain why our negotiations were amicable, but protracted.

It appeared that Riza Ibramović had to go to Macarsca, a town some miles down the coast, on business, which might last a day, a week, a month – he could not say. After that he would be free to travel with me to any part of the globe, provided certain conditions were fulfilled. These were concerned with recompense in event of his failing to sell the horses in Sarajevo; with recompense to his family if, for some reason, he failed to return with recompense; and with recompense to himself, in event of certain imponderables which, he suggested, we might discuss further in a few days time, when, and if, we met in Macarsca, which was a beautiful town anyway.

I saw from all this that I had to do with a real Moslem and I agreed. As a sign of good faith I gave him a thousand dinars and said I would meet with him with his horses two days later in Macarsca. He said that if I was prepared to leave another thousand dinars to satisfy his family, he was sure they would put no difficulty in the way of his accompanying me. In spite of his appearance, I felt there was something honest about him, and I did so. Nor was I to regret it.

Before leaving, however, I became aware of his attitude towards the English, which was hardly encouraging. I asked him to tell me something of this castle of Nechaj, which I had just visited.

He turned and looked at it. 'That,' he said, pointing to the ruin, 'was the work of the Allies.'

'Which Allies?' I asked, wondering if he could possibly be referring to that famous but unnatural alliance by which Turk and Venetian came together to crush the Uskoki.

'*Your* allies,' he said, 'The English.'

'The English! What purpose,' I said, jumping mentally from 1544 to 1944, 'could we have had in destroying that place?'

'When the French were here.'

Such is the variegated history of this coast and its countless oppressors, that it took me several seconds to place this incident chronologically. The Illyrian republic of Napoleon, of course, when Nelson's fleet was bombarding Fiume.

'What will happen now?' he said listlessly. 'Will there be peace? You English know.'

For some reason, I have often noticed, people always think a foreigner better informed about war and peace and the international situation than they are themselves. I am the same myself. So I naturally answered with the greatest confidence, 'Of course there will be peace! Never fear!'

'Because if there isn't,' he said gloomily, 'we Yugoslavs will be in it again. Halfway between East and West.'

Later I was to become familiar with this man's almost Oriental fatalism. It was not surprising. Startling vicissitudes had marked his life. He had fought in both European wars, been wounded by the Austrians in the first, imprisoned and hanged imperfectly by the Italians in the second. He was later enrolled by the Germans for their Russian campaign, in which he got as far as Kharkov. He now cultivated this little plot of land, hoping those times would not return. He took me round the walls before I left, pointing to a large hole at one point which had been made, he insisted, by an English cannon-ball. The hole was encrusted with bracken and twigs which he pulled away, removing a bird's nest in the process; and I saw at the back what might well have been a spherical piece of iron dating from Nelson's day. I could not help looking at it reverently.

'The English.' He looked at me blankly. Such was the sense of depression this man induced that I left feeling I owed him some sort of apology – not for the recent indignities he had suffered, in which we English had clearly played no part – but for my ancestral countrymen who, like all the other foreigners, had harried his coast, jolly British tars no doubt, merrily pumping in shells to the tune of *Rule Britannia*.

Sir Osbert Sitwell
From *Noble Essences: A Book of Characters* (1950)

Gabriele D'Annunzio

Gabriele D'Annunzio! The sound still carries with it a political as well as an aesthetic echo: yet who today remembers him as the Regent of Carnaro, and who, it may be, reads now the great poet who purified the Italian language, and wrote novels and plays which obtained a world-wide reknown? Yet, in addition, D'Annunzio had long been a figure of universal fame, of a kind that scarcely attaches itself to anyone in this age. Indeed, it is difficult to find any just comparison for him, or prototype, except Byron. Like Byron, he had become famous at a very early age – in his own case, in his teens – with his poems. The two men were alike in the shock their books created, in their force of character and their interests: though a great fire shone, too, in the oratory of D'Annunzio – a gift denied Byron. But Byron's personality wielded as powerful an influence as D'Annunzio's, and each left his mark on the world forever, even though his books were for a time not read. Both poets in the end turned men of action and eventually sort refuge, after lives of dissipation, in political adventure. Both men provided innumerable scandals for the boudoir and drawing room: since, again like Byron, D'Annunzio, though he lacked the earlier writer's personal beauty and aristocratic background, was the hero of love affairs that were most eagerly discussed in the worlds of art and fashion. Even those who had read a line by him were interested. To be able to give details of his quarrel with Duse conferred on him or her who announced them a flattering quality of 'being in the know'. If the truth was obscure, then stories, of the most improbable kind, were invented for the consumption of the intimates of the salons of America and Europe... Even today I can recall hearing one of them related: D'Annunzio, it was said, was spending the end of a love affair, and a long Italian autumn, in a decaying castle in the hills. The place was enormous, the scenery appropriate, but as the season dragged on into winter, a bitter dullness invested the castle, no less than the love affair it sheltered, until again the surrounding world of neighbours and peasants was fluttered by the news that a lady in a white cloak rode into the courtyard at midnight and ensuing midnights on a white horse – or should I write white palfrey? – the explanation of this singularly tall story being that the lady in the flowing cloak was D'Annunzio, who had thus clothed himself in order to reawaken interest and induce those who beheld the phantom to believe that a new love was beginning. Such anecdotes were swallowed easily, for undoubtedly an element of sensationalism existed in him, as in various other artists. Inherent even in the name he invented for himself and used – Gabriele D'Annunzio – which attaches itself so easily to the titles of the Archangels of Italian culture, is something of this quality, as well as of the same fondness for the old poetic symbols, which is to be found equally in, for example, his assumption of the pomegranate as his personal emblem, and in the imagery of his books.

This sketch, then, though it too deals with the man more than his work, must yet differ from the other portraits in this volume: for it attempts to paint an atmosphere and a place, and to record a singular episode in European history, as well as to give a necessarily rather fragmentary impression of a great writer. More than that it cannot be, because my contact with him was so brief, whereas his companions in these pages I knew well. But at least, though our acquaintance was so slight, I visited him in his, as it proved, temporary dominion, and that, too, colours the portrait...

One misses so many opportunities, from caution, foresight or the desire for a peaceful life, in consequence leaving modern history and its extraordinary episodes to be described either by those specialists who have developed a nose for news, but no hand with which to write it, or by the hapless beings who write letters signed 'Onlooker' or 'Eyewitness.' The very excuse that these last advance on their behalf is in reality the accusation against them. They chanced, they aver, to have been on the spot when such and such a thing occurred. In short, like Casabianca on the burning deck, they obtusely remained behind when all the more intuitive and sensitive companions had already sought safety. And what do they tell us, subsequently, of what they beheld? Not long ago, for example, I met an officer who had been present at the great catastrophe of the Quetta earthquake. He had been engaged in something he thought to be sport – would it have been pig-sticking? – and at the time had been standing on a hill above the town.

'How extraordinary!' I remarked. 'What a tremendous spectacle and experience it must have been! Tell me what did you see?'

With an air of concentration, he thought for some time, and then, with an outward gesture of his hands, replied:

'Well, first of all, the city was there, and then, the next moment, it sort of wasn't, don't you know?'

Of such are the graphic descriptions usually to be obtained from those accidentally present at events, and the episode of Fiume seemed to deserve more sympathetic, or at any rate professional, study than it would obtain from someone casually stranded there at the time of the poet's escapade. Already there had been great misrepresentation, and it is important to analyse here the causes. Partly they were political, and owing no doubt to a very wise sense of fear of direct political action, as well as the less wise democratic fear of action of any sort, partly they were due to the fact that D'Annunzio was a great poet. The English-speaking peoples, in spite of poetry being essentially their art, have rarely admired poets as individuals: there has been, at any rate of recent centuries, a small and highly specialized audience for contemporary poetry and a popular dislike of it, and of those who write or are likely to write it... In case I should be accused of exaggeration, I must here hurriedly interpose a story of the school days of one famous poet, to which I had listened a few months before I went to Fiume... I had sat next, at luncheon, to an old gentleman who owned to eighty-six years, and a fine impressive machine he looked, as he told me how much he had enjoyed his long life. 'If a man – or a schoolboy for that matter', he continued, 'does not get on well, it's his own fault. I well remember, when I first went to Eton, the head boy called us together, and pointing to a little fellow with a mass of red curly hair, said, "If ever you see that boy, kick him – and if you are too far off to kick him, throw a stone". He was a fellow named Swinburne,' he added. 'He used to write poetry for a time, I believe, but I don't know what became of him.'

A poet, then, of D'Annunzio's type, with his intensely Latin approach to life, will be necessarily more unpopular in Anglo-Saxon countries than even Shelley or Swinburne. Also, usually, there is less chance of kicking him. But D'Annunzio's usurpation of Fiume provided just such a rare opportunity. The press imputed to him not only an imperialistic outlook but a love of money, of power, of sensationalism: in fact whether rightly or wrongly, he was arraigned for those very faults he shared with his accusers. But the real crime he committed in their eyes, but which was seldom mentioned, was that he appeared to be a great artist and as such would naturally be unpopular with the leaders of commercial states, and their businessmen. Only occasionally did the truth peep out in such a heading as *Fresh Attempts on Life of Crazy Poet* – for, in this similar to Lenin, Trotsky, and later to Hitler and his lieutenants, D'Annunzio had been time and time again triumphantly consigned to the asylum or, more effectively still, assassinated in the columns of the world press. No power, one should have known, 'would tolerate for an instant' the vicinity of a ruling poet; whatever might have been the artistic possibilities of his venture, they were killed, though the political and subversive ones were driven back to survive in a more acerbated form in their own country, for a time to conquer, and everywhere for many years to constitute a challenge to the established order that had been responsible for D'Annunzio's defeat: for Fascism was the child of Fiume.

Yet, though D'Annunzio was a poet, one would have expected the world public, or at any rate the Allied public of the 1914-18 war, to have venerated him. By his reputation as a man of genius, and by his altogether exceptional powers of oratory and appeal, he had brought Italy into the war on the side of the Allies. At least, then, those who admired and enjoyed the war should have admired D'Annunzio: no less for the great personal bravery he showed in the struggle, and for the inspiration his courage afforded to his countrymen, than for his success in political persuasion. But having incurred this heavy moral liability, D'Annunzio was soon made to feel that he had brought the Italians into the conflict under false pretences, because, albeit secret treaties between England, France, and Italy guaranteed the Italians certain territories if the Allies won, these conditions, entered into without the knowledge of President Wilson, were never recognized by him, or carried out. And it was D'Annunzio's consequent feeling of being accountable for this failure, his belief that Italy had come out of the war on a par with the defeated nations, that made him risk his life once again at Fiume. Thus, to the Italian people, who know no fear of poetry, D'Annunzio remained not only the man who had done more for their language than any writer since Dante, and the patriot who had alone stood out against what they considered the futilities of the Peace Conference, but – it was a popular claim in Italy – he was supposed, by his seizure of Fiume, to have been the cause of the fall of President Wilson: to whom, in a speech, he had characteristically referred as 'that cold-hearted maniac who sought to crucify Italy with nails torn from the German Chancellor of the Scrap of Paper.'

It was at the end of November, 1920, on the shores of the Neapolitan Bay, that the idea of Fiume first laid hold on us. My brother suddenly remarked to me, as we stood on a terrace overlooking the sea, mountains and islands: 'We never saw Lenin seize power in Petrograd: let us now go to Fiume to see D'Annunzio. It may be the beginning of something else.'

Immediately I realized with what truth he spoke; for here was a small estate seized and ruled over by a poet, and who could tell but that it might develop into an ideal land where the arts would flourish once more on Italian soil (D'Annunzio was wont to claim that Fiume was 'Italian by right of landscape,' and so it was, belonging clearly, as we were to see, to the same order as Naples or Genoa) as they have so often blossomed before? It might even offer an alternative or escape from the Scylla and Charybdis of modern life, Slum-Bolshevism or Democratic Bungalow-Rash, morbid states of the soul that are of no help to the artist.

Whatever, then, may be thought of the results of the Fiume adventure, my brother was right: the moment, the man, the place were of importance. Though he spoke when the last month of the year was so close, as we looked from the terrace, the sun still streamed over the flat roofs, highly coloured tiled domes, feathery palm trees and built-up hills, and glittered on the blue-green waters with an unequalled brilliance and sparkle. All difficulties became minimized under this parade. My father with his ceaseless drive to remodel our careers, and his cautionary refrain of 'Oh, I shouldn't do that!' as if something appalling lurked in the execution of any plan of ours, seemed in our imagination for once to be quite tractable: to journey for a night or two to Venice, and then proceed to the small principality D'Annunzio had established for himself, seemed in itself a small and easy matter. The icy fingers that had already held Northern Italy in their grip were not to be conjured up in the imagination; while such things as passports became totally negligible, mere whims of a genial international bureaucracy, under the rays of the late but glowing sun. I at once telegraphed to my friend Massingham, asking if I might write for the *Nation*, of which he was editor, an account of D'Annunzio's Fiume, and obtained permission to represent the journal. My brother and I then decided to invite Orioli, the

Florentine bookseller, to accompany us, for he was an entertaining and appreciative companion, and his knowledge of the ways of his countrymen, and their language, might prove invaluable. Soon we set off.

We met in Venice; from there, all night long, we sat in a railway compartment, talking and smoking. Orioli, with his emphatically accentuated and fluent foreigner's English, and with his rather lisping gift of vivid phrase, told us, I remember, of his childhood in Romagna, and of how, later, working as a young Italian without means in a shop in Cambridge, he had educated himself by borrowing cap and gown from various undergraduates whose hair he cut, and attending, thus clad, and without making any payment, those lectures he thought would be of use to him. He spoke, too, of his methods of avoiding creditors in those early days – for he realized, when he started his bookshop, that he must have a good suit in order to present a respectable appearance, but he could not pay for it for many years. All these stories he told with an abundance of amusing and well-observed detail... so, with such tales of private enterprise, the night wore on, and indeed, the day following, for the trains in north Italy were still in a chaotic condition after the war, and we arrived in Trieste in the evening, just as dusk had fallen. The harsh north wind with the Greek name blew along the stony streets of the city, and roared in the piazzas. The electric light failed – perhaps, for such was then its way, as a fresh tribute to the anarchist Malatesta – and the fur-capped, flat-faced Slavonic peasants from outlying villages huddled together in clumps, speaking outlandish tongues, within the barren shelter of the great drafty station. No one there, least of all guard or porter, seemed to know when the train would start for Fiume. Italian officers, *Arditi*, Wolves of Tuscany, gesticulated in groups outside an obsolete train. Cloaks, daggers and the feathers of eagles proclaimed rather melodramatically that the Roman legions were assembling once more under a new Caesar, while, further, the flowing black ties of the *Arditi* indicated that the new Caesar was a poet. Through the pervading *braggadocio*

109

atmosphere, through the noisy, vapid chatter, there flickered like a flame an unmistakable enthusiasm, not often at that time to be encountered.

At last the groups broke up, and the individuals who composed them settled noisily into their chosen places in the antiquated train. There was no light in carriages or corridors, but as the train jolted higher into the hills, the snow outside threw a ghostly, almost green illumination on the faces within. Even at this distance, the influence of D'Annunzio was omnipresent and his name scarcely ever left the conversation. Even the somewhat Yugolsav lady in the corner, with eyebrows that even in this pallid obscurity could be seen to meet and intertwine, complained that the cause of Fiume had become a Massacre of the Innocents, a Children's Crusade. And indeed the officer who sat next to me confessed that he was smuggling into the Regency the two enthusiasts of sixteen years of age who accompanied him. They had tried to become legionaries a year before, but on the score of their youth had been turned back by the Italian troops at the border. Both lads were evidently caught in the magic net of D'Annunzio's words, and their pockets were heavy with his speeches, prayers and threats, which, at great labour to themselves, they had copied out in a round but flowing hand. They vowed that if they could not get through to Fiume on the train, they would walk there, over the frozen mountains – and thousands of boys, they declared, would do the same from all over Italy: for Gabriele D'Annunzio remained until his death the idol of young Italy. Even the lady with the eyebrows admitted that, when the Regent rode out through the stony countryside, the people, whether Italian or Croat, would strew the ground with flowers.

We began to approach the rather elusive frontier of an unacknowledged principality. To enter Fiume was by no means easy. The Allies, and the Italian government in particular, did not wish to encourage their nationals to visit the city: while the Regency was also, for its part, strongly opposed to receiving foreigners in a time when there was a shortage of food and necessities. Journalists especially were disliked – and as such I was appearing – because some, who had been received with kindness, had on their return home published attacks of a personal nature on those who had entertained them. Thus it was that, after we had journeyed for some five hours, my own troubles began... The soldier at the border could not read easily, but he could, and did, with some trouble to himself, at last decipher uneasily a name on my passport... Alas, it was not my name, as it happened, but that of the Foreign Secretary who had signed the document. At first the Italian was obviously not sure where he had heard it before, but then, as his eye lighted on the motto under Lord Curzon's coat of arms, *Let Curzon holde what Curzon helde*, and he repeated it in broken English, turning it on his tongue, he received suddenly the full impact of the astonishing plot he had by chance uncovered. Here, he concluded, was Lord Curzon, the chief instrument of English democracy, trying to sneak into the Regency, without informing any of the ministers or officials. He gave a bellow of rage and informed me that I was *not* allowed to proceed on my journey... It was only after moments seemed to have turned to hours that, with the help of Orioli's natural eloquence, and the aid of a Tuscan Wolf with whom luckily a flask of wine had been shared on the cold journey, finally I was permitted my own identity and released.

Eventually we arrived at Fiume. Below us lay the giant warehouses and docks, in plain disproportion to the size of the town. In the harbour was congregated D'Annunzio's by no means negligible fleet. Some of the vessels had been captured by the poet's pirates, others – like the *Dante*, which had deserted to him from the Italian Navy – by his phrases. The leviathan outline of this great ship loomed up into the cold darkness, and its lights, and those of the smaller boats round it, flickered threateningly. Otherwise all was dark, and it was difficult to comprehend the conformation of the port until the next day... Then the sun sparkled and it was possible to appreciate the disposition of the place, with its clustered houses and its bay, a spur of hills sinking into the opalescence of the far seas, and the quivering misty outlines of the islands. The cold, which was intense, crystallised each sound into greater precision. But the human element was here more of interest than the form of the hills or the incidence of climate. Outside our hotel was the chief Piazza, where the Governor had placed two flagstaffs, the idea of which derived from his beloved Venice. And in the Piazza at all hours of morning and afternoon loitered a crowd as fantastic as any – even when one recalls the tumblers and clowns, Turks and Oriental merchants in turbans – ever sheltered by the bubble domes of St Mark's. The general animation and noisy vitality seemed to herald a new land, a new system. We gazed and listened in amazement. Every man here seemed to wear a uniform designed by himself: some had beards, and had shaved their heads completely, so as to resemble the Commander himself, who was now bald; others had cultivated huge tufts of hair, half a foot long, waving out from their foreheads, and wore, balanced on the very back of the skull, a black fez. Cloaks, feathers and flowing black ties were universal, and every man – and few women were to be seen – carried the 'Roman dagger.' Suddenly, as some messenger arrived – it might be an emissary of the Regent himself – on a very palpitating motor bicycle, a stir would pass through the throng so full of swagger and of youth – and yet, as I write this, I recall that, included in the gathering, as if to prove that youth was not universal or eternal, were two Garibaldian veterans with red waistcoats and white hair. But even they seemed to possess some paradoxical secret, and behaved in a manner that gave the lie to their years. For instance, I recall that as, a few days later, we left Fiume, we observed them making a real mess of oysters, crayfish shaped like scarlet aircraft, and cherry brandy, the staple but somewhat exotic foods of this land of youth.

D'Annunzio had detailed, to take us round, as guide, an officer who was gay, enthusiastic, pleasure loving. London in particular – London, which was then truly a city of life and pleasure –

London, which he had never visited, was the object of his most passionate longing. He – for, in his Italian way, he was, though perhaps not consciously to the full extent, a Futurist – dreamt of the tubes and motorbuses and the great stores, the cars in lines, the delicious traffic blocks scented by petrol fumes, the music halls. And the buildings must be beautiful too, he averred. But none finer, I replied, than those to be admired in Italian cities. '*Ma,*' he replied in a voice infused with astonishment, '*il Palazzo di Cristallo.*' He had fought in Poland, and during that time had met many English officers, of whom, however, he retained a singular memory, for he remarked, '*Molto gentili: ma sempre mangiano* jam, jam, jam.'

Our new friend had been ordered to show us the town, the people, the army, and the nightlife of Fiume... The army could be divided roughly into three categories. The biggest consisted of Italian romantic patriots, spiritual grandchildren of Garibaldi, gathered together by the glamour of the Regent's name and words: next was the smaller brand of Futurists, who, whilst disapproving of D'Annunzio as a writer, acclaimed his deeds of bravery and applauded a leader who took no heed of yesterday or for tomorrow; and finally, closely allied to the Futurists, came a little gang of professional fighters, who preferred war at any price to peace. These three divisions it is possible to illustrate for the reader by extreme cases. To the first belonged an officer we met who was a close friend of D'Annunzio's, and a poet himself, and who refused all pay for his services; to the second, Keller the Futurist, a fine-looking bearded giant who somewhat resembled the Augustus John of those years, and had expressed his Futurism in a famous gesture, since he had set out in an aircraft from Fiume for Rome, where he pelted the venerable Giolitti's Ministry with beetroot; to the third, a man like a tiger, with medals instead of stripes, whose very appearance constituted a danger signal. This last individual, by birth a Sardinian, had been in prison for murder at the outbreak of the war, but had specifically been released, it was rumoured, on condition that he promised to devote himself to slaying the enemy. Subsequently he was said to have taken prisoner thirty Austrians in the war, and to have strangled them with his own hands. Yet he was so extremely shocked – as by the way were my brother and I – at the contemporary doings of the Black and Tans in Ireland that, in a nightclub to which we were conducted, he smashed as a protest, immediately behind our heads, the champagne bottle he had just emptied.

Thus, as we walked up the hill to the Palace the following morning, we reflected how, by the singular magic of his personality, D'Annunzio had succeeded in uniting for a time those who loved the past of Italy with those who hated it. Some had been drawn to his cause by the fervour of his words, and by the glamour of ancient and decayed cities such as Torcello, Ravenna or Mantua, while others, who agreed with Marinetti in thinking Venice a city of dead fish and rotting palaces, inhabited by waiters and touts, saw in the policy of the Regent the means of making Italy into a new Roman Empire, mighty in arms, a dangerous and insolent power with skyscrapers and an efficient train service – ideals, as it turned out, afterwards inherited and finally for a time achieved by Mussolini. The hill was steep and we walked up it slowly to the Palace, built in the well-known Renaissance-elephantoid style that is the dream of every Municipal Council the world over – for it had formerly been the Town Hall. Everything was large and square – but in fact not quite large enough. You entered a large square hall, with pillars supporting a square gallery. D'Annunzio's love of the exotic has caused this apartment to be filled with hundreds of pale plaster flowerpots of every size, but all incised with Byzantine patterns or Celtic trellis, and containing palms and succulents. Soldiers lounged among the greenery, and typists rushed furiously through swing doors. In the square gallery, and leading out of the side situated nearest the sea, were the rooms of the poet, always closely guarded: because he would often remain for eighteen hours at a time shut up in his apartment, and during these periods of thought he would take no food and must on no account be disturbed. Today, as it happened, one of these stretches of work had begun, and in consequence, since no one knew when he would return to life, we were forced to pass two days of an incredible monotony, broken solely by a lecture on the political situation of the Regency of Carnaro, which was delivered to us by the Foreign Minister. This gentleman held the unique distinction of being the only bore in Fiume: a fact proclaimed by all who knew him, but which we were destined to find out for ourselves. In looks, he belonged to the small moustachioed, tactical-authority type and, while my brother and I balanced tall frames in agonized positions over diminutive maps, he laid down the law in that flowery French, reinforced with a twang like a guitar, which is the official language of so many Italians and Spaniards... At last, just as the lecture ended, we were informed that the poet would receive us the next day.

At five o'clock the following evening we were, accordingly, conducted to D'Annunzio's study. Our sole interview with him lasted only three quarters of an hour, but it would be impossible soon to forget it. As we entered, I recall a Portuguese journalist was just being shown out, reiterating fulsomely in Italian as he stepped backward out of the presence: 'The Portuguese nation regards you as the Christ of the Latin World – the Christ of the Latin World – the...' When he had gone, in the ensuing silence, the repetition of the words could still be heard from the next room, and then gradually died away... The study was fairly large, and contained little furniture. Its walls were almost entirely covered with banners. On the inner side, supported by brackets, stood stiffly two gilded saints from Florence, their calm, wide-open eyes gazing out over the deepening shades of the Fiumian sea. Near the fireplace, on one of the tables, rose the shape of a vast fifteenth-century bell, made by the famous bell-maker of Arbe, and presented to D'Annunzio by the people of that island. At the central desk sat the Commander himself, with his pomegranate in front of him, behind inkstand and pens.

Often, as I have before emphasized, an analogy in appearance will summon up more effectively for the reader the look of a man than can the most elaborate and precise description. What can one say? That D'Annunzio was small, lightly made, dressed in gray uniform, had a face of rather Arab cast – he came from the south-east of Italy – and streaky mustache and embryo beard. But if I write that – as was the case – the first thing that struck one was that he bore a distinct resemblance to Igor Stravinsky, the admirers of that great genius can picture D'Annunzio more easily. The poet wore many ribbons and on his left shoulder carried the Italian Gold Medal for valor, the equivalent of our Victoria Cross. Though he was completely and grotesquely bald, though only his left eye remained – for he had lost the other in the war – though he was nervous and exhausted, yet at the end of a few seconds the extraordinary charm he possessed, which had enabled him on many occasions to change mobs of enemies into furious partisans, had exercised itself on us... He began to speak. The first words he addressed to us were, 'Well, what new poets are there in England?' (Not, you will notice, 'What new generals are there?' or 'Who plays for Woolwich Arsenal?') Then he went on to talk of our country, and of his fervent admiration for Shelley, whose death he himself had tried to imitate at the age of fifteen in the Bay of Castellammare. In his discourse there was not a little to northern ears of absurdity, but through it ran the hypnotic thread of his eloquence. He switched soon from poetry to sport, and he talked of English greyhounds – which after poetry, he considered evidently the greatest national speciality – 'running wild over the moors of Devonshire.' He proceeded to tell us of the strange conversations which he held with the people. A silent crowd would begin to collect, and then swell quickly outside the Palace. He would go out onto the balcony and demand what it was they wanted. A voice would answer, and thus would gradually build itself up a system of direct intercourse between the people and their ruler. This he claimed to be the first example of such interplay since Greek times. He told us, too, of Fiume and of his intense loneliness there, of how he, who had always loved books and music, had remained in his city for fifteen months, surrounded solely by peasants and soldiers, while the Italian Government, relying on his roving temperament, tried to 'bore him out.' He spoke of the enthusiasm of his legionaries, and declared how difficult it was to keep them at peace: weary of waiting for battle, they would fight one another in some sham contest, and it was by no means unusual for there to be serious casualties from bombs and bullet wounds. Soon after his proclamation, for instance, of the Fiumian Constitution, in which he had announced that music was to be the 'Religious and Social Institution of the Regency of Carnaro,' he had invited an eminent Italian conductor to bring his orchestra over from Trieste and give a series of concerts, and had provided for him a fight for the orchestra to witness. Four thousand troops, among whom were the two Garibaldian veterans whom we had seen – one aged seventy-eight and the other eighty-four – had taken part in the contest, and one hundred men had been seriously injured by bombs. The members of the orchestra, which had been playing during the quieter intervals, fired by a sudden access of enthusiasm, dropped their instruments, and charged and captured the trenches. Five of them were badly hurt in the struggle.

This new principality seemed full of paradox and of hope, as well as of a certain menace: but the Muse of History had decreed that it should fall within a few weeks of our visit. Giolitti showed his native cunning and unrivalled experience by the way in which he brought matters to a head. D'Annunzio had always relied on the fact that feeling in Italy was so strongly in his favour that no Italian Government would dare openly to oppose him, still less to use its forces against him: but the crafty old politician contrived that the whole affair should be over before the Italian people could be aware that it had begun. He waited until the night before Christmas Eve, so that he could be sure that no newspapers would appear for three days, and then sent the fleet to Fiume, with instructions to bombard the place to pieces if the poet remained there. There seemed only one thing for D'Annunzio to do, to leave before the inhabitants were exposed to the fulfilment of this threat... When the news of the fall of Fiume spread, on the morning after Boxing Day, shops and theatres in all parts of Italy were closed as a sign of popular mourning: but it was too late for public opinion to exercise any force – if ever it can in modern conditions.

This rather pitiful end to the poet's adventure was hailed with relief by the press. It was supposed to finish 'an awkward incident': while the poet himself – for whom no word had been good enough when his eloquence had so largely helped persuade Italy to enter the war – was now abused and insulted. In some instances, this frail little genius, who had flown over Vienna during the war, as well as over the most perilous of battlefields and over the Austrian fleet, of which he had destroyed two battleships, was now accused of cowardice in leaving Fiume: a charge that he could afford to spurn... In some cases the writers who attacked him showed hitherto unsuspected powers of imagination. Thus one journalist, in an article published in an English daily paper, headed *Chorus Girls and Champagne*, declared that one could tell from 'the glassy glitter of D'Annunzio's snake-like eye' that he was addicted to cocaine! This compelled me – for D'Annunzio had not many champions at that moment – to write a reply, in which I pointed out that this 'glassy glitter' was not to be attributed to the drug habit, but to the fact that one of the poet's eyes was, in fact, made of glass, since he had lost his own in the war, so recently over, while fighting on behalf of the Allied peoples, among whom the proprietor of the paper in which the libel appeared, and the writer of it, were numbered.

The poet has long been dead, and is today neither insulted daily nor praised. Together with the majority of the great army of the dead, he is out of fashion. Yet truly, though I have here written an impression of an episode in his life, it is his writings, more than his actions, which are of interest, as must always be the case with an author. His novels, so tremendous in their power of evoking emotion, and in their poetic eloquence and rhetoric – books such as *Il Fuoco, Le Vergini Delle Rocce, Il Piacere*, plays like *La Città* – are there for us to reawaken and revive by our interest. In them is to be found often an overwhelming force of imagery, and sometimes a certain quality of lushness – though this does not apply to his poems – that might be cloying, were not its sweetness also contaminated and reduced by the morbidity prevalent at the end of the old century... The public always clamours for a message in poetry or prose: seldom is it more angry than when it gets one. But what words can picture its rage when a poet, having for years preached his message, proceeds, as did Tolstoy and D'Annunzio, for example, to translate it into action? Tolstoy, abandoning wealth and family, finally running off to die in the snow at a wayside railway station, in an attempt to hide from those he had abandoned to their worldly fate, was accused of insincerity; so was D'Annunzio. He had for years preached the importance of being a leader of men, the importance of staying for years immured in the dark strength of your travertine palace, impervious to the light and clamour of the democratic days outside, of waiting for your moment to emerge, armed in the full panoply of your strength, then to act swiftly and with decision. He followed his own advice. For a time he led and acted swiftly. Today his politics belong to the past, so derided by the Futurists who supported his actions, where his written words, which they criticized, belong to the present and the future, and are still there for us to read, their meaning moving and flickering through the immortal phrases, in the same way that a salamander, in part obscured by the smoke of a great fire, might be seen to glow.

Mark Thompson
From *A Paper House (1992)*

Tito's Island

Trips to the archipelago of Brioni leave from Fažana, a fishing village north of Pula. Waiting for the next departure, I sat in the shade of an umbrella pine, facing the islands across a cerulean channel, and rummaged through my pile of guide books.

The 1913 *Handbook* was novelettish. 'Only a few years ago, these islands were very unhealthy, feverstricken, deserted places.' Thanks, however, to one Herr Kupelweiser, an entrepreneur from Merano who bought the islands in 1893, Brioni was transformed into a 'first-class winter resort, answering to all exigencies of modern times.' My Yugoslav guide, published in the '60s when mass tourism along the Adriatic was ballooning, mentions everything about the Brioni except the most salient fact, which glowers behind these sentences like a nightclub bouncer: 'There are hotels on the eastern side of Veliki Brion. These islands are not open to tourists.' This, though, is contradicted by Charles Cuddon's sterling *Companion Guide*, which said the islands were visitable, but not how to reach them. The 1989 *Blue Guide* went further but disdained to grasp the nettle. Veliki Brion 'was the summer residence of President Tito'. True, but there was more to the Old Man's relationship with Brioni than that...

The salient fact – always public knowledge anyway – is that Brioni was Tito's personal archipelago, his Chartwell, Camp David and Kremlin, rolled into one. From 1949 until his death in 1980 it was a summer residence where he withdrew with family and friends, pottered with his hobbies of photography and metalwork, and cultivated his garden. Yet it was also the showcase where he received presidents, princesses, and film stars, as well as a bunker where he could convene Party meetings and orchestrate secret operations with no risk of publicity.

In 1983 Brioni was proclaimed a National Park and Memorial Area. Veliki Brion, biggest of the fourteen islands, was opened to visitors, who flock here through the summer months and can now stay in the hotels once reserved for the nomenklatura. The tourism is packaged, and trippers who hope to nose around Tito's house, stroll in fragrant woods of holm-oak, or swim in the pellucid sea, are bound for frustration. Still, the tour is enjoyable, made more interesting by the organizers' uncertainty whether they are paying homage to Tito and his works or offering a seaside excursion for all the family. The result is a weird combination of the two: a commercial Tito theme-park that defers to the Old Man constantly but less than half-heartedly. Brioni assumes Tito's greatness without trying to demonstrate it, or even caring about it.

Ashore, we were ushered into a motorized train which trundled off towards the safari park at the island's northern tip. We passed the foundations of a first-century *villa rustica*; Brioni was a resort for rich Romans from Pietas Iuliá (Pula). There are Byzantine and Illyrian remains too, but no evidence of Venice's long tenure; the story seems to be one of malaria and neglect down the centuries until Herr Kupelweiser came to the rescue. He built hotels and roads, landscaped the park, planted trees, laid out a golf course, racecourse and tennis courts. The First World War ended Brioni's glittering success as a high-society playground, and when Tito arrived after the Second War, he found only fishing families and a little school that taught in the Italian language. He closed the school, and used army and prison labour to build new villas.

The Serbo-Croatian carriages of our train were full of families and couples; the Italian and German carriages had a few dozen trippers. Besides me, the English-language wagon could only muster a hefty Swedish couple. The publicity promised expert guidance, and our language graduate from Zagreb, neat in drip-dry blouse and navy skirt, looked the part. But she soon lost heart or interest, falling quiet for long minutes. The wagon was stifling;

121

we perspired in silence as the train looped around the inlets and headlands. The Italian language guide never paused for breath; we could hear her babbling like a steeplechase-commentator. Were we too few to warrant the effort? Or too dull? Feeling sorry for our girl and somehow responsible for her apathy, I plied her with questions. No you can't visit Tito's house, that's on a small island in the Memorial Area, for special guests only. Yes, three villas are still kept for the élite politicians.

Then the Swedish man spoke up. What became of the fishing village? Did Tito throw the people off? The guide gazed blankly back. 'Come on now, how was it?' he persisted, winking ripely and nudging his wife. The wife giggled obliquely, which gave our girl a moment to recover her poise. 'Before the war the islands were private property,' she explained blandly, 'and after the war they were nationalized.' The Swede knew all about these euphemisms and he guffawed. 'So that's how he did it, eh!'

Yugoslav visitors to Brioni are told the truth: that the islanders were moved to Fažana at the end of the '60s. Our guide did not enthuse about Tito or defend him with a joke; neither admiration nor irony was detectable. There was no sign that respect for the Old Man made her reluctant to criticize, or that fear held her in check (for criticism of Tito was still outlawed). Nothing as personal as fear. It was as if an enormous, leaden cliché had rattled down like a portcullis of pure habit as soon as the sailor's question was out of his mouth. Hence her reflex obedience to the fading dogma, her lip-service to a cult that persists somewhere far away; to an idol hewn from rock and exfoliating into facelessness upon a distant peak, an idol whose priests have absconded, yet who in the presence of heathens cannot quite be ignored, although too decrepit to require any but token devotions, even at a five-star shrine like Brioni.

Whatever detail is provided about Tito's activity in Brioni has not so much been laundered as bleached. Nothing about the Central Committee sessions convened here to stamp them with Tito's personal authority. Nothing about the 'very strange scene' which occurred in the harbour on the evening of November 2nd 1956, when Khruschev and Malenkov arrived, both seasick in the 'howling gale', for a secret all-night summit about Hungary with Tito, Kardelj, Ranković and Micunović (whose celebrated diaries I am quoting). Khruschev insisted the Yugoslavs should 'understand us properly'; should accept, in other words, that 'counter-revolution' in Budapest was impermissible.

Nor is there any reference to the purges effected here over the years, none more important that July 1st, 1996 when Aleksandar Ranković, federal vice-president and chief of the security services for twenty years, was forced to resign.

If all this, which has long been public knowledge, is omitted, of course the really disgraceful stuff never gets a look-in. It must be said that Brioni's subtropical beauty, and the indolent heat of a summer afternoon, do ease the bleachers' task. At the end of the tour, sitting gingerly on the hot stones of the pier, paddling my feet in the sea as we waited for the return boat to Fažana, I contemplated Tito's cruise-liner yacht moored across the harbour. Try as I might, I couldn't focus my mind on the skulduggery the yacht witnessed one afternoon in 1973 or '74 when – if the scabrous memoirs of the Romanian ex-spymaster Ion Paçepa can be trusted – Tito entertained Nicolae Ceaucescu. He wanted to cajole the Giant of the Carpathians into helping him entrap a troublesome Yugoslav dissident by luring him to Bucharest. The Incarnation of the Highest Aspirations of the Romanian People was chary of bad publicity. Tito, flattering and puissant, prevailed.

By the early '70s Brioni had become thoroughly surreal, hosting an inner-party purge one day, Ceaucescu the next, and Sophia Loren at the weekend. All the other residents had now been removed; Brioni was Tito's domain, and its versatile hospitality reflected the unique chameleon character of its owner's status, both nationally and internationally, which waxed ever greater and more legendary as the years passed and he approached Methuselan realms of old age, it seemed without losing a jot of health or vigour. Of course this status was cultivated by Tito himself, with his superb intuition for his own image-management. For instance, in the '70s he backed two prestige film productions about the partisan war, *The Battle of the Neretva* and *Sutjeska*, both tedious and boasting star-studded casts.

Tito was impersonated in *Sutjeska* by handsome, rakish Richard Burton. Filming was fraught with difficulties, and during a break Burton and Elizabeth Taylor were invited to Brioni. Taking the chance to study his role model, the actor was disturbed by unexpected ambiguities in the atmosphere. According to Burton's diary, the Old Man and Madame Broz regaled their guests with 'long stories which they don't allow their interpreters to interrupt'. Burton noted 'the remarkable luxury unmatched by anything else I've seen and can well believe Princess Marg[are]t who says the whole business makes Buck House [Buckingham Palace] look pretty middle-class.' Yet he also noticed 'the nervousness with which the servants serve us all' on board the yacht. 'Am still worried by the atmosphere of dread which surrounds Tito', runs a later entry in his diary. 'Cannot understand it. Neither can the rest of us.'

His unease was heightened by some surprising news. It seems Tito told him that he had always refused to shoot captured enemies. Burton was impressed, and not surprisingly 'a little put out' when he heard that people in Dubrovnik 'had been shot in the Yugoslavian "purge" in 1948'. He determined to find out if the orders to shoot had come 'from the top. If so I shall be a disappointed man'. Whether Burton settled the question his biographer doesn't say, but his reaction speaks volumes about Western wishful thinking.

Had our guide been told not to disturb our illusions, or was she being spontaneously coy? I couldn't bring myself to ask, but she brightened up when our convoy reached the tiny safari park. Now she could fall back on a neutral ground of data and statistics. The two elephants rubbing their flanks on a wooden stall had been presented by Indira Ghandi. The pair of camels were a gift from Muammar Quaddhafi. Zebra, antelopes and other beasts had been donated by some of 'the ninety state leaders from fifty-eight countries and over one hundred presidents' who had visited the islands. Altogether Tito had hosted 'over one thousand four hundred political meetings on Brioni, including two hundred and fifty foreign delegations, and he set off from here on over fifty peace missions'. By now I was scribbling to keep up.

Last stop on the tour is the 'Tito on Brioni' photographic exhibition, introduced with the caption: 'On these islands the Yugoslav socialist system was created and the foundations of the non-aligned movement were laid.' The islands' credentials as a holy site could not be clearer, but again the ambivalence looms through: there is no information about the System or Movement, not even a chronology or list of achievements. Either the organisers are assuming that the whole world already knows, or they are loathe to profane these institutions by describing them. Or – a third alternative – they were embarrassed by these institutions and decided that the best way of discharging their duty was to keep mum.

Among the scores of photos, there is not a glimpse to be had of Ceaucescu, or for that matter of Burton or Taylor. Quaddhafi is here, strutting in a long cape past a parade of guards on the quayside. And of course the famous photograph of Tito with Nehru and Nasser here in 1956 – the first meeting of non-aligned leaders.

We drifted through the roomful of images of politicians, mostly leaders of non-aligned nations, unremembered by white Westerners. After a quarter of an hour one head of state resembled another, and I went downstairs where stuffed Brioni wildlife poses behind glass amid papier maché scenery. My thoughts retraced our convoy's route to the safari park. I knew from the *Handbook* that imported fauna were nothing new: 'Hagenbeck had a farm built on one of these idyllic spots, where he is elevating ostriches; there is also a game-reserve.' Yet the present safari park is something different. The animals were gifts from member states to the father of the Non-aligned Movement. We had driven bang through Yugoslavia's foreign policy.

Vladimir Dedijer
From *Tito Speaks: his self portrait and struggle with Stalin (1953)*

I was born Josip Broz in May 1892, in the Croatian village of Kumrovec, which lies in a district called Zagorje ('the country behind the mountain'). This is in the north-western part of Croatia, one of the six Yugoslav republics (then part of Austria-Hungary). My village lies in a pretty valley bordered by wooded hills, where the little green River Sutla meanders through woods, past pastel-blue cottages roofed with home-made tiles or shingles green with moss.

Wherever you look in Zagorje you see on the hill-tops the walls of some ancient fortress, castle, or church, the relics of a history that goes back to Roman times, a history full of war and oppression. On one of the hills above Kumrovec, towering like a giant, is Cesargrad, the ragged ruins of the medieval castle of the Counts Erdödy. They were the masters of my village and the surrounding countryside until the middle of the last century, when feudalism was officially abolished in Croatia. They were cruel, and their serfs were often in revolt.

One winter morning in 1573 the serfs of Cesargrad, wearing the cock's feather as a symbol of revolt, stormed into the castle, beheaded the bailiff, burned one part of the castle, and seized several cannon and some muskets. The leader of the rebels was Matija Gubec but the main body was led by Ilija Gregorić who crossed the Sutla from Cesargrad to call the Slovenian serfs to arms. The rebellion spread through the whole of Zagorje and parts of Slovenia; there were tens of thousands of rebels. But the army of the nobility, under the command of Juraj Drašković, Governor of Croatia and Bishop of Zagreb, was mounted and stronger. The poorly clad serfs suffered from the harsh winter weather. Near my home, Gregorić retreated to Zagorje, and at the crossing of the Sutla between St Peter and Kumrovec, below Cesargrad, he was defeated. The following day saw the decisive battle with the main body of the rebel serfs near Donja Stubica, where the serfs were led by Matija Gubec. He was captured. The Bishop-Governor Drašković informed the Austrian Emperor Maximilian:

'As an example to others, with Your Holy Majesty's permission, I shall crown Gubec with an iron crown, and a red-hot one at that.'

And he did. Ilija Gregorić was captured and taken to Vienna, where he was interrogated and after a year returned to the Erdödys in Zagorje, who beheaded him.

The Zagorje serfs were severely punished. Historians say that the bodies of hundreds of peasants hung from the trees in the villages. It is estimated that during this rebellion between four thousand and six thousand serfs were killed in Zagorje. Baroness Barbara Erdödy, who had escaped the sack of her castle, was particularly cruel to the Cesargrad serfs. Three centuries later, whenever as children we awoke at night, out mother threatened that the Black Queen of Cesargrad would take us away if we did not go back to sleep at once.

My forefathers were probably in this famous rebellion, for they had come to Kumrovec from Dalmatia in the middle of the sixteenth century, retreating before the onslaught of the Turkish invaders, and were serfs of the Erdödy family. In later generations there was always at least one of them who became a blacksmith, so that the family came to bear the nickname Kovaći, or Blacksmith. The tradition may later have influenced my own choice of a trade.

My ancestors lived in a patriarchal collective called the *zadruga*. The land was tilled in common, and the whole *zadruga* was under the rule of the *Gospodar* (head man), who was elected. He lived in the biggest house, in which everybody ate together. When a member of the *zadruga* married, the *zadruga* would build him a special little room attached to the big house, so that the whole *zadruga* looked like a beehive. Twice a year the *Gospodar* paid the dues to the Count of Erdödy and to the Church.

Count Erdödy was required to maintain fifty horsemen and two hundred footmen for the army of the Habsburg Emperor. Usually these soldiers were recruited from among the village idlers, for the Count wanted to keep the good workers. As far as I have heard tell there were no soldiers from the Broz family except one, and he was a sentinel on the Drava bridge during the Hungarian rebellion of 1848.

This same year saw the end of the rule of the Erdödys over our village and the beginning of the decay of the *zadruga*. The serfs of Kumrovec received the land, but they had to pay for it, and taxes were increased, especially after the wars of 1859 and 1866, which ended to the disadvantage of Austria-Hungary, which ruled Croatia. As the number of members and the cost of maintenance increased, the *zadruga* began to decline.

Abruptly, the bankers of Budapest and Vienna replaced the Erdödys. The peasants needed land; the firm of Deutsch and Gruenwald bought the entire Erdödy estate, and offered it for sale to the peasants. But the peasants had no money. In a nearby town, Deutsch and Gruenwald established a bank to lend it to them. The rate of interest was nominally eight percent, but commissions and extras raised it to twenty-four percent.

My Grandfather Martin was the last Broz to live in the *zadruga*. In the '60s he left and began to earn his living carting merchandise from Zagreb to nearby towns. He married Ana Blažičko, a tall strong woman who was extremely proud of coming from a family of peasants who had been freemen for more than two centuries. One winter, while Grandfather Martin was driving a cart of salt, a wheel broke and the load crushed the old man. He left a son and six daughters; the son, Franjo, was my father.

At that time a new Hungarian law had been promulgated, according to which the eldest son could no longer be sole heir, but had to share the inheritance equally among all members of the family. This measure was intended to accelerate the disintegration of the peasant holdings. Thus Franjo Broz, reluctant to sell his father's land, was forced into debt so that he might buy out his sisters. Soon the debt was too much for him, and he began to sell one acre after another.

My father was a wiry man with black curly hair and an aquiline nose. The peasants of Kumrovec and the whole of that part of Zagorje used to cross the River Sutla to the wooded Slovene hills where they secretly cut fuel, which they otherwise lacked. Going to the villages across the Sutla, Franjo became acquainted with a sixteen-year-old Slovene girl called Marija, the oldest of fourteen children of Martin Javeršack, who owned sixty-five acres of farm and woodland.

She was a tall, blonde woman, with an attractive face. The wedding took place in January 1881, when my father was twenty-four. It was a very big wedding and my Aunt Ana told me the guests came from Kumrovec on five sleighs.

A hard life awaited my parents. Fifteen acres of land, which dwindled as my father's debts came due, were insufficient to feed the family. When the debts became intolerable, the soft and good-natured Franjo gave it up and took to drinking, and the whole family burden fell upon my mother, an energetic woman, proud and religious.

My father and mother had fifteen children, of whom I was the seventh. In those days, about eighty percent of the children of Zagorje died before the age of fifteen, most of them in infancy. My parents were only a little more fortunate than most. Of their fifteen children, seven survived. When I was ten I fell ill with diphtheria, one of the commonest scourges of our countryside, which had already killed one of my sisters, but I recovered with no ill effects.

Our family lived in house No 8 at Kumrovec, built almost a century ago, solid, with big windows. We shared the house with a cousin. The hall was used by both families; on either side of the hall were two rooms. An open-hearth kitchen, where there was always a stock of firewood, was also shared.

My childhood was hard. There were many children in the family and it was no easy matter to look after them. Often there was not enough bread, and my mother was driven to lock the larder while we children received what she considered she could give us, and not what we could eat. In January my father had to buy cornmeal bread because we could not afford wheat. We children often took advantage of the visit of relatives to beg a slice of bread more than the ration we had eaten. My mother, a proud woman, would not refuse before relatives. But after they went there was a scolding and even an occasional whipping.

One feast-day our parents went somewhere for a visit. We were hungry. Up in the garret hung a smoked pig's head which we were keeping for the New Year. My brothers and sisters were crying, so I brought the head down and dropped it into a pan of boiling water. I added a bit of flour and let it cook for an hour or two. What a feast we had! But the meal was so greasy that we all became sick. When my mother returned we were silent except for an occasional groan. She took pity on us, and that time we got off without as hiding.

Then came the *lukno*, a feudal custom that still survived at Kumrovec in my childhood. After Christmas, for the New Year, friars from Klanjec would appear in every village carrying a cross and followed by a sexton with a sack. A friar would chalk the words 'Anno Domini...' on the door, thus wishing us a happy New Year, and the host would have to give him a few pounds of corn, a bunch of golden flax or two *forints*, which in those days meant two days' wages. You can imagine how we children felt as we stood by, hungry as usual, and watched the sexton pour our corn into his sack.

I remember very well how in my childhood the Hungarian soldiers once entered our village. In 1903 the people of Croatia revolted against the fiscal system which helped Hungary plunder

Croatia, and against Hungarian control over Croatian railways. In our country there were thirty-six thousand railwaymen, all Hungarians, and if a Croat went to a station to buy a ticket, he was compelled to ask for it in Hungarian, or be refused. At a nearby village in Zagorje, peasants removed the Hungarian flag from the station. The police opened fire, killing one and wounding some ten others. Incidents followed throughout Croatia, in which three thousand people were arrested and twenty-six killed. As punishment, the people had to maintain the Hungarian troops. Four Hungarian soldiers were billeted in our house, and we had to feed them a whole month out of supplies that were not enough for our own meagre needs.

The happiest days of my childhood were spent at the house of my maternal grandfather in Slovenia. He was a small stocky man, who called me Jožek (Joey). I looked after his livestock and carried water for the household. His village was in a wood on the steep slopes above the river, and I played in the wood and carved whistles and made whips for the horses I tended.

This was the job I liked best, for as early as I can remember, one of my greatest pleasures was to be with horses. I was already riding bareback when my head barely reached the horse's belly; my father had a horse called 'Putko' that I alone could bridle. I learned in those days that the better you tend a horse, the better he will serve you. During the war I made a point of dismounting from my horse, Lasta (Swallow), when climbing a hill, and I urged my men to save their horses for the plain.

My grandfather Martin was a very witty man and liked practical jokes. From him I inherited the habit which still persists. When my sister was to be married, I, unnoticed by anyone, took her wreath and put it on the chicken-coop. They looked for it all over the house and at last they found it. I no longer remember whether they laughed or not. Let me tell you how the joke was once on me, when I was six. I was on a visit to my Grandfather Martin and often went to a spot where some neighbours were burning lime. One day one of them asked me: 'Josip, would you like to get married?' I said I would, and he promised to find me a bride. He sent me into the hills where my uncle lived and taught me what to say. 'When you get there,' he told me, 'you first say "good evening – good appetite!" Then they will reply, "thanks very much, draw up a chair with us!" Then you say "Thanks, but I've already..." Then they'll ask why you came. Tell them you've heard there is a girl in the house and you would like to get married.' Now that girl was my cousin. I did as I was told. I went, and declared in all earnestness why I had come. I felt ashamed because, being so little I had not the faintest idea what it all meant. My uncle put me on his knees, showed me the girl, and said: 'There is your bride!' Finally I had to tell who had played the joke on me.

But once I caused my grandfather great pain. He always liked to keep the tip of a head of sugar for himself because it was the sweetest. (Sugar was sold in big chunks, the size of a large grenade.) For the same reasons I liked the tip too. One day I took the whole head, small as I was, and carried it off towards a copse to hide it. Unfortunately, as I was crossing a brook the sugar slipped from my arms and fell into the water. It was not fated that I should satisfy my sweet tooth, and Grandfather was equally distressed.

My happy days with him soon came to an end and I returned home.

It was taken for granted in my village that by the time a child was seven he was already a productive worker. I drove the cattle and helped hoe the corn and weed the garden and, I remember well, turned the heavy grindstone that made our grain into flour. Hundreds of times I finished soaked with sweat, and the porridge was the sweeter for that. But the hardest task of all was not physical. It was when my father would send me round the village with his IOU to ask someone to endorse it for him. The other peasants were, like my father, deep in debt, hungry, and with many children. I had to listen to curses and complaints and then, at last, almost always they would endorse the IOU.

One terrible winter when there was no food in the house and no wood for the fire, my father decided to sell our sheepdog, Polak. He traded him to a gamekeeper for two cords of wood. Welcome as the fire was, we children were inconsolable. Polak was our faithful friend who had helped our first steps, for when we could only crawl we would reach up to him, hold on to his thick hair and pull ourselves to out feet, and Polak would then walk slowly round the room. We cried bitterly when we watched our father take him away. Imagine how glad we were when he reappeared even before father had got home. Father took him back to the gamekeeper, and again he returned. This time we hid him in a cave in the woods and fed him secretly for two weeks. By then the gamekeeper had given up hope of finding him, so we brought him out of the woods and father relented and let us keep him. He stayed with us for many years and lived to be sixteen. Polak gave me a lasting love for dogs. I had one with me whenever I could, and later, during the war, a dog called Lux saved my life. In Croatia in those years sixty percent of the population was illiterate. There were few schools, and many peasants resented schooling, for it took their children away from the fields and cost them their labour. But in that respect I was lucky. An elementary school was opened in Kumrovec when I was seven years old and my parents, despite their poverty, agreed that I should go. I had trouble in learning. The lessons were in Croatian and having spent so much time with Grandfather Martin I spoke better Slovenian; and I still had to work. I had little time for study. I would go to the meadow with a book in my hand, but reading was out of the question. The cow would drag me by the tether wherever she pleased. If I let my eye wander from her or dropped the tether, off she would go into someone else's field. I did rather badly in my first year. But gradually I learned and during my fourth year, as I found when I visited my old school recently, my marks were: conduct – excellent; Catechism – very good; Croatian language – good; arithmetic – fair; drawing – good; singing – good; gymnastics – very good; gardening – very good.

There were more than three hundred and fifty boys and girls in our school, and only one teacher for them all. Our teacher had consumption. He would cough and spit blood into his handkerchief, which I would later take and wash in the stream. Then we used to dry it over a fire, because it was the only handkerchief he had and I would return to the school room with it in half an hour. The teacher was very fond of me, and often used to give me bread. One day his mother came and took him away. We all stood at the fence as his cart drove off, and he waved to us with his handkerchief while we all wept.

Then a mistress came, a very severe person, but she married and soon left Kumrovec. Our third teacher was Stjepan Vimpulšek, a mild man, always considerate to his pupils, although he had a large family, a small salary, and many domestic worries.

It was a custom at Kumrovec for children to go to church on Sundays. Whenever the parish priest, Vjekoslav Homostarić, held divine service in St Roko's Chapel at Kumrovec, he took me as an acolyte. Once after the service I could not remove the vestments from the big fat priest, who was in a hurry. He was irritated and slapped me. I never went to church again.

I had many good friends in my school. I remember a cousin called Ivan Broz, who was a bright boy but a little lazy. The teacher recorded in the school register that he was mentally deficient, but later that boy became a very good mechanic.

There are other memories: of playing under the walls of the great Cesargrad castle, where we boys imagined that we were charging against the Black Queen; of fishing and cooking the catch by the river-bank in a bed of charcoal; of hunting for hickory nuts and walnuts and raiding the neighbour's apple orchard; of Pikuša, a game that we played, a combination of hockey, cricket, and golf, played five a side. It involved pushing a wooden ball into a hole in the ground, which one side defended with sticks. We made war on the boys of nearby villages; tended to the flocks in the green valley in the long, hot summer months; sat by the fire in the evening while the grown-ups told stories of the old days of Matija Gubec and talked of far-off places they had seen in their travels when they went out into the world to look for work.

All this ended when I was twelve. At that age it was customary for the boys of Zagorje to choose a means of livelihood, for they were then considered capable of supporting themselves. For a while I worked for my mother's brother tending his cattle. For this I received my food, and a promise from my uncle that he would buy me a new pair of boots at the end of the year. But he did not keep his word; he took my old boots, which had ornaments on them, repaired them for his son, and gave me a pair far worse than my old ones.

He was a stingy man, and I became so dissatisfied with his treatment that at last he realized that we could not go on with our arrangement and he advised me to leave if I wanted to. Soon afterwards a relative called Jurica, a staff-sergeant in the army, came to visit the village. He took an interest in me and told me I should become a waiter; waiters, he said, are always well dressed, always among nice people and get plenty to eat without too much hard work.

Perhaps it was the point about dressing well that interested me most. My ambition when I was a small boy was to be a tailor, a natural result of the wish of every little peasant in Zagorje to have nice clothes. I remember a baron who used to come to our district, an engineer, big and strong. He had a car that looked like a carriage and could do about fifteen miles an hour. The children would gather around it screaming when he stopped. But he lost every bit of respect in our eyes because the seat of his trousers was mended. We said: 'What kind of baron is he supposed to be with trousers mended like ours?'

My father received Jurica's idea coldly at first, for he was hoping to be able to send me to America. All Croatia was going through bad times. To protect itself against the flood of American grain, the Austro-Hungarian government set up customs tariffs on imported grain, which was of advantage chiefly to large

135

landowners and richer peasants; while the village poor, the greater part of the rural population, were scarcely able to survive on their own grain. Grain, and food in general, were extremely dear. Two hundred pounds of grain cost eighteen crowns in America and twenty-four in Austria. There was no work to be found in the villages. Large-scale emigration developed in Croatia, mostly to America. But such a journey could be made only by peasants who had enough money for the transatlantic journey. Perhaps two hundred and fifty thousand people went from Croatia to America between 1899 and 1913. Many more would have gone if they had had the money, but the journey cost about four hundred crowns, which was a great deal in those times. My father tried to collect the money for my passage, but such a sum was beyond him and finally he agreed to Jurica's suggestion.

And so at fifteen I set off with my relative, Staff-Sergeant Jurica Broz, for a little town about sixty miles away called Sisak. I looked with wonder at the old castle, a witness of the great history of this town, which in Roman times had some one hundred and thirty thousand inhabitants and was the capital of the whole province. Situated at the confluence of three rivers, it became a great stronghold against Turkish onslaughts. Its fame revived for a time during the last century when a branch of the Vienna-Trieste railway line was extended as far as Sisak, and all goods going east to Belgrade were reloaded into small vessels; but when the line was extended beyond Sisak, the little town fell again into obscurity.

For me it was a wonder after my own village. What most excited me was undoubtedly the railway engine that carried us to Sisak. How I envied the engine driver! However, I had to take a job, not with engines but in a restaurant belonging to some friends of my cousin.

It was a pleasant place, with a garden and a skittle alley where the officers and non-commissioned officers of the 27th Home Guard Regiment, whose camp was nearby, would come in the evenings and bowl under the big chestnut trees by the light of bright acetylene lamps, while a gipsy band played lively music. Nevertheless my new profession soon disappointed me, for I learned nothing and found that I had to do all sorts of jobs, including dishwashing. After my day's work I had to set up the skittle pins until late at night and be on my feet until the last guest had left.

Soon I met some apprentices who worked for a man called Nikola Karas, a locksmith. At that time a locksmith in my country not only made locks but was a sort of general mechanic in a town. He mended bicycles, shotguns, threshing machines, and repaired the hand-rails on stairs. Locksmithing was considered a craft. My friends told me that locksmithing was a form of engineering and that engineering was the most beautiful trade in the world; that engineers built ships and railways and bridges. With my family tradition of blacksmithing this appealed to me, and I went to see Karas, a kindly man of sixty, who told me I must send for my father because only he could sign the contract for my apprenticeship. My father came and reached an understanding with Karas under which my master was to give me food and lodging, my father clothes. But my father had no money, so from the small amount I had saved from tips in the restaurant, I bought blue overalls and began the career I was to follow for many years. Karas' locksmithy had one or two journeymen and three or four apprentices; for those times in Croatia it was one of the larger workshops. This very vividly illustrates how the economic development of my country was impeded, being restricted to supplying the industries of Vienna and Budapest with raw material. In all Croatia the annual production of iron and steel amounted to no more than three pounds to an inhabitant.

Life as an apprentice was an improvement over life in the restaurant. Our workshop was not large, consisting of two rooms in the cellar. In the middle of the shop was the block with the anvil. In winter months the apprentices slept on a long table, and in summer they went out into the yard and slept on the hay in the stable. Work began at six o'clock in the morning and finished about six in the evening. About midday, Karas' daughter Zora would come to the shop and bring the boys' food, and the work would go straight on.

The food was not bad. In the morning we used to get a pint of milk and coffee and a three-kreutzer roll.

I recall those years with pleasure because I had a great opportunity to learn. Twice a week I went to the apprentice school from five to seven o'clock in the evening, where we were taught geography, history, languages and general subjects. There was one teacher, Feliks Despot, whom I did not like at first. True to his name, he was very severe, and never smiled. One day I learned why. He had been married to a girl who had died in childbirth. Once as I was going past the cemetery I saw my teacher lying prostrate over his wife's grave and crying like a child. I quickly withdrew so as not to be seen and after that I had a strange respect for him. For three whole years we had never seen him smiling.

On Sunday afternoon we apprentices from different workshops would meet while our masters were having their nap after a heavy Sunday dinner. My brother Štefan was also one of Karas' apprentices, and he and I would bring our pigeons and white rabbits, like the other boys. This was actually an apprentices' pigeon and rabbit exchange. I remember a saddler apprentice called Miho Merkos, and a boy barrel-maker called Mirko Špoljar, who were my good friends. They gave me their performing pigeons and I gave them my fat white rabbits, which I had been secretly feeding with scraps of which I had deprived myself.

One day, all Sisak was excited. The river-bed near Sisak was being dredged, and the workers discovered the foundations of old Roman buildings, long submerged. Roman pots, vases, busts, and even an occasional gold piece were brought up from the river-bed. One and all rushed to the river to search in the mud, hoping to find gold pieces. We apprentices went to search for the Roman treasure in the river while Karas was away. We came back empty-handed and got a severe scolding from our master.

Twice I found myself in trouble during my apprenticeship. There was another teacher I did not like very much and on April Fool's Day I smeared some ink on the black chair he sat on. But instead, our school director, Ferdo Kefelja, came in, and in white trousers. I was too stunned to open my mouth. I wanted to tell him what I had done and kept hoping he would not sit down. He made straight for the chair, however, and when he left it there was ink on his white trousers. Afterwards I confessed and told him truthfully whom I prepared the ink for, and being a good-natured man he forgave me.

The other episode was more serious.

Going to the apprentice school had awakened in me a passion for reading. I seized everything I could lay my hands on: histories, both classical and modern novels, travel stories, adventure serials, Sherlock Holmes. It took me a long time to get money, mostly from making keys or repairing locks for neighbours, and there was not much time for reading: twelve hours in the workshop, school twice a week, and the lamp only allowed on long enough to get ready for bed. So I read during working hours. Once I was working on a lathe with a new drill, reading aloud while the other apprentices listened. They usually set a guard to look out for Karas, but Sherlock Holmes' adventures were so absorbing that the sentry forgot all about his watch. Karas came into the shop and crept behind my back; and as ill luck would have it, the drill cracked just at that moment. Karas flew into a rage and slapped my face.

I felt very bad about the slap and decided to run away, although it was the last month of my three-year apprenticeship. From Sisak I fled straight to a nearby brick factory, but Karas reported my escape to the authorities, and the gendarmes came to the factory and escorted me to the prison in Sisak. Old Karas had a good heart, though. He sent dinner to me in prison, and arranged for me to be released to complete my training and to do my first job on my own: making rails for the staircase of the District Court in Sisak.

One day a journeyman called Schmidt came to Karas' workshop from Zagreb. He was a good-looking lad who wore a red scarf, and had a friendly, cheerful nature. Unlike most of the other journeymen, he never slapped or beat us. He could talk about all sorts of things, about Halley's comet and the aviator Farman and other marvels, while we listened open-mouthed. On the eve of May Day, 1909, he told us that it was the workers' holiday and that we must bring green boughs and flowers to decorate our workshop. I had many talks afterwards with Schmidt and learned more. To my regret he soon moved on, in the usual journeyman's way, but then another one came – Gasparić. He was a strong fellow and taught us to wrestle in the Græco-Roman style. Gasparić was even more militant than Schmidt. He and some other workers, particularly carpenters and printers, began to meet at the Lovački Rog (Hunter's Horn) beer-house to discuss organizing unions. Although trade unions in Croatia had been formed far back in the middle of the last century, and the Social-Democratic Party was organized in 1894, they were persecuted. In one year, twenty-three out of twenty-four issues of a socialist paper were banned. In Sisak there were no trade unions, for they were banned by the local authorities.

We apprentices were not allowed to go to the beer-house for ourselves, but often Karas would send us to fetch him beer and then we used to peep inquisitively into the room where Gasparić and his friends met. They held their talks under difficult conditions. The innkeeper would not allow them to stay unless they ordered something to drink. Within an hour they would become mellow and gay, and thereafter nothing serious was accomplished. This sort of trouble was common, and resulted in the building of workers' halls. There was already one in nearby Brod, but none in Sisak.

Gasparić did what he could, which consisted of indoctrinating us apprentices. At his suggestion I collected donations for *Free Word*, the socialist newspaper, and sold 'workers' matches', five percent of the proceeds going to the paper. I read the pamphlets he brought to the shop for us, especially the book *Looking Backwards* by Edward Bellamy and, of course, *Free Word*, which gave us news of workers' movements in other countries. I remember especially the stories of the persecutions in Russia, of the twelve Japanese socialists who had been sentenced to death by the Mikado and of the 'Socialist Republic' that was being formed in Milwaukee, where the socialists had won the election.

In Croatia, where because of the property qualification only seven percent of the people could vote, the Social Democrats had only one deputy in Parliament. In my own village there were only three voters. I was filled with ambition to do something about these conditions and was ready to set out from Sisak into the world on my own. I was, as it will be easy to understand, an ardent sympathizer of the Social-Democratic party and looked forward eagerly to joining a trade union.

Another important reason for leaving Sisak when I became a journeyman was my desire to perfect my trade. At that time there was no specialization, and a locksmith was obliged to know all kinds of engineering work. On the other hand, it was the custom for a master to keep all knowledge of precision work from his apprentices, to prevent competition when they in turn became masters, and Karas was no exception to this rule.

So in my eighteenth year the world lay open before me.

III: Cities

THE COAST OF DALMATIA, with its spectacular scenery, venerable maritime history and political significance, is the location of some of the most interesting cities and towns of the Mediterranean. The coast has long been of strategic importance, both militarily and economically, and its wonderful cities and towns have always attracted travellers and merchants from overseas. From Split, built around the grand palace of a Roman emperor, to Dubrovnik, the jewel of the Adriatic, Croatia's maritime cities were the crucial link between Italy, central Europe and the empires of the East. Spread out along the rugged landscape of the coast, sheltered behind the myriad islands of the Dalmatian archipelago, these cities and towns are steeped in the history of Mediterranean travel, trade and power.

Diocletian, the Illyrian-born Roman emperor who ruled from 284AD until 305AD, is credited with the shoring up of Roman power during a period when the Empire was becoming increasingly stretched in Africa and the east, and simultaneously coming under heavy barbarian attack in northern Europe. His solution was to divide the administrative burden in two and assign a senior and junior emperor to each half, a system that became known as 'the Tetrarchy'. Diocletian is also remembered for his part in the extreme repression of Christianity, the so-called 'Great Persecutions', which began in 303 and lasted to around 313. So many Christians were killed that the period is known in the Christian tradition as 'the time of martyrs'. After his abdication in

305, he retired to the monumental palace which had been constructed for him in the province of his birth. While the innovation of the Tetrarchy was initially successful, it foundered in civil war after Diocletian's departure, and Constantine emerged from the resulting chaos as sole emperor in 306, setting the stage for the collapse of the Western empire and the eventual rise of Byzantine power in the city he refounded as Constantinople. The selection from Edward Gibbon's monumental *The Decline and Fall of the Roman Empire* concerns Diocletian's retirement to what is now the city of Split, and the extraordinary palace which was his home in the twilight of his life.

Spalato and Trau is an edited extract from Robert Smythe Hichens's *The Near East: Dalmatia, Greece and Constantinople*, published in 1913, a travelogue which gives a lively and closely observed account of a trip to parts of the Mediterranean world which at that time were still relatively unknown to most Western Europeans. Hichens (1864-1950), who published widely and successfully during his life, is now best remembered as a writer of supernatural tales, the most famous of these being *How Love Came to Professor Guildea*, the story of cold-hearted scientist who is persecuted by the affections of an unseen being. In the passages below, Hichens's novelistic eye for detail and atmosphere is at the fore, and his section on the beautiful seaside town of Trau rhymes well with the extract we have chosen from Ann Bridge's 1935 novel *Illyrian Spring*. Bridge (1889-1974) published prolifically and successfully as a novelist during her life. Her first novel, *Peking Picnic*, was widely acclaimed when it appeared in 1932, winning the Atlantic Monthly Prize, and several of her later novels, including *Illyrian Spring*, were Book Society Choices. *Illyrian Spring* tells the story of a successful but sad painter, Lady Kilmichael, who journeys to Yugoslavia to escape an increasingly frustrating home life. On the sparkling coast of Dalmatia she strikes up a friendship with Nicholas, a precocious young painter with problems of his own. Bridge's richly detailed evocation of Dalmatia includes some delightful passages set in Trau, and her descriptions of the town and landscape are themselves marvellously painterly, a mirror of the activity of her protagonists. The overall effect is of shimmering colour in the intense and changeable light of the Adriatic.

The third extract is by the distinguished archaeologist sometimes known as the 'father of egyptology', Sir John Gardner Wilkinson (1797-1875). Wilkinson made his first trip to Africa in 1821. Having left Oxford without getting a degree, he departed from England in poor health to spend some time in Europe. It was in Italy, under the influence of the egyptologist Sir William Gell, that he developed his passion for the archaeology of Egypt. His first trip was to last over ten years, during which he travelled widely in the country, learned Arabic and Coptic, and contributed very significantly to the archaeology of the ancient kingdoms. His system for the numbering of tombs is still in use, and he provided the first full chronology of the New Kingdom, as well as mapping the entire site of the ancient city of Thebes (not to be confused with the Greek Thebes made famous in the myth of Oedipus). Wilkinson had a passion for travel, and was a meticulous observer. *Dalmatia and Montenegro*, an account of his journey through the area in 1844, was first published in 1848; it contains a wealth of detail about the country and its history as well as its inhabitants and their customs. The extract chosen here describes the fair at Salona (now Solin, near Split), and gives the reader a strong impression of the happy excitement of the crowd and noisy hubbub of this annual event in the Dalmatian calendar.

The final selection in this chapter is a pamphlet by one Leonard Green, of whom there is little certain information. *A Memory of Ragusa*, which we reproduce in full, is an example of that unusual class of documents, the completely private publication. We can assume it was produced in a tiny edition for a small number of people known to the author, since the only publication information provided by the author is the name of the printing house, and he states that it has been produced by him 'for his friends' as a Christmas greeting, something which he seems to have done more than once since there are some other similar holdings kept at the British Library. Perhaps these friends are those same people who were with him in Ragusa (now Dubrovnik) to witness the extraordinary scenes described in his pamphlet. The occasion was the funeral of the murdered Croatian politician Stjepan Radić ('Raditch' as Green has it). Radic, born in 1871, was the celebrated leader of the Croatian Republican Peasants' Party, which had argued for the creation of a unified Balkan peasant federation incorporating Slovenia, Croatia, Serbia and Bulgaria. In June 1928 he was shot in the parliamentary chamber at Belgrade by a Montenegrin politician, and he died two months later. His funeral in Zagreb was attended by one hundred thousand people; Green and his companions saw the marking of this event in Ragusa, and his decision to write this account of it and publish privately gives us a marvellous insight into the character of public events in the Dalmatian city during the interwar years. The Nettuno Convention to which Green refers was a series of treaties aimed at improving economic relations with Italy; negotiated in 1925, they had remained unratified by the Yugoslav government until 1928, when they were signed by the then foreign minister Vojislav Marinkovic.

Edward Gibbon
From *The History of the Decline and Fall of the Roman Empire (1875)*

Diocletian in Split

Diocletian, who, from a servile origin, had raised himself to the throne, passed the nine last years of his life in a private condition. Reason had dictated, and content seems to have accompanied, his retreat, in which he enjoyed for a long time the respect of those princes to whom he had resigned the possession of the world.

It is seldom that minds, long exercised in business, have formed any habits of conversing with themselves, and in the loss of power they principally regret the want of occupation. The amusements of letters and of devotion, which afford so many resources in solitude, were incapable of fixing the attention of Diocletian; but he had preserved, or at least he soon recovered, a taste for the most innocent as well as natural pleasures, and his leisure hours were sufficiently employed in building, planting and gardening. His answer to Maximian is deservedly celebrated. He was solicited by that restless old man to reassume the reins of government and the Imperial purple. He rejected the temptation with a smile of pity, calmly observing that if he could shew Maximian the cabbages which he had planted with his own hands at Salona, he should no longer be urged to relinquish the enjoyment of happiness for the pursuit of power.

Before we dismiss the consideration of the life and character of Diocletian, we may, for a moment, direct our view to the place of his retirement. Salona, a principal city of his native province of Dalmatia, was near two hundred Roman miles (according to the measurement of the public highways) from Aquileia and the confines of Italy, and about two hundred and seventy from Sirmium, the usual residence of the emperors, whenever they visited the Illyrian frontier. A miserable village still preserves the name of Salona, but so late as the sixteenth century, the remains of a theatre, and a confused prospect of broken arches and marble columns, continued to attest its ancient splendour. About six or seven miles from the city, Diocletian constructed a massive palace, and we may infer from the greatness of the work, how long he had meditated his design of abdicating the empire. The choice of a spot which united all that could contribute either to health or to luxury, did not require the partiality of a native. 'The soil was dry and fertile, the air is pure and wholesome, and though extremely hot during the summer months, this country seldom feels those sultry and noxious winds, to which the coast of Istria and some parts of Italy are exposed. The views from the palace are no less beautiful than the soil and climate was inviting. Towards the west lies the fertile shore that stretches along the Hadriatic, in which a number of small islands are scattered in such a manner, as to give this part of the sea the appearance of a great lake. On the north side lies the bay, which led to the ancient city of Salona; and the country beyond it, appearing in sight, forms a proper contrast to that more extensive prospect of water, which the Hadriatic presents both to the south and to the east. Towards the north, the view is terminated by high and irregular mountains, situated at a proper distance, and, in many places, covered with villages, woods, and vineyards.'

Though Constantine, from a very obvious prejudice, affects to mention the palace of Diocletian with contempt, yet one of their successors, who could only see it in a neglected and mutilated state, celebrates its magnificence in terms of the highest admiration. It covered an extent of ground consisting of between nine and ten English acres. The form was quadrangular, flanked with sixteen towers. Two of the sides were near six hundred, and the other two near seven hundred feet in length. The whole was constructed of a beautiful free-stone, extracted from the neighbourhood quarries of Trau or Tragutium, and very little inferior to marble itself. Four streets, intersecting each other at right angles, divided the several parts of this great edifice, and the approach to the principal apartment was from a stately entrance, which is still denominated the Golden Gate. The approach was terminated by a *peristylium* of granite columns, on one side of which we discover the square temple of Æsculapius, on the other the octagon temple of Jupiter. The latter of those deities Diocletian revered as the patron of his fortunes, the former as the protector of his health. By comparing the present remains with the precepts of Vitruvius, the several parts of the building, the baths, bedchamber, the *atriumi*, the *basilica*, and the Cyzicene, Corinthian and Egyptian halls, have all been described with some degree of precision, or at least of probability. Their forms were various, their proportions just, but they were all attended with two imperfections, very repugnant to our modern notions of taste and conveniency. These stately rooms had neither windows nor chimneys. They were lighted from the top (for the building seems to have consisted of no more than one storey), and they received their heat by the help of pipes that were conveyed along the walls. The range of principal apartments was protected towards the south-west, by a portico five hundred and seventeen feet long, which must have formed a very noble and delightful walk, when the beauties of painting and sculpture were added to those of the prospect.

Had this magnificent edifice remained in a solitary country, it would have been exposed to the ravages of time; but it might, perhaps, have escaped the rapacious industry of man. The village of Aspalathus, and long afterwards the provincial town of Spalato, have grown out of its ruins. The Golden Gate now opens into the market place. St John the Baptist has usurped the honours of Æsculapius; and the temple of Jupiter, under the protection of the Virgin, is converted into the cathedral church.

Robert Smythe Hichens
From *The Near East: Dalmatia, Greece and Constantinople (1913)*

Spalato and Trau

Bora, the wind of the dead, blew when our ship rounded the lighthouse of Spalato long after darkness had fallen. And the following day was the '*giorno dei morti*.' The strange cathedral, once the mausoleum of the Emperor Diocletian, was crowded with citizens and peasants devoutly praying. Incense rose between the dark, hoary walls, the columns of granite and porphyry, to the dome of brick. Outside in the wind the black hornblende sphinx kept watch on those who came and went, mourning for their departure. The sky was a heavy grey, and the temple was dark and looked wrinkled and seared with age, and sad despite its pagan frieze showing the wild joys of the chase, despite the loveliness of its thirteenth-century pulpit of limestone and marble, raised high on wonderfully graceful columns with elaborately carved capitals.

Spalato is the biggest, most bustling town of Dalmatia. Much of it is built into the great palace of Diocletian, which lies over against the sea, huge, massive, powerful, once probably noble, but now disfigured by the paltry windows and the green shutters of modern dwellings, by a triviality of common commercial life, sparrows where eagles should usually be. When nature takes a ruin, she usually glorifies it, or touches it with a tenderness of romance. But when people in the wine trade lay hold upon it, hang out their washing on it, and establish their cafés and their bakeries and their butchers' shops in the midst of its rugged walls, its arches and its columns, the ruin suffers, and the people in the wine trade seem to lose in value instead of gaining in importance.

Spalato is a strange confusion of old and new. It lacks the delicacy of Zara, the harmonious beauty of Ragusa. One era seems to fight with another within it. Here is a noble twelfth-century *campanile*, nearly a hundred and eighty feet high, there a common row of little shops full of cheap and uninviting articles. Turning a corner, one comes unexpectedly upon a Corinthian temple. It is the Battistero di San Giovanni, once perhaps the private temple of Diocletian. For the moment no one is near it, and despite the icy breath of the *Bora* raging through the city and crying, 'This is the day of the dead!' a calm of dead years enfolds you as you enter the massive doorway and pass into the shadow beneath the stone wagon-roof. A few steps, and the smell of fish assails you, hundreds of strings of onions greet your eyes, and the heavy rolling of enormous barrels of wine over the stone pavements breaks through the noise of the wind. You have come unexpectedly out through a gateway of the palace onto the quay to the south, and are in the midst of commercial activities. The

149

contrasts are picturesque, but they are rough, and, when complicated by the *Bora*, are confusing, almost distressing. Nevertheless, Spalato is well worth a visit. It contains a small, but remarkable, museum, specially interesting for its sarcophagi found at Salona and its collection of inscriptions. The sarcophagus showing the passage of the Red Sea is very curious. Apart from the now disfigured palace, the Battistero, the very interesting and peculiar cathedral, with its vestibule, its rotunda, and its Piazza of the Sphinx, like nothing else I have seen, the town is full of picturesque nooks and corners; and its fruit market at the foot of the massive octagonal Hrvoja Tower, which dates from 1481, is perhaps even more animated, more full of strangeness and colour, than Zara's Piazza delle Erbe. Here may be seen turbans of crimson on the handsome heads of men, elaborately embroidered crimson jackets covering immense shoulders and chests, women dressed in blue and red, white and silver, or with heads and busts draped in the most brilliant shade of orange colour. When the *Bora* blows, the men look like monks or Mephistopheles; for some – the greater number – wrap themselves from head to foot in long cloaks and hoods of brown, while others of a more lively temperament shroud themselves in red. They are a handsome people, rustic-looking, yet often noble, with kind yet bold faces, steady eyes, and a magnificent physique. Their gait is large and loose. There are giants in Dalmatia in our days. And many of the women are not only pretty, but have delightful expressions, open, pure, and gay. There seems to be nothing to fear in Dalmatia. I have driven through the wilds, and over the flanks of the mountains, both in Dalmatia and Herzegovina, in the dead of the night, and had no unpleasant experience. The peasants have a high reputation for honesty and general probity as well as for courage. And beggars are scarce, if they exist at all, in Dalmatia.

Trau has a unique charm. The riviera of the Sette Castelli stretches between it and Spalato, along the shore of an inlet of the sea which is exactly like a blue lake. And what a marvellous blue it is on a cloudless autumn day! Everyone knows what is meant by a rapture of spring. Those who traverse that riviera at the end of October, or even in the opening days of November, will know what a rapture of autumn can be.

Miles upon miles of bright-golden and rose-red vineyards edge the startling blue sea. And the vines are not stunted and ugly, but large, leafy, growing with a rank luxuriance. Among them, with trunks caught as it were in the warm embraces of these troops of bacchantes, are thousands of silver-green olive-trees. And peasants in red, peasants in orange colour, move waist-deep, sometimes shoulder-deep, through the glory, under the glory of the sun. Here and there in a grass-grown clearing, like a small islet in the ocean of vines, appears a hut of brushwood and woven grasses, and under the trees before it sit peasants eating the grapes they have just picked warm from the plants. Now and then a sportsman may be seen, in peasant costume, smoking a cigarette, his gun over his shoulder, passing slowly with his red-brown dog among the red-gold vines. Now and then a distant report rings out among the olives. Then the warm silence falls again over this rapture of autumn. And so, you come to Trau.

Trau is a tiny town, set on a tiny island approached by bridges, medieval, sleepy, yet happy, almost drowsily joyous, in appearance, with that air of half-gentle, half-blithe satisfaction with self which makes so many Dalmatian places characteristic and almost touching. How odd to live in Trau! Yet might it not be a delicious experience to live in dear little Trau with the right person, separated from the world by the shining water, – for who comes over the bridges, when all is said? – guarded by the lion and the statue which crown the gateway, cradled in peace and mellow fruitfulness?

The gateway passed, a narrow alley or two threaded, a corner turned, and, lo! a piazza, a loggia with fine old columns, a tiled roof and a clock-tower, a *campanile* and a cathedral with a great porch, and underneath the porch a marvel of a doorway! Can tiny Trau on its island really possess all this?

The lion doorway of the *duomo* at Trau is certainly one of the finest things Dalmatia. The *duomo* dates from the thirteenth century, but has been twice enlarged. It is not large now, but small and high, dim, full of the smell of stale incense, blackened by age, almost strangely silent, almost strangely secluded. In the choir is a deep well with an old well-head. There are many tombs in the pavement. The finely carved pulpit, with its little lion, and the fifteenth-century choir stalls are well worth seeing, and the roof of the chapel of St Giovanni Orsini, which contains a great marble tomb, has been made wonderful by age, like an old face made wonderful by wrinkles. But Radovan's doorway is certainly the marvel of Trau. In colour it is a rich, deep, dusty brown, and it is elaborately and splendidly carved with two big lions, with Adam on a lion and with Eve on a lioness. The lioness is grasping a lamb. There is a multiplicity of other detail. The two big lions, which stick out on each side of the round-arched doorway, as if about to step forth into the alleys of Trau, have a fine air of life, though they both look tame. Their mouths are open, but almost smiling.

When you leave the *duomo*, wander through the Venetian streets of this wonderful little island city, where Gothic windows and beautifully carved balconies look out to, lean forth to, the calm, blue waters, edged by the red and the gold of the vines. For this place is unique and has an unique charm. Peace dwells here, where it lingers, and will linger, I hope, for many centuries yet, girdled by olive groves, by vineyards, by sun-kissed waters, guarded by the lions of Venice.

Ann Bridge
From *Illyrian Spring (1935)*

'Yes, but I still don't quite like it, Nicholas. All that foreground is too flat; it's too much the same quality as the wall and the tower. You want to make more difference between flowers and stone.

Why don't you use another brush for that part? And I think you'd do better with a little green in the paint for that – there's always a green tone about the white of flowers. I don't like that shadow from the column either.'

'What's wrong with it?'

'You've got it too like the tower shadow – don't you see? It's nearer – well, then bring it forward.' She waved her hand at it. 'And I should get some red into the picture, here, and here – that will help pull the whole thing together and warm it up. If you can get all that better I think it will really be rather good.'

'You're a hard task-mistress, Lady K! I was rather pleased with it.'

'No, I don't feel you've quite got it, my dear child. It wants pulling together. I know it's difficult, all that white on white – but you *did* choose it!'

'And you *did* think I couldn't do it didn't you?' said Nicholas, screwing himself round on the camp-stool to grin up at Lady Kilmichael, as she stood behind him, studying the canvas on the easel. 'And you're quite surprised that Little Nicky has done it even as well as he has!'

'Yes – but it's not in the least use for Little Nicky'– the warmth of an imperceptible smile came into her voice on the two words – 'to half-paint things. You must *see* a subject properly, the essentials of it; and then get them into a picture. It's no good painting shapeless unselected masses of objects.'

They were on the broad *fondamento* at Trau, outside the Porta Marina, over which the Lion of St. Mark, in his little penthouse, presides with such a singularly coy and lamb-like expression. Immediately to the right a projecting piece of the city wall cuts off the view abruptly – to the left the sea, the hills and shores beyond showed blue and pearl-like as a milky opal, faintly traced with masts of ships moored at the quayside; the long vista was closed at the further end by the creamy polygonal mass of the Camerlengo tower, part of the old Venetian fortifications, its heavy crenellated battlements crumbling here and there – in the foreground that white column rose, abrupt and solitary, from the pavement. That view up the *fondamento* is at all times one of the loveliest aspects of the lovely little island town, but in the month of May a strange enchantment is added. The inhabitants of Trau then cut, in their mainland fields, the harvest of the starry white *Chrysanthemum cinerarioefolium,* from which insect-powder is made, and spread them out on mats to dry in the sun all along the *fondamento,* so that whole immense space is floored, not with cobbles or flagstones, but with flowers. There was something incredibly lovely about that pale pavement of blossom, spreading up to the foot of the white column, and stretching away towards the creamy mass of the tower beyond, under the tender blue of the North Adriatic sky – a strange blue, washed with silver, as if it had taken its tone from the silvery white of the limestone hills, the pale rocks of that arid coast. And it was this aspect of Trau that Nicholas had elected to paint.

It was his second picture, and he had already spent a couple of days on it. He had begun with a brilliant little painting of three women in the pottery market outside the former Porta Aenea at Spalato, which he had finished in a day – a painting so good that Grace was astonished. It seemed that he really could make a picture as well as a sketch; make a whole out of his subject, with the solidity of the actual somehow welded and fused into the significance of the design. This, for her, was the essential thing, and it looked as if Nicholas had got it. Technical accomplishment of course he still lacked, except for his draughtsmanship, which was already astonishing; his sense of colour seemed to her weak too. But that he was worth helping she felt sure. After that first picture she insisted on going to Trau, to get fresh material for her own sketches for the American contract. She found plenty. The little medieval town, filling its island to the brim like one of those toy cities in ivory with painted roofs, set in a border of looking glass, was so full of delicious things to draw that she hardly knew where to begin. And there Nicholas had fixed on the view from the *fondamento,* with the flowers, the column and the tower, as the thing he would and must paint next. Grace had thought it over-ambitious, and said so; lovely in itself, all those different planes and tones of creamy white, in the soft clear light, might be difficult to make anything of, she considered. But Nicholas had persisted, and had tackled it with a measure of success that surprised her. It gave, indeed, just the measure of his success that she was now become so critical – was forcing him towards such a high degree of excellence, of completeness. If he had failed, as she expected, she would have encouraged him and left him alone.

They had fallen into a sort of routine of work, quickly and almost without noticing it. The buses from Spalato to Trau were slow, and at awkward times; the hire of a car and chauffeur was exorbitant. Nicholas, suddenly displaying a quite unexpected resourcefulness, had thereupon routed out, through the agency of one of his sitters in the pottery market, a rather dilapidated Peugeot car which he managed to hire without a driver for quite a reasonable sum. Every day, in this, they drove over to Trau, where he parked it on the small piazza by the bridge; they worked all the morning, took a long luncheon interval at the little restaurant on the quay, sitting under the shade of the awning, and then, if they had the energy, filled up their sketchbooks for an hour or so in the afternoon. At four or thereabouts they knocked off, and armed with Grace's tea-basket drove somewhere for a picnic and a little sightseeing, only returning at dark to Spalato, to dine at the restaurant in the Piazza, and then to sit outside it, drinking coffee or beer, watching the shadows flung by the street-lamps repeating the grace of the colonnades in black along the white pavement, and the octagonal lantern of Diocletian's mausoleum grey against the stars.

Grace loved these expeditions. The landscape of Dalmatia, as they gradually revealed it to her, was a perpetually renewed enchantment. She could not get over the fact that the prevailing colour of that coast should be white. Shades, gradations of tone of course there were, but the impression was of a white landscape; and the summits of the mountains, above the last traces of vegetation, where really white, like paper or cream. And in what subtle ways these white hills took their colour from the light and atmosphere about them! On lowering days they showed a sullen grey, featureless and dull; at noon, in sunshine, they had the warmth of ivory; there was a moment at evening when, most strange of all, as the light left the sky all the solidity of rock and stone deserted them, and they melted into the sky, became invisible, lost in one incredibly tender tone, like a shadowy pearl. She was charmed too with the near-at-hand details of the landscape – the grace of olive trees, the patches of bright flowers, goats browsing among ruins, the dark flame-like shapes of cypresses round some monastery – and for a background, always, that delicate, opalescent blue of the sea and the shores of bays and islands.

Sir John Gardner Wilkinson
From *Dalmatia and Montenegro (1848)*

A great fair is held every year at Salona, on September 8th, to which all the people of the neighbourhood look forward, with anticipations of feasting, business and amusement.

It is a curious sight, and the concourse of people is very great. The costumes are numerous and varied; among which the most remarkable are those of the pretty Castellane women, of the townspeople and peasantry of Sign and Sebenico; and of the peasantry, and the *borghesi*, of Spalato. Many come from the Turkish frontier; and sometimes a few Turks from Herzegovina, whose dress differs not very much from that of the Morlacchi who wear the turban. The costumes of the women are the most numerous and remarkable, those of the men varying much less, in the different districts of Dalmatia; but the colours in both are striking, are admirably suited for a picture. Blue and red are most predominant.

All Spalato is, of course, at the fair: and the road to Salona is thronged with carriages of every description, horsemen and pedestrians. The mixture of the men's hats, red caps, and turbans, and the bonnets and Frank dresses of the Spalatine ladies, contrasted with the various costumes of the country-women, present one of the most singular sights to be seen in Europe; and to a stranger the language adds in no small degree to its novelty.

Some business is done, as well as pleasure; and a great number of cattle, sheep and pigs are bought and sold, as well as various stuffs, trinkets and the usual goods exhibited at fairs. Long before midday, the groups of peasants have thronged the roads, not to say streets, of Salona; some attend the small church, picturesquely placed upon a green surrounded by the small streams of the Giadro, and shaded with trees; while others rove about, seeking their friends, looking at, and looked at by, strangers as they pass; and all are intent on the amusements of the day and the prospects of a feast.

Eating and drinking soon begin. On all sides, sheep are seen roasting whole on wooden spits, in the open air; and an entire flock is speedily turned to mutton. Small knots of hungry friends are formed in every direction: some seated on a bank under the trees, others in as many houses as will hold them, some on the grass by the roadside regardless of sun and dust, and a few quiet families have boats prepared for their reception.

In the meantime, the hat-wearing townspeople from Spalato and other places, as they pace up and down bowing to an occasional acquaintance, view with complacent pity the primitive recreations of the simple peasantry; and arm-in-arm civilisation, with its propriety and affectation, is here strangely contrasted with the hearty mirth of the unrefined Morlacchi. At the fête of Bubastis in Egypt, more wine was said to be consumed than during all the rest of the year; and the same may, perhaps, be said of the fair of Salona; but some years ago the resemblance of the two fêtes was still more strikingly like, and the fights that 'came off' were worthy of Bubastis, or of Donnybrook. This was 'in the good old times' of Venetian rule, when anyone was allowed to take the law into his own hands and settle with his enemy, without troubling a magistrate. The Morlacco then waited for the fair of Salona to pay off old scores of revenge, and on this day of retaliation many scenes of bloodshed took place.

The Austrian government has put a stop to the barbarous system; all now passes off with good-humoured conviviality; and if some *sirdárs*, or rural police officers, attend, with their armed *pandoórs*, to prevent irregularities, this is the only precaution taken on an occasion, which formerly required the presence of a military force. The dress of these *pandoórs* is the same as of the other Morlacchi, who are all armed; and their sole distinction is a small flat plume of brass feathers, worn in the turban.

The dance of the Morlacchi is the most interesting sight at the fair. It sometimes begins before dinner, but is kept up with greater spirit afterwards. They call it *Collo*, from being, like most of their national dances, in a circle. A man generally has one partner, sometimes two, but always at his right side. In dancing, he takes her right hand with his, while she supports herself by holding his girdle with her left; and when he has two partners, the one nearest him holds in her right hand that of her companion, who with her left takes the right hand of the man; and each set dances forward in a line, round the circle. The step is rude, as in most of the Slavonic dances, including the *polka*, and *radovátschka*; and the music, which is primitive, is confined to a three-stringed violin.

The distance that many people have to go, and the early habits of the people, prevent the 'festivities being kept up to a late hour;' which, with the regulations of a cautious police, ensure the quiet termination of this lively scene.

Leonard Green
From *A Memory of Ragusa (1929)*

I

It is August, 1928. Wherever one goes in that fortified city of Ragusa – that gave its name to those fabled 'argosies' of our childhood – there is abundant display of the national tri-colour. The city seems to rise white from the dazzling sea, its grey walls and bastions one with the rocks that are their foundation, and the air is filled with an aromatic tropical scent of pine, rosemary and oleander. The narrow paved streets that admit no traffic but the passenger by foot, and an occasional donkey with laden panniers, are bright with flags, and then one notices that every other windowsill, and every one of those stone Venetian balconies over which a vine has been trained to act as roofing, carries a wide piece of black cloth or silk. The flags are all seen to be at half-mast, and before where all seemed gay with colour, now black is seen to predominate. On the lintels of private doorways and on all public buildings are placards deeply edged in black; outside the newspaper shops are the Zagreb papers with funereal borders and headlines; the electric lamps in the Stradone give out a weeping radiance through the crepe shrouds that envelop them. Why?

Because Raditch is dead, and the Nettuno Conventions have been signed by 'bloody Belgrade'.

II

Photographs of the dead leader fill every shop window. Peasants from the mountains who have come into market, picturesque in their national dress, stand looking at the newspaper photographs of that great funeral in Zagrab. The are no orchestras in the cafés, no concert in the Brsalje, that beautiful piazza shaded by mulberry trees, under which the whole town sits gossiping in the evenings with its Turkish coffee and its *Slivovitz*, the great fourteenth-century stone tower, seventy feet high, at one side, and the blue Adriatic, that cage of sunlight, stretching away to infinity. In the midst of this national mourning for a political leader, whose elevation to the rank of hero is due in part, perhaps, to the spectacular circumstances of his tragic death, the celebration of the popular festival of the Assumption of the Sainte Vièrge is something of a relief, though shorn of the jollities that normally conclude it. For two days the great beaten silver plaque of the Madonna and Child, their faces copper-coloured like the bodies of their sun-dyed worshippers, has been set up on a kind of palanquin in one of the chapels of the Cathedral, and unceasingly women have come to pray and kiss the Madonna's silver robe.

But it is in the late afternoon of the holiday that evidences of the day's interior preparations are seen. About five o'clock the Stradone, that paved street that runs from west to east of the walled town, is filled with a throng of men and women in their national dress. The men wear breeches with scarlet sash, and, in the case of many of the older men, from its ample folds peep out the chased silver handles of knives and pistols, for the brigand sleeps only just beneath the surface of your older Dalmatian. Over the snow-white linen shirt, with its ample episcopal sleeves, is the waistcoat embroidered in many colours and crowning all, the round red cap with its golden or coloured tassel.

III

The women come walking in twos or threes, their long wide skirts billowing like a ship in full sail, caught tightly at the waist by an embroidered girdle, and above the wide sleeves of their bodice emphasising the gorgeous colours of their waistcoats; on the head a tall white cap with wings. They walk, swinging rhythmically from the hips, some part of the lilt being due perhaps to the habit in the daytime of carrying heavy loads upon their heads, leaving the arms free to swing with the rest of the body.

We all make our way down the Stradone, past the church of St Biagio, and past the Rector's Palace, reminiscent in a diminished form of the Doge's Palace at Venice, to the Cathedral, founded by Richard Coeur de Lion in 1192.

The great doors on the north, and the south, and the west are wide open, and through these the whole town streams. There is an entire absence of formality. There are a few benches and a few praying desks, but we mostly stand, the women flirting with their fans, the men using their straw hats to make a little breeze in the intense heat. Some old priests sit around the High Altar saying their office, but no one pays much attention to them. The devout are saying their own prayers, none so enthralled that she cannot greet a neighbour. One chapel is filled with Franciscans, in brown habits with white girdles, grouped picture-like round the altar and engaged in their own devotions until it is time for them to take part in the procession.

IV

Small boys in fluttering white surplices stand about in groups, or run on little errands, in and out of the crowd. Old men in their national dress, carrying huge candles, one of them staggering under an enormous wooden crucifix, push their way to the centre of things. And the lads of the town are there too, fresh from a day on the sea, their copper-coloured bodies gleaming through their thin white linen shirts, open at throat and chest. They stand in groups, friends with their arms around each other's necks, others holding hands, all of them groups of statuary breathing and alive.

Suddenly the organ blares out – the air grows heavy with incense, groups of priests are seen to have robed and assembled round the High Altar. The procession is about to begin. Out we all dash into the Piazza to get a good view, and after some slight waiting, there is a clangour of bells and we see the foremost banner come round the west side of the Cathedral Church of Madonna Maggiore. Immediately there is a whirring of wings and the sky is darkened momentarily by a great flock of pigeons that have risen from the marketplace and fly off to Heaven to tell Madonna that her procession has started.

Behind the first banner, and leading the procession, come two long lines of small children, five or six years old, shuffling along in their sandalled feet, very solemn and well-behaved, their dignity hurt from time to time by some elder brother or father in the crowd, who pats the small head encouragingly as the procession goes by.

V

Then come the Franciscans and the Dominicans, then a band of small girls scattering roses and oleanders from ribboned baskets, and then the great silver Madonna and Child riding on a blue silk palanquin carried by old, gnarled men in their embroidered clothes, the disengaged hand mopping the profuse perspiration, a bodyguard carrying lighted candles. Then the priests, smothered in great copes of white damask with bright Dalmatian colours.

After this there is no more colour: all the colour has been grouped around the Madonna. Now follow the men's guilds, the men in black, with white linen shirts relieving the opacity, then a crowd of nuns, and then all the mothers and widows of the town, over their heads long black lace scarves.

The procession winds along the narrow street that runs parallel with the Stradone, and turns into the latter, down which it comes to return to the Cathedral. As it passes the Church of the Franciscans their bells ring out and the Dominican and Jesuit bells join the chorus, until all the bells in the town are ringing, just as all the people in the town have joined the procession. Back we pour into the Cathedral for Benediction and the Exposition of the Host.

VI

The harsh, strong voices of the women chant an interminable litany, with a gay, waltz-like flavour about the tune, and then the great moment arrives, the focus of all this explicit devotion. From a golden haze of innumerable candles and incense smoke, the gorgeous figure of the priest is seen holding up the Host. We all drop to our knees; for one brief moment there is silence, and then – all is over – we rush helter-skelter through the big doors, leaving the nuns still singing that waltz-like litany, so that almost we dance out into the piazza and normally a secular jollity would replace the religious. But Raditch is dead and the national mourning checks the exuberance.

But what are the boys shouting and why are they running down to the old harbour? We all crowd down and, standing at the quay, pressing close to each other, we see the hillside above the town ablaze. The great heat of the past days, or perhaps a chance match, has set the pinewoods alight, and fascinated, we watch the great natural bonfire, the resinous perfume of the burning pine making the whole air odorous. The Madonna has arranged a fitting end to the *festa* after all. Or perhaps it is a funeral pyre for the dead leader, and out of the ashes there will arise another to maintain and strengthen Yugo-Slav unity.

IV: War

I T HAS BEEN CROATIA's misfortune to find itself situated at one of the great strategic points on the European map. As a crucial part of the Balkan gateway to the East, and controlling some of the key cities on the Adriatic, it has been important as a buffer zone, a staging post and a trading point. As so it has also been a vital interest in any clash of greater powers, whether local or remote, and this has brought war to the country many times throughout history. It was a flash-point during the Second World War, and several of the extracts here are concerned with the Allied support for Tito's anti-Fascist Partisans, which was initially staged from the inhospitable islands of the Dalmatian archipelago. Croatia was the scene of brutal fighting again in the disastrous aftermath of the collapse of Yugoslavia, as nationalist ambitions which had been suppressed under the previous regime came to the surface across the Yugoslav Balkans.

The Fourth Crusade has been described as 'the unholy crusade'; certainly the sack of Zara (now Zadar) was censured by the Pope who had raised the armies of the Cross, but it deserved this name for more than that. Although the original intention had been an assault on Islamic power in order to help take the Holy Land back for Christendom, the Crusade was diverted from its planned attack on Egypt (then the seat of Muslim power) by clever politicking, initially by the Venetians, and then by exiled Byzantines. The result was that the Crusader army ended by attacking, laying seige to, and finally sacking the Christian city of Constantinople, precipitating the definitive split between the Eastern Orthodox and Catholic Churches.

Innocent III had called for a Crusade in 1198; after some difficulty, an army, mostly from northern France, was raised. Contacts had been established with Venice, and the departure for Egypt was to have been staged from the city. The Venetians had been contracted to provide boats, provisions and so on. However, when the Crusaders arrived, their army was less than half the size they had projected and, to the dismay and anger of the Venetians, they were unable to honour their contracts. The doge, Enrico Dandolo, by then ninety and completely blind but still a shrewd and wily politician, suggested that the Crusaders could go some way toward fulfilling their obligations to Venice by assisting in the recapture of the strategically important city of Zara, which had shaken off Venetian rule, and was under the control of the (Christian) King Emeric of Hungary. With little choice open to them given their debts to the Venetians, and against the will of the Pope, who expressly forbade the attack on the Christian city, the Crusaders agreed to help Venice; and in October 1202 a mixed force of holy warriors and Venetians – including the blind doge himself, at the head of fifty galleys – sailed for Zara. The city was reached in November, and the forces laid seige. A last-minute missive from the Pope underlining the illegality of the attack, combined with meddling from Crusaders who themselves did not wish to attack the Zarans, resulted in the botching of the peaceful handover of the city to the doge; the result was that the Venetians determined to attack the city, and most of the Crusader force concluded that it would be worse to dishonour their agreement with the Venetians than to participate in the conquering of the city. After a seige, the city was overtaken. The Pope was furious and threatened the entire army with excommunication; however, following an alarmed delegation from the Crusade's nobles, he went back on this, and, in the second missive reproduced below, merely suggests the Crusaders ask the forgiveness of King Emeric. The prize of the Holy Land was too great to be lost over a Dalmatian city.

The Crusaders wintered at Zara; there they received the envoys of Duke Philip of Swabia, who was the feudal lord of the leader of the Crusaders, Boniface of Montferrat. This marked the beginning of a process that would see them embroiled in the intrigues of the Byzantine princes, the abandoning of the original object of Innocent III's Crusade, and would finally result in the brutal and rapacious sacking of Christianity's eastern jewel, Constantinople.

We reproduce here two missives from Innocent III to the Crusaders at Zara. We also present an extract from the *Devastatio Constantinopolitana*, an eyewitness account of the entire Fourth Crusade, from the preaching of the Cross in France to the division of the spoils of the Byzantine city. Written by an unknown Crusader, it contains some short passages concerning the sack of Zara (a section from the first papal missive was reproduced exactly in the second missive; the square brackets indicate this section of text).

The second extract is by Vladimir Dedijer, who featured in Chapter II. This piece is from *The War Diaries*, a book that covers his time fighting as a Partisan alongside Tito during the Second World War. A long-time Communist, he had served time in prison for his views before coming to prominence during the war. With Tito's ascension to power after the war, he became the editor of the Communist newspaper *Borba*, but broke with the Communists in 1954 over the 'Djilas Affair' – the censure and excommunication by Tito of another former Partisan, Milovan Djilas, over a series of articles he wrote for *Borba* and other publications which were critical of the way the Yugoslav political system was developing. Dedijer subsequently wrote and taught in many countries, and campaigned for human rights until his death. As well as the authorised biography *Tito Speaks*, he wrote an investigation of Catholic complicity in Croatian atrocities, *The Yugoslav Auschwitz and the Vatican: The Croatian Massacre of the Serbs During World War II*.

It has long been rumoured that Sir Fitzroy MacLean was the original on whom James Bond was modelled; if so, the original was far more interesting than Fleming's fictional copy. MacLean (1911-96) was a diplomat, soldier, writer and politician. Educated at Eton and Cambridge, he was posted to the British embassies in Paris and Moscow during the '30s, and whilst in the Soviet Union explored remote parts of the country which were forbidden to foreign nationals, often chased by the NKVD, the secret police force which was the forerunner of the KGB. When war broke out in Europe, he was still in the Diplomatic Service, but left in 1941 to join the Cameron Highlanders with the rank of private; in the same year he was elected Conservative MP for Lancaster. He was in the SAS by 1942. Often participating in missions behind enemy lines, he was personally briefed by Churchill before his famous mission to Yugoslavia to fight with Tito's Partisans. During this period he struck up a personal friendship with Tito which endured after the end of the war. The Croatian mission and others are recounted in *Eastern Approaches*, from which the extract included here is taken. MacLean remained in politics as MP for Bute and Ayrshire until 1974. Other books by him include *Tito: A Pictorial Biography; All the Russias;* and *A Person from England and Other Travellers.*

Bill Strutton is probably best remembered for his prolific script writing for British television, contributing to many long running series including *The Saint, The Avengers,* and *Dr Who.* Many of his novels, including *Island of Terrible Friends,* draw on his experiences during the Second World War. Born in Australia in 1923 into a large family, he left his university to work as a clerk in Adelaide before joining the Australian army in 1939. He was deployed in the eastern Mediterranean, and it is on these experiences that *Island of Terrible Friends* is based. He was captured by the Germans in Crete and imprisoned at Stalag VII, where he learned to speak three languages; on his release at the end of the war he entered journalism. His first novel, *A Jury of Angels,* was published in 1957; *Island of Terrible Friends* appeared in 1961. He died in 1978.

The events in Evelyn Waugh's *Sword of Honour* trilogy are based on his own time at war, and the episodes which take place in Croatia draw closely on the time he spent there during 1944-45. Waugh (1903-66) arrived in Croatia in 1944 as part of the Allied mission to aid the Yugoslav Partisans, an operation which had been spearheaded by Fitzroy MacLean. Stationed with Randolph Churchill, son of Winston, in the small town of Topusko (Begoy is a fictional location), Waugh saw little action, and appears to have spent his time very much as his protagonist, Guy Crouchback, spends his: assisting the Partisans as far as was possible, liaising with the local Partisan and Communist leaders, and helping with the evacuation of Jews fleeing persecution and internment. The rather unfavourable portrait of the Partisans he draws here is often considered to reflect the sceptical attitude he held towards them, an attitude which came out of not only his right-wing political views, but also from the Catholicism to which he converted into in 1930, and which he rightly viewed to be under threat from the authorities in a newly Communist Yugoslavia. He certainly did not share Fitzroy MacLean's admiration and respect for Tito's forces.

Sword of Honour, in the form of a single work, was the last novel of a famous career which had begun in the late 1920s with a biography of Dante Gabriel Rossetti, shortly followed by his acclaimed first novel *Decline and Fall* in 1928. It had been previously published in three parts: *Men at Arms* in 1952, *Officers and Gentlemen* in 1955, and then a gap of six years before the final part, *Unconditional Surrender*, which appeared in 1961. The extract below is taken from the latter book.

The island of Rab, mentioned in the extract as the site of a camp from which the Jewish refugees had escaped, was indeed the location of an Italian concentration camp. Established in 1942, it may have held as many as fifteen thousand people, mostly Croats, Slovenes, and Jews. The inmates suffered very poor living conditions, surviving on starvation rations, and a large number died. After the Italian capitulation in 1943, the prisoners overran their captors, took their weapons, and drove them off the island. As the Germans advanced in the wake of the Italian collapse, the Partisan authorities helped to evacuate the Jewish prisoners onto the mainland, while the armed men of the 'Rab Brigade' were mostly absorbed into Partisan units.

American journalist Brian Hall arrived in Yugoslavia shortly after the killings at Borovo Selo, an event which is covered in this extract and which would prove one of the crucial catalysts at the beginning of the disaster that unfolded in the Balkans in the 1990s. He spent the following months travelling through the republic as it splintered and disintegrated, and talked to the ordinary people of what was once Yugoslavia as they reaffirmed the regional identities that the former Communist state had tried, with such little success, to erase. The book that came out of this experience was *Impossible Country: A Journey Through the Last Days of Yugoslavia*. Other books by Brian Hall include the novels *The Dreamers* and *The Sakaid*, and the non-fiction works *Stealing from a Deep Place* and *Madeleine's World*. He lives in New York.

Following this is a piece by Misha Glenny, an international authority on the Balkans, who made one of the most outstanding English-language contributions to the reporting of the crisis unfolding in Yugoslavia. He had previously covered the area for the *Guardian* newspaper, before being made Central European correspondent for the BBC World Service. Stationed in Yugoslavia from 1991 onwards, and speaking five languages including Serbo-Croat, he reported fearlessly and knowledgeably throughout the disastrous collapse of the Balkans. As in the extract below, taken from *The Fall of Yugoslavia*, he routinely reported from on or near the frontlines in a war which had no respect for civilians, and precious little for journalists. As well as being excellent reportage, his accounts are at once factual and also outraged at the appalling horror and criminality of the war, giving the reader a vivid sense of the sheer brutality and lawless chaos into which much of the former Yugoslavia had descended. His detailed historical study *The Balkans: Nationalism, War and the Great Powers 1804-1999* provides an overview of the area from the 1804 Serb uprising against their local Ottoman rulers onwards, and sees the terrible events at the close of the twentieth century as the most recent in a long series of conflicts over ethnicity, territory and power.

From *The Registers of Innocent III, the Fourth Crusade*

December 1202

To the counts, barons and all the crusaders without greeting:

We sorrow not a little and we are disturbed that in those instances in which we have been accustomed to grant the grace of remission and to offer the promise of an increase in eternal recompense, now (and we do not say this without a great deal of grief) we are compelled to deny the consolation of our salutation and the protection of an Apostolic blessing. For behold, your gold has turned to base metal and your silver has almost completely rusted since, departing from the purity of your plan and turning aside from the path onto the impassable road you have, so to speak, withdrawn your hand from the plow and looked backward with Lot's wife. For when, as you were fleeing Egypt, you should have hastened to the land flowing with honey and milk, you turned away, going astray in the direction for the desert. There you recalled to mind how in Egypt you sat amongst the fleshpots, and you hungered not only for garlic and melons, but you thirsted after the blood of your brothers. We are mindful, indeed, of the serpent of old: how God established enmity between the seed of the woman and its offspring following the fall of the first human. Because it was ineffective against the head, it lay in ambush for the heel. It hid itself along the path so that it might at least strike horses' hooves and might bring down the rider along with the horse, seeing to it (by virtue of the usual craft of deceit and the malice of accustomed evil) that insofar as you offended in one matter, you destroyed the merit of your entire labour – even as a trifle of leaven spoils an entire mass and they who are guilty of one action [against the law] are guilty of all. Inasmuch as that ancient enemy, who is the Devil and Satan, the seducer of the whole world, is mindful of the fact that no one has greater love than one who lays down his life for his friends, in order to deprive you of the reward and good will for such love, he caused you to make war against your brothers and to unfurl your battle standards initially against people of the Faith so that you might pay him the first fruits of your pilgrimage and pour out for demons both your own and your brothers' blood. Having the appearance of going not to Jerusalem but rather of descending into Egypt, you went down into Jericho on your way from Jerusalem and consequently fell in among thieves. Although they stripped from you the mantle of virtues and laid on you, once you were despoiled, the blows of sin, nevertheless, so far they have not wished to depart or leave you half alive, because up to now afflictions are visited upon you by evil angels, with the result that, just as you turn aside to the islands for your necessities and turn spoils taken from the Christians into your own income, so also (we learned) you recently did [the same] at Zara.

For when you arrived there by ship, after first unfurling your battle standards in challenge to the city, you set up tents for a siege. You surrounded the city on every side with trenches and undermined its walls, not without a good deal of bloodletting. When ever the citizens wished to submit, along with the Venetians, to your judgement (and not even in this could they find any mercy in you), they hung images of the Cross around the walls. But you attacked the city and the citizens to the not insubstantial injury of the Crucified One, and what is more, by violent skill you compelled them to surrender. Yet, reverence for the Cross you took up, or devotion to our most beloved son in Christ, Emeric, distinguished king of the Hungarians and to that nobleman, Duke Andrew, his brother, who have assumed the sign of the Cross for the aid of the Holy Land, or, at least, the authority of the Apostolic See, which took care to prohibit you strictly from attempting to invade or violate the lands of Christians unless either they wickedly impede your journey or another just or necessary cause should, perhaps, arise that would allow you to act otherwise in accordance with the guidance offered by our legate, should have deferred you from such a very wicked plan. Lest indeed the forgoing prohibition be heard with little zeal, should there be those who presumed to contravene it, we ruled they would be bound by the chain of excommunication and denied the benefit of the indulgence that the Apostolic See granted to the crusaders. In other respects, although our beloved son Peter, cardinal priest of the church of San Marcello, legate of the Apostolic See, had taken care to explain to some of you the meaning of our prohibition and, finally, our letter was publicly presented to you, you submitted to neither God nor the Apostolic See but compelled the pitiable Zarans to surrender. The Venetians, therefore, knocked down the walls of this same city in your sight, they despoiled churches, they destroyed buildings, and you shared the spoils of Zara with them.

Lest, therefore, you add sin to sin and there be fulfilled in you, as it is written, 'The sinner values little when he has arrived in the depths of vice,' we admonish all of you and exhort you more intently, and we command you through this Apostolic letter, and we strictly order under the threat of anathema that you neither destroy Zara any more than it has been destroyed up to this point nor cause it to be destroyed (or permit it, insofar as is in your power). Rather, arrange to restore to the envoys of that same king all that has been taken.

Moreover you should realize that you lie under the sentence of excommunication and cannot share in the grant of remission promised you.

Issued at the Lateran.

February 1203

To the counts, barons, and other crusaders without greeting:

We are inwardly touched by a pain in the heart and are not a little troubled by grief that you, soldiers of Christ, who have left your respective homes, along the way (indeed, on an impassable road) were, to the contrary, made minions of Satan, and you who put your hand on the plow, having turned back, you are now not fit for the Kingdom of God, according to evangelical teaching. For when you vowed to go up from Egypt to Jerusalem, to the contrary you descended from Jerusalem into Egypt and you looked back, along with Lot's wife, for which, along with her, you were transformed into a pillar of salt. This is not the salt prescribed for use in every sacrifice but rather the salt of which the Lord gives witness when He says, 'If salt loses its saltiness, it no longer has any use save for being thrown out and tread under foot by all.' Well, although you bore the Cross for Christ, you later turned your arms against Him, and you, who should have attacked have learned that, when you arrived there by ship, after first unfurling your battle standards...

[in challenge to the city, you set up tents for a siege. You surrounded the city on every side with trenches and undermined its walls, not without a good deal of bloodletting. When ever the citizens wished to submit, along with the Venetians, to your judgement (and not even in this could they find any mercy in you), they hung images of the Cross around the walls. But you attacked the city and the citizens to the not insubstantial injury of the Crucified One, and what is more, by violent skill you compelled them to surrender. Yet, reverence for the Cross you took up, or devotion to out most beloved son in Christ, Emeric, distinguished king of the Hungarians and to that nobleman, Duke Andrew, his brother, who have assumed the sign of the Cross for the aid of the Holy Land, or, at least, the authority of the Apostolic See, which took care to prohibit you strictly from attempting to invade or violate the lands of Christians unless either they wickedly impede your journey or another just or necessary cause should, perhaps, arise that would allow you to act otherwise in accordance with the guidance offered by our legate, should have deferred you from such a very wicked plan. Lest indeed the forgoing prohibition be heard with little zeal, should there be those who presumed to contravene it, we ruled they would be bound by the chain of excommunication and denied the benefit of the indulgence that the Apostolic See granted to the crusaders. In other respects, although our beloved son Peter, cardinal priest of the church of San Marcello, legate of the Apostolic See, had taken care to explain to some of you the meaning of our prohibition and, finally, our letter was publicly presented to you, you submitted to neither God nor the Apostolic See but compelled the pitiable Zarans to surrender. The Venetians, therefore, knocked down the walls of this same city in your sight, they despoiled churches, they destroyed buildings,]

... and you shared the spoils of Zara with them.

Although we have been troubled not a little regarding this, nevertheless, we rejoice in the Lord that you recognize your guilt and you propose to expiate it by penance, as our venerable brother, the bishop of Soissons, and the others who came with him from your camp humbly intimated to us. Although, when in our presence, they minimized your deviation, still they did not wish to obstinately excuse it away – because they could not. For we learned through them that you proceeded to the storming of Zara moved not by your own will but compelled, so to speak, by a certain necessity. Although this does not excuse the boldness of such cruelty, inasmuch as you persuaded yourselves that you were in a crisis of this sort and inasmuch as [one gives] 'a hide for a hide,' then a person should surrender all that he has for his breath of life.

In order, therefore, that your crime be completely purged, we admonish all of you and carefully exhort you and through this Apostolic letter strictly charge you by direct order that, to the extent that you repent such a great aberration and there are suitable reparations for the sin, you take care to make atonement to the Lord through penance and suitable satisfaction, returning all that came to you by way of spoils at Zara and in the future fully abstaining from similar acts. Because, indeed, no one may, except by our authority, set aside the sentence handed down by the Apostolic See that you incurred for the recent deed - although it has been unheard of up to now that anyone whatsoever attempt to absolve those whom the Roman Church has bound, except perhaps those who are at the point of death (as that Church permits) – it follows that the absolution that the bishops travelling with your army conferred on you had no validity. Therefore, we have given orders to our beloved son Peter, cardinal priest of the church of San Marcello, a legate of the Apostolic See, to demand and receive such an oath from those who have not yet vowed to obey our orders, either in person or through another prudent man. Moreover, they are to demand from those who have already taken oaths that they acknowledge in their presence they have so sworn themselves. And so, supported by our authority, they may bestow upon you the bounty of absolution in accordance with the Church's procedure. Next without violating our mandate in other matters, they are to enjoin you under the obligation of the oath that you, the counts and barons, by means of a letter patent with attached seals, pledge both yourselves and your heirs to the Apostolic See that, in accordance with its mandate, you will take care to render satisfaction for such high-handed action. Moreover they are to warn everyone in the host that you fully guard against similar actions in the future: neither invading nor violating the lands of Christians in any manner unless, perchance, they wickedly impede your journey or another just or necessary cause should, perhaps, arise on account of which you would be empowered to act otherwise according to the guidance offered by the Apostolic See. As for the rest, we have placed in the mouth of the said bishop certain words, which he can faithfully relate to you.

Therefore we instruct all of you and exhort in the name of the Lord and order through this Apostolic letter that you humbly beseech the aforementioned king of Hungary that, out of his innate regal clemency, he deign, for God and because of God, to show mercy to you for the offense you committed against him.

Issued at the Lateran.

Anonymous
From *Devastatio Constantinopolitana*

The fleet began to move out on the Kalends of October. As they left the harbour, Lord Stephen of Perche's ship, Viola, was lost. The Venetians, in company with the pilgrims, made their way across the sea and arrived in Istria. They forced Trieste and Mugla into submission; they compelled all of Istria, Dalmatia, and Slavonia to pay tribute. They sailed into Zara, where their [crusader] oath came to naught. On the feast of Saint Martin they entered Zara's harbour. They besieged Zara from every side, both on land and water. They erected more than one hundred and fifty machines and mangonels as well as ladders, wooden towers, and numerous instruments of war. They also undermined the wall. After the citizens of Zara saw this, they surrendered the city on the fifteenth day, with the result that, saving only their persons, they placed everything they owned in the possession of the *doge* of Venice. The *doge* reserved half of the town for himself and his own people; the other half he gave to the pilgrims. They looted the city without mercy.

On the third day following entry into Zara, a quarrel arose between the Venetians and the pilgrims, in which almost one hundred people were killed. The barons kept the city's goods for themselves, giving nothing to the poor. The poor laboured mightily in poverty and hunger. Consequently, when they complained greatly about the barons, they managed to get ships to ferry them to Ancona, and one thousand departed with leave and, in addition, more than a thousand without leave (For there was an order that no one dare to release anyone from the army). Out of the transports ferrying them, two were lost. The army wintered in Zara. The Venetians so completely razed the walls and houses of the city that not one stone remained on another. While the ships were in the harbour at Zara, three of the great vessels were lost.

From *The War Diaries of Vladimir Dedijer 1941-43*

Tuesday November 24th: Bihac

We must quickly rid ourselves of old habits, of the old carelessness. For instance, this morning we found the November 14th issue of *Borba* in a garage – Stalin and Tito's speeches – unsent. Nine hundred copies for Croatia. The comrade drivers said 'the auto could not get through.' But what they did not realise is that *Borba* is sent by horse, by wagon. So, the people are going in two directions at once. How we distributed our literature in the illegal period. I remember the first *Proletar*, printed in Beograd. With how much enthusiasm we rapidly distributed from Beograd into Croatia...

The forty of us, members of AVNOJ [Anti-Fascist Council of National Liberation of Yugoslavia], sat in a bus and drove towards

Bihac. The trip was easy up to Vrtoc but hit snow there. We all climbed out and pushed the bus. When we passed the Ripac gorge, in front of us opened up the Una valley. Fertile, warm. Not a sign of snow. On the left side in the fog rises Pljesivica like a wall. Ruined, charred houses all around, everywhere. We look at the old fortress of Sokolac, which recently surrendered in battle. There were sixty Ustasha in it. We cross through Zegar, a series of barracks with thick walls. This was among the last strongholds conquered. Bihac is a large city. We go through Prekounke; old Muslim houses. We pass by 'Slasticarna' – the Ustasha's last stronghold on the left bank of the Una. Now we are on the bridge. On one side runs a wide, concrete canal through a park, above rise bulwarks, towers, and churches. On that side of the bridge, in the houses behind the corner stood four Ustasha machine guns, and above, on the tower, two more. They rained down deadly fire. Zoran points to the iron fence on the bridge. Every two meters a rod, two fingers wide, and in each rod twenty holes. On the other bank there are five or six pine trees and a hedge – cut open by shells. Behind the corner, where an Ustasha machine gun stood, I see children standing almost knee deep in spent cartridges. We were quartered in the Bosna Hotel. I again walked through the city. These men with ties around their necks, with hats, made-up women with silk stockings seemed strange to me. The streets were rather crowded. My first glances almost always hit on the signs of battle. From the square in front of the church – where earlier an Orthodox church had stood, but which had been destroyed and even its foundations razed – an Ustasha howitzer struck the cloister, at a hundred meters, where our machine guns were situated. The first shell struck the roof, covering the machine gun with plaster and temporarily silencing its firing, but the Partisan cleaned up the machine gun and began firing anew. The second shell did not hit it. All of the surrounding houses were riddled with bullet holes. I dropped in at the former district office. This building had once belonged to a rich Jew. He had once ransomed it for money but the Ustasha later slaughtered him. The Ustasha settled in the house. I returned to the hotel after dark. The streets were quiet. Across from the Kula – a tall medieval fortress, in which the Ustasha tortured our people – a turbe with its greenish light had a ghastly effect. On this turbe stood the signs, 'Viktor Gutic Street,' 'Dr Mile Budak Street.'

I found my comrades from AVNOJ by the radio. We all were waiting hopefully to hear what Moscow would report tonight. Old Cica Luka Pavicevic, a peasant from Mojkovac near Valjevo, when he heard that the Red Army had again advanced said:

'It would be our shame, if they reach our Serbia before we do!'

Wednesday, November 25th: Bihac

This city once numbered over twelve thousand inhabitants. Three thousand of them were Serbs. Now, there is not one Serb left. All were slaughtered, except some forty who escaped to Beograd. In the Bihac district a total of around twelve thousand Serbs were killed, one of the greatest losses suffered by our people. They were slaughtered mercilessly. The Ustasha did all of this. The former district head in Bihac, a certain Vucic, whom we released because many Serb townspeople confirmed that he had saved them, said that this massacre was performed by the former Veliki Zupan, Ljubivoje Kvaternik. The district head received the following orders from Kvaternik:

'The Ustasha will execute certain actions. You are not to interfere. Only, if you find corpses – bury them!'

We have now learned precisely how this terrible massacre was performed. Today, I saw one of these criminals. This is Jusuf Pasagic, who slaughtered over two hundred people with his own hands. This man was a porter in Belgrade for twelve full years. He greatly loverd his *rakija*:

'No joke, I could drink a half an oke,' he said

With the coming of the Ustasha to power, this alcoholic, an illiterate, took up his rifle, goaded by the Zupan, the noble Kvaternik, and the 'man of letters,' Mile Budak, who said at various assemblies, 'There are those who do not want to slaughter Serbs. I want to show them how it is done!'

Fascism made a brutal executioner out of this Jusuf – one of the thousands who are burning and torching around Europe. This man in front of me is not a pathological product. He is the product of Hitler's 'new order.' There is no difference between this one and Radan Grujicic, Becarevic, Vujkovic, Heydrich, Terboven in Norway, Dorrieau in France and many others.

Jusuf committed his first atrocity in Bosanska Krupa. With a certain Husein Grandula, who is now a legionnaire on the Eastern Front, he robbed the merchant, Ilja Smiljanic, took sugar and coffee from him and then took him out into the street. Captain Himzo Biscevic shot him with a pistol, and Jusuf and Husein began to butcher him with an axe. They cut him up in pieces and then went drinking in the Krupa cafés.

This same group continued killing throughout Bihac. Himzo arrested Bude Mileusnic from the village of Hrgara, Bojic and a certain Dizija from Meljenica. These executioners first got drunk, and then took their victims to Zegar. Himzo ordered their rifles aimed at the peasants ten times and on the eleventh they fired!

Jusuf is a thirty-year-old man. His sunken nose showed that he suffered from tertiary syphilis. He had horrible, long hands and pale green eyes.

The atrocities began on June 23rd, immediately after Germany's attack on the USSR. This was a signal for the general extermination of all of our people. They allegedly called the peasants to work. There were summonses in all of the Serbian villages, the women prepared their men *pogace* for the road, *brasnjenike* as the people here call them. Even songs were heard from somewhere, the last songs in this region, songs which have fallen silent, here, already for eighteen months, up until today.

Instead of 'work' a massacre, the likes of which had never been seen, took place. Every night trucks took the people out to the Garavica field, a mile from Bihac towards Licko Petrovo Selo, at Crno Jezero.

It is difficult to confirm the precise number of victims. Our comrades in the city command in Bihac estimate the number of dead serbs as:

1 Jankovac: all of the peasants save two
2 Zavolje: 850 souls slaughtered and thrown in a pit, which was then covered with concrete
3 Zalozje: 40 persons
4 Gata: 300-400 persons
5 Zapoljac: 300-400 persons
6 Vrata: all of the Serbs were killed
7 Lick Petrovo Selo: all of the Serbs were killed
8 Vaganac: all of the Serbs were killed

Most of the victims, around eight thousand five hundred, were killed at Garavica. Jusuf said that the massacre lasted around twenty nights. The trucks each carried thirty persons.

'Each night I killed five to six people. Over two hundred in all!' He said coldly.

The Ustasha committed still another atrocity. They ordered the Croatian village to bury the dead Serbs! They wanted our two people to be enemies for all time to come. The peasants came at night with lanterns and hoes and buried the victims. And there were criminals among them. One of them was captured, Tomo Jankovic, from Kran, an old man over seventy. He acknowledged that he killed people who were still alive with blows delivered to the head with a pickaxe. Others were buried alive.

'It was easy to butcher them! You place their head over your knee and then you do it!' he said.

First the people were killed with a machine gun, and later they were slaughtered with pickaxes in the back of the head. The victims were ordered to lie down, stomach on the ground, and so were killed.

This Hitlerite student, Jusuf, was captured by our Partisans from Bihac. One of them, Mehmed Micic, told me:

'This same bandit came to me in a café with a bloody knife ... Meho Salihdzic, known as "Strasni," came with a human brain in a box and demanded *rakija* to drink along with 'this snack.' Nikita Vivkovic, a student, an infamous Frankovac, while walking during the *corso* pointed out some girls, one whose ear had been cut off and the other whose nose had been severed. I saw the worst horrors while I was in jail in the Kula. Hasan Bajremovic met the prisoners at the doors and immediately cut them with a knife in the side. Many fell dead from the blow. The fat postal clerk, Ivan Mazar, crammed people into trucks and then trampled on them. The worst thing I saw was when Miro Matijevic, a café owner from Vrhpolje, first cut off a peasant's index finger and then gave it to him to eat. I saw through the window how the peasant placed his own severed finger into his mouth. Afterwards, another of his fingers was cut off. This was at night, shortly before that great massacre ...'

The criminal, Jusuf, was shot tonight. A mild punishment. Our forces are searching for one of his namesakes, Jusuf Pasagic, who killed two thousand people.

So far, around one hundred Ustasha have been condemned to death and shot in Bihac ... [this was followed by a list of names]

Forty-eight hours after our entrance into Bihac, the Ustasha took a group of people to Jasenovac. Thirty-two people were on the list: fourteen Catholics, nine Orthodox, nine Muslims! These people will probably be killed.

During the slaughter at Krupa at Crno Jezero, the peasant, Vukobratovic, jumped out of the truck in which the Ustasha drove their victims to the slaughter, beat them, and stabbed them with bayonets. He jumped into the water and remained there for a full four hours. Later, he escaped.

This is just one small part of the horrors which Bihac, the old city on the Una, underwent. I walked for a long time through its dark streets and empty parks ... I looked at the Una, which at this spot is as wide as the Sava in summer at our Cukarica.

Saturday, November 28th: Bihac

Vesa, Paja Sevic, and I dropped in on the town command this morning and there Pavle Pekic invited us to attend the interrogation of Mirkec Golubovic, a gymnasium dropout from Bihac, who had participated in Ustasha crimes. He had dropped out of gymnasium before the war, and up until 1941 had been supported by his mother, who ran a hotel in the city. Mirkec's brother, Dragan, was a totally different man. Dragan had joined the Partisans in the first days and actively worked against the Germans and Ustasha. In Zagreb he began to organise the assassination of a German general, but was arrested and killed. However, over twelve thousand Serbs from the city and outlying districts had been killed. Mirkec had participated in the atrocities with the Ustasha youth, David Prsa, Nikica, and Ante Vickovic and Pera Simic.

Pavle Pekic told us before they brought in Golubovic what this criminal had done. Immediately after the attack on the Soviet Union, the Ustasha in Bihac had arrested many of our youth. At the end of June 1941, Maks Luburic arrived in Bihac and began to teach the local Ustasha how to commit atrocities. Mirkec Golubovic himself explained at the interrogation what Luburic had told them. He did not acknowledge that he had done anything, only that he had watched:

'Luburic showed how ten men could be killed with one bullet. He learned that in Italy. The victims were lined up one behind the other, head to head and then he placed a bar along their heads. If someone was a little taller than the others then his head had to be 'tapped' with a hammer to make him bend, so a straight line of heads could be had. After that the bullet was fired into the first victim's head and it would pass through all the skulls. Ammunition could be conserved in this way ...'

Golubovic spoke further about the instructions given him by Luburic for slaughtering people:

'Luburic noted that it was more practical to butcher people than shoot them, because the matter could be performed quicker and cheaper. To butcher a man, you needed to slit his throat, and then take all of his identity papers and documents, and finally, cut open his stomach and throw him into the water ...'

Pavle Pekic asked Mirkec Golubovic why it was necessary to cut open the stomach, to which he replied smiling:

'I asked Luburic just that question, and he told me you had to do that so the corpse wouldn't float back up to the surface!'

After these theoretical exercises Luburic went to Bihac with his pupils to commit the atrocities. The jailed members of the Communist Youth, Milan Obradovic, Dusan Kuga and Braco Kavezon, students from Bihac, as well as Braco Radetic, a member of the Town Committee in Bihac and one of the best youth leaders in this region, served as the subjects for the first experiment. Besides the four of them, tens of peasants from Grmec were arrested. They were taken by truck to Zavalj, a village beneath Pljesvica, where the mass killing of our people later took place. Dusan Kuga managed to free his hands and jump out of the truck. He was a courageous man who had participated in the demonstrations in Beograd on December 14, 1939 and had been injured there. The Ustasha chased Kuga, but he managed to escape. The other comrades were killed that night and thrown into a pit. Since this was the first time anyone had escaped from one of Luburic's shootings, he spared no effort in trying to find Kuga. Ustasha patrols combed the vicinity of Bihac night and day. Kuga had taken refuge with some workers on the Bihac-Knin line in the village of Strbacki Buk. He succeeded in making contact with the party organization in Bihac. He asked for a revolver and forged papers so that he could cross into Serbia because it had been heard in this region that the battle against the occupier was already being waged in Serbia. Luburic was furious. He remained in Bihac, although according to his plans he was already to have left, and said that he would not quit the town until Kuga had been caught. He managed to do just this through Mirkec Golubovic, who exploited the acquaintances of his brother, Dragan, and came into contact with our comrades. He masqueraded as our sympathizer, told the comrades about Ustasha raids and when he had gained the trust of some comrades, he suggested to them that he could obtain papers for Kuga from the Ustasha. His plan succeeded. The comrades were under surveillance, could not leave the town, and so entrusted the task of taking Kuga's revolver and papers to Mirkec. Golubovic accepted, but brought with him Luburic's right-hand man, Esad Kapetanovic, one of the most infamous cutthroats in the Krajina, whom he had left with an Ustasha ambush at a site where he would bring Kuga. This is how Kuga was captured. The Ustasha tied him up to bring him to Luburic in Bihac. But the brave student from Beograd University, Dusan Kuga, did not allow himself to fall into Luburic's hands alive. When he was crossing the gorge between Luskan and Strbacki Buk with his guard, he jumped into the Una. He could not make a run for it because his hands were tied. The Ustasha fired after him. This was how he died.

This was not Mitkec Golubovic's only deed. He joined in the raping of our comrades Stana Sucevic and Nada Beokovic in the Kula's jail, and then sliced up their vaginas with his bayonet. Comrades from Bihac who survived testified during the investigation how Mirkec would carry human eyes in his pockets. These he obtained by mutilating peasants from Podgrmec and, showing them off on the *corso*, said, 'I have weak eyes and carry these in reserve, because it makes no sense that they take such eyes to the grave.'

Pavle Pekic recited the many other crimes committed by Mirkec Golubovic and described how the criminal had been captured. He, together with some Ustasha, had fled to Zagreb after the liberation of Bihac. Here, fortunately, he met one of our comrades, who had just been released from a concentration camp. They saw each other several times and our comrade decided to try to lure Golubovic to Bihac. He began to tell them that since his brother, Dragan, was a Partisan hero, Golubovic had nothing to fear, that there was always a place for him with the Partisans, that he should return to Bihac. Mirkec finally agreed, and came to Bihac ten days ago. Pavle Pekic had not asked him one direct question about his crimes until today, but had let him talk on his own. But today all of the material had been finally put together, and Pavle Pekic decided to question him directly.

Golubovic was brought into the room. He was a tall young man with blond, curly hair. He wore a sweater with padded shoulders, two ski emblems on the chest, and a red necktie was thrown over the sweater. His movements were exaggereated, theatrical; when he smoked he licked his lips and blew the smoke out into the air. A typical dandy from the Beograd *corso*. There was nothing special about him. Ljotic and Pavelic had pulled hundreds of similar young men into their ranks and made criminals out of them. He was a real Hitlerian robot. A stupid man, crime had become the law for him, and he murdered as coldly as he blew smoke into the air.

Pavle Pekic asked Mirkec Golubovic how the atrocities at Garavica and the other execution sites around Bihac had been committed, and Mirkec calmly replied: 'One day I was walking on the streets toward the Kula when Kapatanovic, the Ustasha captain, stopped me and asked me to take his place since he was busy and lead a transport to the execution. It was around noon; around forty men, who had been beaten and tortured, were crammed one atop another in the truck. We drove them to the Klokot, a tributary of the Una. I wanted to shoot the men by the book, to line them up and then to shoot them, but the Ustasha attacked them like wild men and began to butcher them, to stab them with knives. The men screamed and yelled, but the Ustasha just kept hitting those who showed any signs of life. They even threw some individuals who were still alive into the freshly dug mass grave ... I could not watch this, but decided to put an end to the misery of these wretches and so I fired one bullet each into their heads ...'

'And how many people did you "put out of their misery" in this way?' Pavle Pekic asked him calmly.

'I don't remember; I had fifty to sixty bullets in my case, and I spent them all. I had to go to the next transport since all of my ammunition was gone ...'

Paja Sevic suddenly interrupted Golubovic:

'You are a criminal, you are a bandit, you must pay for all of these murders!'

Paja ruined Pekic's investigation. Mirkec blanched and began to fumble with his necktie. Then Pavle Pekic posed his first direct question, and then a second. There were also witnesses: Mehmed Midzic, who saw what Mirkec Golubovic did with the peasants from Grmec from the Bihac Kula where he was imprisoned. The Ustasha had lined the peasants up in a circle in the Kula's courtyard, gave each peasant a club and forced them to run in a circle. If anyone tired and slowed down, the one behind him had to hit him with his club. The Ustasha stood beside the peasants, and if one of them stopped, they struck him or sometimes stabbed him with a knife.

'It's not true,' said Mirkec, 'that I beat them to make them run faster ... I stood outside the circle and sometimes tapped the legs of those running. Eh, there was one funny fellow. Whenever I tapped his legs he would crumble like a sack. He had nothing sporting about him ...'

When Midzic said that they had torn out the peasants moustaches and forced the peasants to eat them, Mirkec again denied the story. He refused to acknowledge that along with the criminal Pasagic he had drenched the priest Tintar's beard with gasoline and then set fire to it. When Pavle asked Golubovic why he had taken the truck to Garavica and the other killing fields, he calmly replied that he was just putting those men whom the Ustasha were torturing out of their misery. He simply did not understand why the responsibility for these acts was being put on him.

'I'm not guilty of anything,' he said. 'All of this was the work of others; I tried to rescue the people. Nikica Vickovic was the worst. Once, when I had returned from a shooting, I went beside the former Yugoslavia Hotel and heard a frightful screaming. I rushed inside to see what was happening. The "Honor Work Service" was inside. Middle schoolers were screaming and yelling. They were eating jam on bread and Nikica joked that he had thrown a human finger into the jam ...'

New witnesses entered: Slavka Zardina and Raza Kovacevic. Mirkec had tortured these two women. He denied everything, only admitting that he had slapped Reza a couple of times, but that 'had been friendly and a joke.' We could stand no more. Vesa, Paja and I went outside. Paja said that he thought he would see someone like Lombroz, but this was a common *corso* dandy. Vesa explained that this type of criminal was really characteristic of fascism. There were thousands just like Mirkec in Europe. Stupid wretched Hitlerian robots. But today justice will have its due. The investigation will end tonight, and Mirkec Golubovic will be brought in front of a tribunal. It seems he will be publicly hanged.

Later I looked through the Ustasha documents captured during the liberation of Bihac. From them it could be seen that the Ustasha considered using poisonous gas against us. In the report of the special emissary of the government's vice-premier, whose task it was to report on conditions in Bihac, it was said:

'The mood of the population is very gloomy, and is worsened by the appearance of six thousand refugees from the villages of Cukovi, Klisa, Orasac, and Kulen Vakuf ...

'According to the plan of General Rumler, who has been selected to lead the operation in the south and south-east, the present force in Bihac amounting to three thousand men is fully insufficient for any important activity ...

'General Rumler suggests that he be allowed to use poison gas to clear out the forests which are inaccessible to military units, since this is a hilly and forested region, and we, in general, share this opinion.

'Besides the above measures, according to both the Zupan's and my opinion, it is necessary to convince the German military command to send four or five armoured cars with their crews to this region in order to secure the roads in the regions of the upcoming military operations ...'

In another document the Ustasha acknowledge that the peasants, both Croats and Muslims, do not approve of the slaughter of the Serbs, and thus the Ustasha suggest that the killings be performed in secret:

'With the arrival of the mentioned Black Legion company in Vilus, the following families were slaughtered ... [there follows a list of names]

'Because of this slaughter of the Orthodox population, complaints among the Croatian Catholics and Muslims have increased because they fear retaliation, that is they are afraid that those who have escaped will bring the Partisans down upon them, and that they will kill them ... It is necessary that the necessary authorities issue orders that women, children, and the elderly are not to be killed publicly in such a manner.'

Fitzroy Maclean
From *Eastern Approaches (1949)*

Road to the Isles

We were to travel as far as Arzano. After we had gone a very short distance it became evident that our driver did not know the way. This was disturbing, for the situation was still extremely fluid and no one seemed very certain of the exact extent of the enemy's advance.

The next village which we entered at full speed turned out to be still occupied by the Italians. With the exception of the Colonel at Livno they were the first I had seen since the capitulation and for a moment the sight of their grey-green uniforms, so long the mark of an enemy, took me by surprise. Then they flocked forward, clenching their fists in the Communist salute and I remembered that we were amongst friends or at any rate co-belligerents.

I talked to several of them while the driver once again asked the way. They were the usual friendly peasants whose chief concern was to get out of Yugoslavia, with its unpleasant memories, and back to '*la Mamma*' in Italy. I felt somehow that, despite the heroic echoes of their name, the Garibaldi Brigade which the Partisans were trying to form would not be an unqualified success from a military point of view. They had clearly not much enjoyed fighting for the Germans and the prospect of fighting against them filled them with alarm and despondency.

Meanwhile, the nature of the country through which we were passing had begun to change. The grey rocks and crags of Dalmatia were gradually taking the place of the wooded hills and green valleys of Bosnia. Everywhere there were traces of the recent fighting. The bridges were down and, scattered along the road and in the stony fields were burnt-out tanks and armoured cars with German, Italian, and Croat markings. Towards evening, after a good deal of casting about, we came to Arzano, a few tiny whitewashed houses, clinging to the side of a hill. Across the valley, dark against the setting sun, rose the first of the ranges of hills, which lay between us and the coast.

We were made welcome by the local Brigade Commander and his Political Commissar, two hilarious characters with heavy moustaches, almost indistinguishable the one from the other. Brigade Headquarters were sitting down to their evening meal. We pulled out our mess tins; they were filled with stew and black bread and a bottle of *rakija* was opened.

While we were eating, we explained who we were and what we were doing and broached the subject of our onward journey. To my relief the Brigade Commander seemed to take it as a matter of course that people with urgent business to transact should slip through the German lines at night. For the greater part of the way, he said, it was simply a question of knowing the lie of the land and dodging German patrols. There was only one place where we were likely to run into trouble. That was a road which we should have to cross and which was strongly held by the enemy.

We produced our map. He gave us in some detail an account of the latest fighting, and a plan was made without further ado. We were to be given two dozen men who would act as guides and escort during the first part of the march. When we reached the road, they would cause a diversion while we slipped across. Thereafter we would make our way by ourselves to a house in a certain village, where we would find reliable men who would put us on the right road to the coast.

This seemed a good plan in the best Fenimore Cooper tradition and before we set out a good many healths were drunk to the success of our venture. Then some songs were sung; plaintive Dalmatian folk songs, rousing Partisan marching songs, bitter Communist political songs, and, in our special honour, 'Tipperary' in Serbo-Croat by an old gentleman who remembered (rather dimly) hearing it sung on the Salonika front in 1917.

The last chorus was still ringing out as our little party wound down the hillside in the gathering dusk. From the west, where the daylight was dying away behind the hills for which we were making, came the flash and boom of some fairly large guns. The fighting was flaring up again.

At first our way lay through the cultivated land of the valley. Then we started climbing, still through muddy fields, up the long slope opposite. At the top we had our first halt. We had been going for about three hours and from now onward we would have to march as silently as possible. Hitherto a couple of pack-ponies had carried our kit and the wireless set. Now, to avoid making more noise than was essential, we sent these back and divided the load amongst the members of our own party. After we had started on our way, we could still hear for some time the gradually fading sound of hoof-beats in the distance.

Soon we were over the crest and picking our way down a precipitous track towards the next valley. Somewhere beneath us lay the road with its German patrols. Under foot the loose jagged stones clattered noisily against each other. There was no moon and in the dark there could have been no worse surface to walk on for heavily laden men trying not to be heard. In single file the long procession wound its way painfully downwards in the pitch darkness, stopping from time to time to listen.

After several false alarms of enemy to the front, to the rear and on both sides, and many whispered confabulations, we reached the bottom, and there parted with our escort who filed off to create their diversion.

How they fared, we never knew. After some time had elapsed, there were 'noises off' from which those of us who remained concluded that the attention of the enemy was fully engaged elsewhere, and, taking advantage of the opportunity thus offered us, slipped down to the road and across its broad white dusty surface.

Once we were all safely on the other side, we mustered our diminished force and continued on our way, this time through dense bushes and scrub. All of a sudden a new obstacle blocked the way; a fast flowing river, too wide and too deep to be fordable. By now we had been marching for six or seven hours over rough country in the dark, and we were glad to sit down while someone was sent to look for a means of getting across. But waiting was a cold business, and we were not sorry when, half an hour later, our scout returned to say that further downstream there was an old man who would put us across on a raft.

The raft, when we got to it, was a minute, flimsy affair, not much larger than a big soap box, on which there was barely room for one passenger besides the aged ferryman, who, grumbling to himself as he went, propelled it across the rapid current with vigorous but erratic strokes of his pole. Eventually, after a series of individual journeys, each of which landed the passenger, soaked to the skin, at a different point on the opposite bank, we were all across. We bid farewell to the boatman, still grumbling to himself in the darkness, and set out to look for our next target, the village where we were to find reliable guides.

The need for guides was already beginning to make itself felt. We had not gone far when there was the usual hoarse whisper of 'enemy'. As usual we all stopped dead in our tracks and held our breath, but this time, instead of silence, we heard the unmistakable sound of men making off at full speed through the scrub. This was too much for the Partisans. On all sides I heard the rattle and click of sub-machine guns being cocked and I reflected with alarm that, in our present formation, at that moment a rough semi-circle, an attempt to shoot it out in the darkness with an unseen and possibly imaginary enemy, besides rousing the entire neighbourhood, would almost certainly inflict heavy casualties on our own party. But fortunately more prudent councils prevailed and, while we inflicted, it is true, no damage on the intruders, we at least succeeded in preserving our anonymity.

The incident had convinced me of the advisability of finding our guides as quickly as possible and then continuing our journey to the coast by the most direct route. Somebody, probably, to judge by his behaviour, the enemy, now knew where we were, and, if we continued to wander about aimlessly in the dark, would almost certainly come back in force to deal with us. Mitja, who was in charge of navigation, was accordingly summoned, maps and an electric torch were produced, and a more direct route plotted. Then, hoisting our packs back into position, we started once again to pick our way upwards over the ever-shifting scree of the hillside, our feet sliding back half a yard for every yard that we advanced.

The village for which we were bound lay on some flat ground at the top of the next range of hills. There were, it appeared, Germans quartered in it. The house we were looking for was a farm on the outskirts of the village. The rest of us lay behind a hedge while one of the Partisans went and knocked on the door. For a time nothing happened. Then the door opened a few inches and a whispered conversation took place. Clearly nocturnal visitors were regarded with suspicion.

Finally, after much whispering, a tall, gaunt, elderly man in a cloth cap emerged, with long drooping moustaches, and a rifle slung over his bent shoulders. He was, it seemed, the Partisans' chief contact-man in the village, where, under the noses of the Germans, he conducted his own miniature underground movement. Should the Germans be driven out, he would come into his own and probably become mayor. Meanwhile, he led a clandestine, surreptitious existence, full of nerve-racking episodes such as this. He took the lead and we moved silently off. The going – loose, sharp-edged stones – was as bad as ever.

After another hour or two of marching it began to get light. By now we were out of the danger zone and our guide turned back to his village; we only had to follow a clearly marked track which plunged downwards into the valley. There was not much further to go and the knowledge that we were nearing our destination suddenly made us feel tired and sleepy. We plodded along in silence. Dawn, coming up over the hills we had just crossed, was beginning to light the topmost pinnacles of the great range which rose like a jagged wall on the far side of the valley, the last barrier between us and the sea. As the rays of the rising sun touched them, the mountain tops turned to gold. The mist still lay thick in the valley beneath. We wondered, with an increasing sense of urgency, what, if anything, there would be for breakfast.

The country which we were now traversing was almost incredibly rugged and desolate. In some places, amid the great whitish-grey boulders, the stones had been cleared away to form tiny patches of cultivated ground, not large enough to merit the name of fields, where the vivid green of the vines contrasted vividly with the drab background of the rocks. Here and there stood the remains of a peasant's cottage, its blackened stones an eloquent reminder of the results of Italian military government. Then, rounding a corner, we came upon a church, with three or four houses round it, and a group of Partisans with tommy-guns standing in the roadway. We had reached Zadvarje – our immediate destination.

We asked for Brigade Headquarters and were taken to an upper room in the priest's house, the largest in the village, where we found the Brigade Commander, a young man in his early twenties, sitting down to a breakfast of black bread and captured ersatz coffee made from roasted grain. He asked us to join him and eagerly we did so. It was not the breakfast I should have ordered from choice, but it was very welcome all the same, and was rendered doubly so by a bottle of *rakija* which was produced to wash it down. By now it seemed the most natural thing in the world to gulp raw spirits at breakfast.

By the time breakfast was over we felt as if we had known the Brigade Commander (and the dozen or so other people who had flocked in to watch us eat) all our lives. Each of them had told us his or her life-story and we, in response to a volley of questions, had reciprocated with a great many personal details of an intimate and revealing nature. The Brigadier, who in civil life was an electrician's mate and who had been one of the first Partisans in Dalmatia, could not take his eyes of us. To him we seemed, as indeed in a sense we were, beings from another world. How, he wanted to know, had we got here? We explained. What did it feel like to be dropped out of an aeroplane? Had we been sent or had we come because we wanted to? What were we going to do, now that we were here? Might our Government send in arms, and ammunition, and boots, and greatcoats, and food? And would some be sent to Dalmatia?

It was all that we could do to stem the flood of questions and bring the conversation round to our onward journey. This, according to the Brigade Commander, presented no great difficulty. Standing outside the door, he showed us our route. As far as the river at the bottom of the valley, we could travel in a truck which they had captured a few days before. From there onwards – over the last great ridge of Biokovo, and down to the sea – we should have to walk, for the next bridge was down and there was no means of getting the truck across. If we left at midday, we should reach the pass over Biokovo at dusk, which would enable us to complete our journey to the sea under cover of darkness. This was advisable as practically the whole coast was now in German hands, save for the tiny harbour of Podgora, for which we were bound and where we hoped to find some kind of craft to take us across that night to the island of Korcula.

Having thus planned our route, the Brigadier next turned his attention to the truck and was soon hard at work at the head of a gang of amateur mechanics. I asked him what was the matter with it and he answered that it had been shot up by a Henschel the day before. 'The driver was killed,' he added, 'but the engine was not badly damaged, and we will soon get it right again.' He asked us if there was anything we would like to do in the meantime. We said there was: we would like to lie down and go to sleep.

When we woke the sun was high, the truck was ready, and it was time to start. We said goodbye to the electrician turned Brigadier. We had only been his guests for a few hours, but I still remember his efficiency, his friendly straight-forwardness and his obvious gift of leadership. He was, it seemed to me, a good man by any standards. I tried afterwards to get news of him, but there was bitter fighting in the coastal areas in the months that followed and it seems likely that he and most of his men were killed.

Before we started, someone took a group photo with a camera taken from a German officer, a copy of which was, much to my surprise, to reach me by a courier months afterwards. Then we climbed in to the truck; everybody pushed, and we rattled off down the hill in fine style.

The length of the ride hardly justified all the trouble that had been taken to put a vehicle on the road. We had scarcely started when we reached the demolished bridge and it was time for us to get out again and walk. But at least our friend the brigadier had been able to assert the claim of his Brigade to be regarded as partially mechanized, a great source of prestige amongst the Partisans.

Just before we reached the summit of the ridge, we were overtaken by a thunderstorm and torrents of drenching rain, and for a few moments we sheltered in a peasant's hut by the roadside, full of smoke and smelling of garlic, like a mountaineer's hut in the Alps.

Then the rain stopped as suddenly as it has started, and a few minutes later we reached the top and were looking down on the Adriatic, with the islands in the distance, the jagged outline of their mountains grey-blue against the fading red of the sunset. Neither Mitja nor my bodyguard had ever seen the sea before, and so we waited while they accustomed themselves to the idea of so much water. Then the sun sank behind the islands, and we started on our way down.

Below us on the right we could see the lights of Brela, where there was an Ustasha garrison. Further to the north, out of sight, lay Split, where the Germans were now firmly established. Immediately to the south, on our left as we descended, was Makarska also held by the enemy, and beyond it stretched the peninsula of Peljesac, along which German troops from the garrisons at Mostar and Metcović were beginning to advance, in preparation, no doubt, for an invasion of the islands. Somewhere in the darkness at our feet lay Baska Voda, still, for the moment, in Partisan hands.

Once or twice on the way down we were challenged by Partisan patrols, gave the password, and went on. Then, at last, we heard the dogs barking in Baska Voda, were challenged once more, and, passing between high whitewashed walls, found ourselves on a narrow jetty, looking out over a tiny harbour.

There was no time to lose if we were to reach Korcula before daylight. While we made a frugal meal off a bottle of Dalmatian wine and a couple of packets of German ship's biscuits, two Partisans in bell-bottomed trousers and fishermen's jerseys started work on a fishing smack, fitted with an auxiliary engine, which was to take us across.

Soon everything was ready. The storm had cleared the air and it was a fine night. The wireless set and our kit were put aboard; we followed them; I made myself comfortable in the bows with my pack under my head for a pillow, and, with the engine spluttering away merrily in the stern, we set out across the smooth star-lit waters of the Adriatic.

I have seldom slept better. When I woke, we were some way out and, looking back, we could see the lights of Markaska and of the other villages along the coast twinkling across the water. All around us, an unexpected and rather startling sight for one waking from a deep sleep, the dazzling white acetylene lights which the Dalmatians use for fishing flared and flickered from dozens of little boats. In war as in peace, black-out or no black-out, they continued to make their living in their own way, unmolested by Germans or Partisans. I asked our crew whether the Germans made no attempt to keep a check on what was going on. 'Yes,' one of them said, 'they patrol these waters regularly,' and as he spoke, as if in answer to my question, there came the louder, more regular chugging of a more powerful engine, and a strong searchlight went sweeping over the surface of the sea a mile or two away.

The course which we followed was perforce a roundabout one, in and out amongst the islands. Once we stopped to drop a message at Sucuraj on the eastern extremity of the island of Hvar, half of which was held by the Partisans while the other half was occupied by a force of Ustasha, who had landed on it and were digging themselves in. As we approached Sucuraj, one of the crew, muttering 'Signal!' started fumbling in the locker and eventually produced a small lantern, which he lit, and then, standing up, waved a couple of times in the direction of the shore.

The response was immediate; a shower of machine-gun bullets ploughed up the water all round us. 'Wrong signal,' said our Partisan gloomily and waved his lantern three times instead of two. Once again the machine gun opened up, this time with a rather better aim, and I began to wonder whether we had not perhaps struck the wrong part of the island and were not signalling to Ustasha. Meanwhile we had kept on our course and were by now within hailing distance of the shore. '*Partizani!*' we shouted hopefully.

To my relief the sentry did not give us another burst. 'Is that you, Comrade?' he shouted. 'I thought it must be, but why did you give the wrong signal?' And an argument started which was still in progress when, after delivering our message, we once again put out to sea. Soon I was asleep again and when I next woke the sun was coming up behind the mountains of the mainland and we were nearing our destination.

Bill Strutton
From *The Island of Terrible Friends* (1961)

The Landing Craft Infantry (LCI) crew were a bit disdainful about taking medical supplies aboard. Guns for Vis made a more direct appeal to their imaginations and they were ill-disposed to get moving with the rolls of lint and bandages which Rickett and company started heaving out. They enlisted a port officer to prove that the landing craft had no room left, and while Rickett argued that he was not going to be separated from the precious little pile of gear he had fought for by allowing it to be put aboard a schooner, to follow them across to the Yugoslav coast at its leisure, Dawson whistled up a couple of Italian dock workers, pointed to their supplies with a commanding finger, and with a curious combination of gibberish and mime, terrified them into carting it aboard.

By the time Rickett and several opposition officers had exhausted themselves in debate, it was all loaded on deck and snugly secured under canopies against the rain.

A wind laden with stinging drops tugged and whipped at their caps. Dawson cocked an ear in the all-but-total darkness to the sounds of weather which rolled ominously in to the quay from seaward. 'Tell you one thing,' he said, as though a comforting thought occurred. 'We'll all be sick as dogs...!'

He hawked, spat into the darkness where the sea slapped at the quay, and jerked his head towards the heaving silhouette of the LCI.

If reputations can be made overnight, Dawson's renown as a prophet was established then and there. He, Major Rickett, and the fair-haired Captain Clynick had just sorted themselves out their resting places below when a raucous gang of Raiding Support Regiment troops came stumbling down over them, straight from their farewell revelries, and proceeded to pitch their gear about and fight for space, cursing and lurching as the LCI got under way and rose to breast the sea which came surging out of the darkness to meet her.

Soon everybody was being sick, for they were battling into a full gale. Dawson, stricken by his own prophecy, lay prone, sheet-white and retching helplessly, his condition worsening till he was unconscious.

It was no time to think about food, but a tipsy youth in the Raiding Support Agency did, with querulous irrelevance. He stood up, swaying, and demanded to know why they had come away with no rations; immediately a row blazed and spread throughout the deck as the recriminations flew back and forth. A couple of violent rolls as big waves smacked the LCI abeam put an end to it, and as the boat began to hit the real weather, the combatants began subsiding like reaped corn. A general groaning started. Even the durable Rickett loosened his tie, wiped a cold film from his face, bethought himself of getting up on deck for air. He had thought he was a good sailor and it angered him to be sick.

An officer came clattering down in glistening oilskins. He took off his cap and shook the drops from it. He looked around him at the stricken troops.

'Running for Bari. We can't get anywhere in this. Try again tomorrow.'

He vanished up the companionway. Somebody raised a cheer.

The next night was little better, but Rickett was cheered by a very profitable raid ashore at Bari which yielded them two primuses – gifts of the British Red Cross. He and Clynick returned hugging them as though they were made of beaten gold. The bravoes of the Raiding Support Regiment had mostly been subdued by seasickness and hangovers into quietness – all except a large Glaswegian, vociferous and unintelligible, who had from his own triumphal sortie into the low life of the town, fought a rearguard back to the boat against a vengeful crowd of Italians and was now nursing a bloody hand. They brought him to Rickett. A couple of tendons in his wrist had been severed. He cursed thickly as Rickett put him off the ship and into an ambulance. It started off for the General Hospital as the LCI warped away from the mole. From the back of the wagon their first casualty brandished a white-bandaged fist and screeched, to cover his dismay.

'I'll be seein' you, Jack! Ye'll be back in a week with yer goolies shot off! The whaul bloody lot of ya!'

The storm escorted the little craft relentlessly up the eastern coast of Italy, taking almost as heavy a toll among the soldiers on board as on the night before. The LCI wallowed along in a tattered sunset which limned the distant monotony of the shore whenever the swell lifted them high enough to perceive it. It was bleak and without comfort, but they would hug it until night fall. The boats nourishing Vis and its handful of defenders only ventured out to it across the Adriatic during the dark period. The waters of the Yugoslav coast were alive with enemy patrol boats, and even on moonless nights the clashes were frequent.

The darkness walled in around them, muttering with fretful winds, almost palapable in its density. The LCI turned to run them into its darkness.

It was about two o'clock when Rickett stirred at a hand on his shoulder. He wiped a hand over his face. He no longer felt sick. Frank Cynick was bending over him.

It had grown calm. The boat was throbbing steadily through a lagoon stillness.

'Come up and have a look,' Clynick whispered.

He got to his feet and followed the stocky outline of Clynick up the companionway. They rose into total blackness on deck, groping like blind men towards the gunwale. There he stared about him. Stars shone in the water. Now he could see the shapes of sailors moving about him, the huddle of the deck cargo, the line of the gunwale – and a great shadow, blotting out a vast expanse of star-powdered sky, rearing above them, as suddenly and completely present as a revelation.

The boat thrummed slowly forward into its engulfing gloom. Now the faintest shapes were wheeling past them. Was that a bollard? A dockside hut? A soldier, standing quietly there, as immovable and unseeable as granite against the black arras of cliffs?

A match flared and lit a face – only a few yards away, a face without a body – then died.

Abruptly a voice shouted an alien command, almost in Rickett's ear, so that he turned. '*Stoi!*'

Almost immediately a machine gun opened up a little above them, with a morse of flame tongues, and the bullets screamed through the rigging. The dark hills took up the sound and threw it back. Out of the darkness a fruity English voice on the quay roared irritably: 'Stop that, you silly bastard! Get the ruddy gangway up!'

The LCI touched. A gangway bumped heavily down on the gunwale. A figure rose out of the shore darkness on it and stood poised there, hands on hips. A torch flicked on and travelled over the canopied lumps of cargo.

'Right, get it off!'

A dozen beret-topped Commando silhouettes came swarming aboard in time to meet the Raiding Support Regiment which came surging up to the deck. Rickett shouldered his way through a confusion of disembarkers versus unloaders to the English port officer up on the gangplank. As he did so an irate shout above the din arrested him.

''Ere! What's all this? *Bandages*! 'Oo asked for bandages?'

'Cripes, look at this! A bedpan!'

'Well, chuck it off, then! Just get the guns!' the port officer roared.

Rickett reached him, 'Those bedpans are mine,' he said with dignity, and stepped aside to dodge the unloading chain.

'They're on top of our guns,' the figure of the port officer said. 'Get 'em off before my blokes heave 'em into the sea. What's this?'

The torch rested on the carboy of methylated spirits, and the voice grew interested. 'Vino?'

'Medical supplies,' Rickett said. 'We're a surgical team.'

The port officer paused and flashed the torch over him. A couple of the Commandos halted. One of them muttered: 'Blimey, *RAMC**!'

'It'll be ENSA** girls next.'

Rickett ignored that and aimed at the dark bulk of the port officer. 'They said you'd be needing us,' he said.

There was a brief pause while that registered.

'Evans! Brown! Help the major here with his gear!'

The port officer's name was Le Bosquet. He reached out a hand and introduced himself. 'It's not the Jerries we have to worry about so much as these Jugs***. They're getting automatics from us now, first they've seen. Trigger happy as kids, Slovenka!'

A dark outline standing at Le Bosquet's elbow moved forward. It was a woman. Her face shone faintly in the nimbus of the torch as her dark eyes inspected Rickett. She was aquiline and toughish to look at, with lank strands of hair flapping beneath a forage cap, but the eyes were deeply alive.

* Royal Army Medical Corps
** Entertainmet National Service Association
*** Yugoslavians were nicknamed 'Jugs' which comes from the variation of spelling – Jugoslavians

'Yes sir?' Her accent was strong.

'Can you fix Major Rickett up with a place to sleep?'

'I will see.' She turned and walked down the gangway. Rickett looked after her until she was swallowed in the blackness. The port officer turned from watching them unloading. He was sardonic. 'You can look. But that's about all.'

'Are there many of those?'

'Women? About a third of the partisan army. About the only way you can tell them from the men is, they've got bigger bottoms.'

'Rather rough place for them to be isn't it?'

Le Bosquet laughed. 'If you think of them as women, you're going to be in trouble,' he said.

The surgical pannier had a pretty rough trip ashore but the Commandos doing the unloading were as gentle with Rickett's carboy of methylated spirits, under his pleading, as with a baby. He needed it to fire his precious Red Cross primuses. Gingerly they manoeuvred it across the gangway and stumbled safely on to the mole with it. There it stood teetering, breathing a little under its weight.

'Hey, sir! Where shall we put it?'

The port officer murmered: 'There'll be a truck along for your stuff.' Aloud he yelled: 'Just put it down there!'

'Right!' The answer floated back cheerfully. Then Rickett heard the thump and the awful splintering of glass.

Out of the ensuing silence one of the Commandos growled: 'You bloody twerp, Jonesy! *When I say ready!*'

Rickett came groping forth across the gangway and on to firm land. He stood looking down at the wrecked carboy, and he groaned.

But he was not able to mourn it long. Somebody said: 'Listen!' They all heard the truck at the same time, growing louder. Rickett turned and saw it looming along the narrow mole towards them. It was coming suicidally fast in the dark, 'Scarper! It's the Professor!'

The three Commandos turned and fled up the gangplank.
Twenty yards away the truck scattered the dark forms of several
partisan soldiers who turned and hurled strange curses at it. It
bore down upon Rickett standing there deserted on the mole
until he, too, gathered his wits and leaped for the side. The big
shadow of the truck hammered past him in a flurry of wind,
completed the demolition of the carboy, and drew up with a
screech at the dim gangway. A stocky figure climbed down,
followed by a woman partisan. The driver walked around the
front, and peered underneath. 'Bits of broken glass,' the figure said
happily. 'Well, well!'

'A colleague of yours,' the port officer said. 'Captain Heron,
Major Rickett.' Heron, in the darkness, gave an impression of
broad shoulders, a straggling moustache, an air of bland
devilment, and he whiffed of a strange liquor. He ran a Field
Ambulance, and when they confessed to their identities, it was
Rickett's which shook him.

'A surgical unit! I say! They don't mean to forget us after all!'
Heron brought out a flask, had a nip, and passed it on. 'By the
way, who left that big bottle there for me to smash into?'

'That bottle,' Rickett said bitterly, 'was a carboy of meths. It
cost me two hundred cigarettes on the black market in Bari.'

'You can't drink meths,' Heron observed, 'Though after the Jug
rotgut, one wonders. Here.' He thrust the flask towards him.

A guff of wild spirit from it did not entirely comfort Rickett. 'It
was all I had to boil my instruments with,' he said.

Heron caressed his wide moustache and inspected him. 'What
General Hospital are you from? You sound like a worrier to me.'
He said it pleasantly.

It was Heron – the Professor – who conducted Rickett and his
helpers, Captain Frank Clynick and J J Dawson, to the place where
they were to spend their first night on Vis. The fact that he and Le
Bosquet had been whiling away with some gentle tippling the
long night spell of waiting for a possible supply boat to arrive did
not seem to have impaired their efficiency a whit. They worked

stoically and hard, cursing and joking in the blackout, with occasional recourse to the Professor's warming flask of *rakia*. Heron whistled up another truck and took aboard the mixed surgical equipment with high good humour and with no further losses. He drove off the leading truck with a dramatic lurch and a clanging as of an enormous xylophone as they scraped the quayside bollards.

The truck bringing up the rear was driven by a cockney orderly who spoke almost entirely in rhyming slang. He and his ten comrades had been with Heron's ambulance right through the desert from Alamein. They had campaigned with the Long Range Desert Group and had seen lots of pretty lively action. Their job with battle casualties had been patch-up-and-shift-back, and for all they knew, that was where the matter ended, for they looked with suspicion upon anything as high-falutin' as a surgical team, which smacked somehow of base. It was clear that they wanted nothing to do with that.

Nevertheless the cockney driver took pity on Dawson, aghast as they careered along the quayside after Heron's swerving truck.

'Don't worry, mate,' he said. 'The time to look out is when he's on the wagon.'

Heron pulled up before a dark building and motioned Rickett out. They started to walk towards the door, when a figure leapt from its shadow with a levelled gun.

'*Stoi!*'

They had no time to reply before the sentry fired, and the roar and the surprise nearly floored Rickett where he stood.

'*Engleski!*' Heron yelled, and grabbed Rickett to halt him.

They both remained stock still while the partisan came forward, his rifle never wavering, until he was within a yard of Rickett and Heron. He glared at them both intently, then with an abrupt gesture of his gun motioned them to pass.

They started unloading the truck.

'Stand-to every night,' Heron explained. 'When they yell *stoi*, for heaven's sake stop. Every night's a panic now. They don't know

which night Jerry's coming – only that it's any night now, and
then –' He shrugged.

Under the light of Heron's torch the house turned out to be an
empty butcher's shop. It still smelled of meat and fat.

'Dump your supplies in here till morning. I've got you a billet
farther down the waterfront.'

'Leave my gear unguarded?' Rickett protested. 'This place
hasn't even got a lock on it!'

'Nobody'll touch it,' Heron assured him. 'These are not Eyeties.
Besides, the island operates an excellent insurance against theft.'

'It does?'

'Yes. If anybody lifts anything, he's shot.'

Like the other buildings along the waterfront, their billet was in
total darkness, partly shuttered, but breathing that indefinable
awareness that told of watchers in the shadows. Sure enough, they
had not walked three paces before they halted at a rapped
challenge from the shadows. A partisan lounged forward, vetted
them, and let them pass.

In the hall they stepped around a mounted anti-tank gun. Two
partisan youngsters manned it, smoking, very awake, at the open
door. A broad, iron-balustraded stair reached up from the
cavernous ground floor room, with its wine barrels and its litter
of sleeping soldiers, into a landing. Heron shepherded them into
the first upstairs room, stumbled around a table to close the
shutters, and switched on the light. After a whole night of groping
in blackness it had the brilliant suddenness of a blow. Under its
dazzle Heron's face, till now briefly sculpted by shadows and
starlight and an occasional furtive match, was disappointingly
absolute. He was fair, short, broad, with a sandy moustache. But
there were sun wrinkles around his eyes and they were careless,
amused, and a little sleepy.

He gestured and said: 'Must be the housekeeper's day off.'

The room was a shambles, its long table crammed with bully
and other rations, some of them open and half-emptied among

the litter of dirty plates. It was as though they had surprised an enemy, not an ally, at a midnight meal, and he had fled in the middle of it.

Dawson had already reconnoitred the food and had selected himself a tin. Rickett lowered himself into a chair, fished in his haversack for some treasure. He might as well show some goodwill, he thought, and brought a bottle of *Johnnie Walker* to light.

He plumped it on the table, and reached for some mugs.

'Have a drink.'

Heron's sleepy eyes widened a little at the sight of that. He switched on his grin. 'Christ, whisky! Now I know you're from base!'

The dawn woke Rickett, as it always did. He stretched, wiped his face, and swung his feet over the bed, groping with his toes for his boots. The light filled the whitewashed bedroom. In contrast to the mess room and the lower floor shambles it glowed spotlessly clean.

In one corner Captain Clynick lay with his cherubic face turned innocently to the ceiling. Dawson slumbered shapelessly under a blanket in another corner. Rickett shuffled to the window and looked out.

The peace of the place was as pristine as the first dawn on a new planet. There was the harbour, vaster than a lagoon, but entirely still, opalescent in the half-light. It was totally empty – void even of a fishing boat, a dinghy. The mole was uncannily silent. The boat which had brought them had vanished. For a moment he felt deserted. With the sight of this meaningless emptiness, with the light slowly beginning to gild the stonework of the houses fringing the quiet water, the reality of Vis and the uneasiness of it began slowly to invade him. But it was beautiful, and he felt for a cigarette to flavour his comtemplation of it. The sunlight was spreading on the waterfront. He would go down and walk in it.

Rickett was about to reach for his boots when he saw the shape in the sky winging down noiselessly, growing in his eye until it was large, yet silent except for a sigh, a whining of wind. It flashed past him, and rattled. Abruptly the hills rattled back. From its markings he saw it was a Messerschmitt. It rose lazily out of its swoop and its engine coughed into life for the first time with a roar. It turned in the sun, the gold rippling along its belly, and skimmed serenely over the hill in a manoeuvre as effortless as a gull's. Its sound vanished, but another rattling floated faintly above the hills which now hid it. It was as though it was saying its good morning, shaking the island's sleepers with contemptuous intimacy, and getting a grunt here and there in return.

He took his overcoat and clattered downstairs, past the anti-tank with its still-watchful crew, and out into the brightening air. The harbour front was stirring. A three-tonner moved into sight and ground to a stop. Some Red Cross orderlies clambered down – Heron's boys. They treated Rickett's approach with reserve and directed him towards their CO's* billet as though they didn't know whether they were doing the right thing.

In spite of a heavy night, Professor Heron was up, sitting at a well-laid table, and submitting somewhat bleakly to the ministrations of a black-clad housekeeper who fussed about him with dishes. He looked at a big plate of bacon and eggs and pushed it over to Rickett.

'Here. Have some breakfast.'

'I wouldn't want to deprive you.'

'You are not,' Heron said dryly, and poured himself a large mug of tea. 'Any ideas where you're going to set up shop?'

'I was thinking of doing a reccy –'

'Better see the man in charge,' Heron said. 'I'll take you there.'

The island of Vis, like its neighbours, is one of several exposed peaks in a submerged mountain chain. It rises sheer out of an intense green sea to some three thousand feet. Two of its bays, Vis and Komisa – where Rickett landed the previous night – are almost landlocked by the steep mountainsides and form magnificent natural harbours. They lie at opposite ends of Vis, and though only

* Commanding Officer

five miles apart on the map, they are joined by a narrow, stony, tortuous mountain track which wanders over half the island before descending dizzily again to the sea.

In the centre of the island the rocky hills dominated by Mount Hum enclose a small central plateau, nourishing it with their rains and their siltings, which the natural chemistry of time and weather have transformed into rich, red earth. On it grow vines whose grapes fill the wine vats in every house on the island.

It was the second time that the British had come to Vis. In 1810 the Royal Navy garrisoned the island to hold its ports open for trade which flowed into the heart of Europe, in defiance of Napoleon. Its ships also held a French fleet bottled up in Trieste – until, stung to action by an enraged Emperor, eleven French warships stocked with troops sallied out to capture Vis and destroy the small British squadron of four men-of-war.

Captain William Hoste, sighting the French, signalled his captains to 'remember Nelson' and led them forth to rout the French in a furious and brilliantly skilful engagement.

The British built two forts on Vis, one beneath the topmost peak, and governed the island until it was ceded to Austria in the peace of 1815.

Now, once more to keep a foot wedged in this tiny back door to Europe, the British have landed troops on Vis – or rather, a troop: fifty Commandos.

It was an impertinently confident gesture, and a little belated, for the other islands in the Dalmatian cluster lying opposite Split on the Yugoslav coast had already fallen to a drastic German sweep of the coast. Nevertheless, the tiny band of men in green berets had joined up with the Titoist partisans manning Vis amid flowers and handshakes and embraces and sonorous speeches of welcome, and much firing of guns, to which the Yugoslavs – 'the Jugs' – were dangerously addicted. It was a joyous *entente* between utter strangers, spiced with high peril, and for these reasons, romantic. It was to abate somewhat in the ensuing months in the face of political, tactical, racial and material realities.

More Commandos would be following – if they arrived in time. In the teeth of its threatened engulfment, Vis was pouring clandestine supplies across into the Yugoslav hinterland, where saboteurs kept the railway lines constantly cut and rendered road communications so hazardous that now the sea lanes between the islands bore the heaviest enemy traffic of all.

While this small hump of craggy stone remained uncaptured, it kept at bay a fantastic number of the enemy. Its harbours were naked by day, but every inlet and creek, under the steep protective shoulder of the hills, swarmed with camouflaged small craft, both partisan and British, which emerged at night to hound the German shipping. British MGB's* were boarding, bombarding, burning freighters, tackling the E-boats in running fights, even taking prizes in tow back to Vis.

Of the twenty-eight German divisions drawn and pinned down in the Balkans by partisan ebullience, the cream of these were now gathered around Split and these offshore islands. In their vanguard was the crack 118th Jaeger Division. Korcula and Brac, close island neighbours to Vis, briefly snatched by partisans after the Italian collapse, had already been overwhelmed by big German forces a month before.

On New Year's Day, 1944, the Germans mounted *Operation Freischutz* – designed to mop up the remaining three islands defying them and to wipe the tiny garrison of Vis off the map. Away to the south-west, Lagosta fell. In a little over a fortnight the Germans had blasted the partisans off their last, and closest neighbour – the long narrow island strip of Hvar.

Rickett had landed on Vis with his bedpans and his primuses at a moment when, with an advance troop of Commandos and a couple of thousand ill-armed partisans, it now faced the Germans alone. His arrival put a clear emphasis on the *no retreat* order. There was no evacuation plan even for the wounded. He would operate on the battlefield.

* Machine Gun Boats

His advisor on where to set up shop was Lieutenant-Colonel Jack Churchill, Commanding Officer of the British troops, lovingly known as Mad Jack. He was fair, quiet and fierce, and whenever he stood opposite the Germans, they were in for a surprise. At times he piped his troops into battle; at others, led them, waving a claymore. On several occasions he had gone into action with a bow and arrow and there were several astonished but very dead Germans to bear mute witness to his archery.

'No use putting your hospital down in the harbours,' he told Rickett. 'They're the first places Jerry'll go for. Find a place up top somewhere. And, I say – none of this rot about marking the place out with Red Crosses, unless you want to be a priority target. Camouflage *everything*.'

It was on the lofty central plateau of the island, just under the peak of Mount Hum, that Rickett at last found and commandeered a house. It was a square, dilapidated farmhouse and it stood aloof from a cluster of stone buildings called Podhumlje. The tiny hamlet sat at the southern end of the plain, halfway between sky and sea. Away on one side a track wound over the island's back. On the other the rock-strewn earth ran a few yards into space before crumbling vertically away into the sea. They reached Podhumlje from the port by a mean and tortured ascent which allowed them, in its hugging of the mountain walls, a few grudging inches between the truck wheels and a majestic eternity of far rocks and water. It would not be an ideal path up which to bring the wounded, but it was the only one.

Even in the sober early morning Captain Heron's slap-happy driving style was not suited to nervous passengers. He tackled the mountain track with the insouciance with which he had ploughed through the blackout the night before. Heron must have noticed his uneasiness when they slithered on the loose stones, for he said airily: 'The time to worry is when you meet somebody coming the other way.'

They reached the plateau and got out at Podhumlje.

Around them, in a tender morning sea streaked with ripple shivers, the enemy islands basked blandly in the morning sun. In this light they were so close that it seemed he would only have to fire a shotgun to startle any roosting birds among their dark, vegetable tumble, and then pick them off, one by one, as they rose. The sides of Korcula were as lucid of texture as the marks on a reptile, slumbering close and apparently unaware. How else did one reconcile this malign proximity with this quiet?

Closer still loomed Hvar, north of them. He could see the roads which veined it with white. He could pick out the bleached clusters of houses. Beyond it, across a soft expanse of watered silk, Brac reared a prehistoric spine, its crags clear-etched. Less than twenty miles off, the snow caps of the Dinaric Alps, the mainland itself, serrated the skyline. The morning sun iced them pink.

For the soldiers there might be profit in meditating how the wrath stored so close around would awake and fall upon them. For him, there was only a strange wonder, and his own task. He had to turn an old house that was little more than a bare stone shell into something like a hospital.

Their second journey to Podhumlje was to take possession of it. They undertook it recklessly at dusk, after a wearying day of negotiating to requisition it, and of begging stores from an amiably helpless quartermaster.

As if darkness were not hazard enough for taking the cliffside track, the road was choked with partisans winding their way up on foot to night action-stations. A fresh rumour had come blowing across the water that the German attack would come this night, and the expectation of it thrilled dangerously through the mass of partisans like some high-powered narcotic.

The army their truck crawled past was curiously exalted. The men and women, clad in their motley of Italian, American, British and captured German uniforms, topped with a sidecap and its Tito star, waved and grinned at them. They staggered under heavy machine-guns, prodded at their donkeys bearing goatskins of wine, and gave themselves entirely to their harmonic battle chanting. The singing rang from the stone mountainsides. The truck, clinging desperately round the hairpins, the driver's face a pale, alert blob beside Rickett, ran suddenly into a great wave of their voices – Aeolian, gusty, tremendous, as if borne on a wind. It blew in their faces from a chasm ahead, washing them through, in spite of themselves, with a sudden heroic intoxication, a shudder, almost, of delirium. It breathed into their defiance a majestic beauty, and such was its contagion that in the splendid moment of coming upon this sudden glory of voices, it would almost not have mattered if they had gone over the cliff. It was as mighty as that, as terrible, as moving.

This was the way the partisans sang when they went into battle, but whether such sound as this gave those ragged soldiers the courage that was theirs, or whether their courage gave them this sound, Rickett did not know.

The house of Podhumlje had belonged to a priest who had fled on the day the partisans set foot on Vis. Whether he had pursued too guilty a relationship with the Nazis, or simply felt religion to lie too dangerously at variance with the partisan outlook, remained a mystery. The reality he left behind was a large shambling building whose lower floor was one square store-room, stone-paved, unlit by any windows, containing several great barrels of wine higher than a man, an untidy cluster of smaller racks of dusty bottles, and a wine press.

Dawson tapped a barrel and gave a rare grin when he found it full. So were all the other barrels. The fat gallon-sized bottles proved to hold *Procek*, rich and fruity like Madeira, quite possibly sacramental. There was enough, if this were so, to provide religious comfort for several generations of peasantry to come.

To come into this place was to telescope time. One stepped straight through the double wooden doors into a bible scene, with the goatskins hanging from the rafters, the crude wine-grower's implements rusting against the wall, the donkey nuzzling in at the door, the old woman gowned in homespun black who peered at them uncertainly from a crumbling window of the next house down a lane. A goat stumbled among the rocks, grazing and lifting its head to complain.

Once it became clear that Rickett, though senior and a surgeon, was unconcerned with rank or bossing it over them, Heron and his somewhat ruffianly crew surrendered the independence they would otherwise have fought to the death to preserve.

A little guardedly, they elected to work close to him at Podhumlje, and brought their own outfit up to move in a couple of houses away. It involved them in evicting a handful of partisans, which was not easy, and exhausted most of their tact. The other houses swarmed with Jugs and were patently impossible to occupy.

It was intensely gloomy inside the hospital. Rickett chose the brightest upstairs room for the theatre, and set up the portable operating table. Dawson, rummaging about with the zeal of a pioneer, found an ancient dressing table and detached its mirror. He strung this on wires over one end of the operating table to help spread the light coming in from the small window. At the other end of the table they hung their precious Tilley lamp. With the mirror, it might provide just enough light to see by, when it came to operating at night. That is, if they ever got any fuel for it...

Next door the primuses were set up for sterilising.

'All I need is some meths to light them,' Rickett said. 'And for the lamp.' He sighed and damned the men who had dropped his carboy.

They invited Heron and his men in to christen the place. Heron accepted rather touchingly. Though there was all the wine in the world in the vats downstairs, he bought over a bottle of *rakia* with which to toast the hospital. Rickett accepted a mug of it from him, drank, and gasped for air. It was explosively strong and it tasted vile. He shook his head at Heron, who, jeering, tilted the bottle invitingly to offer him some more.

Then an idea struck Rickett. He changed his mind and reached out his mug.

'Say when,' Heron said, and raised his eyebrows as the mug filled and Rickett forebore to speak. He hesitated.

'Don't be stingy,' Rickett said. 'There's no ration on this stuff, is there?'

Heron shrugged and filled it up.

Rickett took the mug to the primus, uncapped it, and poured some of the *rakia* inside. Then he brimmed the cup-like primer.

'Stand back,' he said, and struck a match to the *rakia*. It burned with a wobbly, almost transparent blue flame.

In a few moments the primus was roaring. Occasionally it actually hiccoughed but then it would roar into life again.

'Thanks,' Rickett said.

Heron overcame his wonderment quickly, for he was a firm believer in the beneficent power of alcohol.

'I told you, didn't I?' he said. 'People can worry too bloody much!'

Evelyn Waugh
From *Sword of Honour (1952)*

Summer came swiftly and sweetly over the wooded hills and rich valleys of Northern Croatia. Bridges were down and the rails up on the little single-track railway-line that had once led from Begoy to Zagreb. The trunk road to the Balkans ran east. There the German lorries streamed night and day without interruption and the German garrisons squatted waiting the order to retire. Here, in an island of 'liberated territory' twenty miles by ten, the peasants worked their fields as they had always done, subject only to the requisitions of the partisans; the priests said Mass in their churches subject only to the partisan security police who lounged at the back and listened for political implications in their speeches. In one Mohammedan village the mosque had been burned by Ustasha in the first days of Croatian independence. In Begoy itself the same gang, Hungarian-trained, had blown up the Orthodox church and desecrated the cemetery. But there had been little fighting. As the Italians withdrew the Ustasha followed and the partisans crept in from the hills and imposed their rule. More of their fellows joined them, slipping in small, ragged bodies through the German lines; there were shortages of food but no famine. There was a tithe levied but no looting. Partisans obeyed orders and it was vital to them to keep the good-will of the peasants.

The bourgeois had all left Begoy with the retreating garrison. The shops in the little high street were empty or used as billets. The avenues of lime had been roughly felled for firewood. But there were still visible the hall-marks of the Habsburg empire. There were thermal springs, and at the end of the preceding century the town had been laid out modestly as a spa. Hot water still ran in the bath house. Two old gardeners still kept some order in the ornamental grounds. The graded paths, each with a 'view-point', the ruins of a seat and kiosk, where once invalids had taken their prescribed exercise, still ran through boskage between the partisan bivouacs. The circle of villas in the outskirts of the town abandoned precipitately by their owners had been allotted by the partisans to various official purposes. In the largest of these the Russian mission lurked invisibly.

Two miles from the town lay the tract of flat grazing land which was used as an airfield. Four English airmen had charge of it. They occupied one side of the quadrangle of timbered buildings which comprised a neighbouring farmhouse. The military mission lived opposite, separated by a dung heap. Both bodies were tirelessly cared for by three Montenegrin war-widows; they were guarded by partisan sentries and attended by an 'interpreter' named Bakic, who had been a political exile in New York in the '30s and picked up some English there. Both missions had their wireless-sets with which to communicate with their several headquarters. A sergeant signaller and an orderly comprised Guy's staff.

The officer whom Guy succeeded had fallen into a melancholy and was recalled for medical attention; he had left by the aeroplane that brought Guy. They had ten minutes' conversation in the light of the flare-path while a party of girls unloaded the stores.

'The comrades are a bloody-minded lot of bastards,' he had said. 'Don't keep any copies of signals in clear. Bakic reads everything. And don't say anything in front of him you don't want repeated.'

The squadron leader remarked that this officer had been 'an infernal nuisance lately. Suffering from persecution mania if you ask me. Wrong sort of chap to send to a place like this.'

Joe Cattermole had fully instructed Guy in his duties. They were not exacting. At this season aeroplanes were coming in to land at Begoy almost every week, bringing, besides supplies, cargoes of unidentified Slavs in uniform, who disappeared on landing and joined their comrades of the higher command. They took back seriously wounded partisans and allied airmen who had 'baled out' of their damaged bombers returning from Germany to Italy. There were also 'drops' of stores, some in parachutes – petrol and weapons; less vulnerable loads, clothing and rations – falling free as bombs at various points in the territory. All this traffic was the business of the squadron leader. He fixed the times of the sorties. He guided the machines in. Guy's duty was to transmit reports on the military situation. For these he was entirely dependent on the partisan 'general staff'. This body, together with an old lawyer from Split who bore the title 'Minister of the Interior', consisted of the General and the Commissar, veterans of the International Brigade in Spain, and a second-in-command who was a regular officer of the Royal Yugoslavian Army. They had their own fluent interpreter, a lecturer in English, he claimed, from Zagreb University. The bulletins dealt only with success; a village had been raided; a fascist supply wagon had been waylaid; mostly they enumerated the partisan bands who had found their way into the Begoy area and put themselves under the control of the 'Army of Croatia'. These were always lacking in essential equipment and Guy was asked to supply them. Thus the General and the Commissar steered a delicate course between the alternating and conflicting claims that the partisans were destitute and that they maintained in the field a large, efficient modern army. The reinforcements excused the demands.

The general staff were nocturnal by habit. All the morning they slept. In the afternoon they ate and slept and idled; at sunset they came to life. There was a field telephone between them and the airfield. Once or twice a week it would ring and Bakic would announce: 'General wants us right away.' Then he and Guy would stumble along the rutted lane to a conference which took place sometimes by oil-lamp, sometimes under an electric bulb which flickered and expired as often as the headquarters in Bari. An exorbitant list of requirements would be presented; sometimes medical stores, the furniture of a whole hospital with detailed lists of drugs and instruments which would take days to encipher and transmit; field artillery; light tanks; typewriters; they particularly wanted an aeroplane of their own. Guy would not attempt to dispute them. He would point out that the allied armies in Italy were themselves engaged in a war. He would promise to transmit their wishes. He would then edit them and ask for what seemed reasonable. The response would be unpredictable. Sometimes there would be a drop of ancient rifles captured in Abyssinia, sometimes boots for half a company, sometimes there was a jack-pot and the sky rained machine guns, ammunition, petrol, dehydrated food, socks, and books of popular education. The partisans made a precise account of everything received, which Guy transmitted. Nothing was ever pilfered. The discrepancy between what was asked and what was given deprived Guy of any sense he might have felt of vicarious benefaction. The cordiality or strict formality of his reception depended on the size of the last drop. Once, after a jack-pot, he was offered a glass of *Slivovic*.

In mid-April a new element appeared.

Guy had finished breakfast and was attempting to memorize a Serbo-Croat vocabulary with which he had been provided, when Bakic announced:

'Dere's de Jews outside.'

'What Jews?'

'Dey been dere two hour, maybe more. I said to wait.'

'What do they want?'

'Dey're Jews. I reckon dey always want sometin'. Dey want see de British captain. I said to wait.'

'Well, ask them to come in.'

'Dey can't come in. Why, dere's more'n a hundred of dem.'

Guy went out and found the farmyard and the lane beyond thronged. There were some children in the crowd, but most seemed old, too old to be parents, for they were unnaturally aged by their condition. Everyone in Begoy, except the peasant women, was in rags, but the partisans kept regimental barbers and there was a kind of dignity in their tattered uniforms. The Jews were grotesque in their remnants of bourgeois civility. They showed little trace of racial kinship. There were Semites among them, but the majority were fair, snub-nosed, high cheek-boned, the descendants of Slav tribes judaized long after the Dispersal. Few of them, probably, now worshipped the God of Israel in the manner of their ancestors.

A low chatter broke out as Guy appeared. Then three leaders came forward, a youngish woman of better appearance than the rest and two crumpled old men. The woman asked him if he spoke Italian, and when he nodded introduced her companions – a grocer from Mostar, a lawyer from Zagreb – and herself, a woman of Fiume married to a Hungarian engineer.

Here Bakic roughly interrupted in Serbo-Croat and the three fell humbly and hopelessly silent. He said to Guy: 'I tell dese people dey better talk Slav. I will speak for dem.'

The woman said: 'I only speak German and Italian.'

Guy said: 'We will speak Italian. I can't ask you all in. You three had better come and leave the others outside.'

Bakic scowled. A chatter broke out in the crowd. Then the three with timid little bows crossed the threshold, carefully wiping their dilapidated boots before treading the rough board floor of the interior.

'I shan't want you, Bakic.'

The spy went out to bully the crowd, hustling them out of the farmyard into the lane.

There were only two chairs in Guy's living room. He took one and invited the woman to use the other. The men huddled behind her and then began to prompt her. They spoke to one another in a mixture of German and Serbo-Croat; the lawyer knew a little Italian; enough to make him listen anxiously to all the woman said, and to interrupt. The grocer gazed steadily at the floor and seemed to take no interest in the proceedings. He was there because he commanded respect and trust among the waiting crowd. He had been in a big way of business with branch stores throughout all the villages of Bosnia.

With a sudden vehemence the woman, Mme Kanyi, shook off her advisers and began her story. The people outside, she explained, were the survivors of an Italian concentration camp on the island of Rab. Most were Yugoslav nationals, but some, like herself, were refugees from Central Europe. She and her husband were on their way to Australia in 1939; their papers were in order; he had a job waiting for him in Brisbane. Then they had been caught in the war.

When the King fled, the Ustasha began massacring Jews. The Italians rounded them up for their own safety and took them to the Adriatic. When Italy surrendered, the partisans for a few weeks held the coast. They brought the Jews to the mainland, conscripted all who seemed capable of useful work, and imprisoned the rest. Her husband had been attached to the army headquarters as an electrician. Then the Germans moved in; the partisans fled, taking the Jews with them. And here they were, a hundred and eight of them, half starving in Begoy.

Guy said: 'Well, I congratulate you.'

Mme Kanyi looked up quickly to see if he were mocking her, found that he was not, and continued to regard him now with sad, blank wonder.

'After all,' he continued, 'you're among friends.'

'Yes,' she said, too doleful for irony, 'we heard that the British and Americans were friends of the partisans. Is it true, then?'

'Of course it's true. Why do you suppose I am here?'

'It is not true that the British and Americans are coming to take over the country?'

'First I've heard of it.'

'But it is well-known that Churchill is a friend of the Jews.'

'I'm sorry, signora, but I simply do not see what the Jews have got to do with it.'

'But we are Jews. One hundred and eight of us.'

'Well, what do you expect me to do about that?'

'We want to go to Italy. We have relations there, some of us. There is an organization at Bari. My husband and I had our papers to go to Brisbane. Only get us to Italy and we shall be no more trouble. We cannot live as we are here. When winter comes we shall die. We hear aeroplanes almost every night. Three aeroplanes could take us all. We have no luggage left.'

'Signora, those aeroplanes are carrying essential war equipment, they are taking out wounded and officials. I'm very sorry you are having a hard time, but so are plenty of other people in this country. It won't last long now. We've got the Germans on the run. I hope by Christmas to be in Zagreb.'

'We must say nothing against the partisans?'

'Not to me. Look here, let me give you a cup of cocoa. Then I have work to do.'

He went down to the window and called the orderly for cocoa and biscuits. While it was coming the lawyer said in English: 'We were better in Rab.' Then suddenly all three broke into a chatter of polyglot complaint, about their house, about their property which had been stolen, about their rations. If Churchill knew he would have them sent to Italy. Guy said: 'If it was not for the partisans you would now be in the hands of the Nazis,' but that word had no terror for them now. They shrugged hopelessly.

One of the widows brought in a tray of cups and a tin of biscuits. 'Help yourselves,' said Guy.

'How many, please, may we take?'

'Oh, two or three.'

With tense self-control each took three biscuits, watching the others to see they did not disgrace the meeting by greed. The grocer whispered to Mme Kanyi and she explained: 'He says will you excuse him if he keeps one for a friend?' The man had tears in his eyes as he snuffed his cocoa; once he had handled sacks of the stuff.

They rose to go. Mme Kanyi made a last attempt to attract his sympathy. 'Will you please come and see the place where they have put us?'

'I am sorry, signora, it is simply not my business. I am a military liaison officer, nothing more.'

They thanked him humbly and profusely for the cocoa and left the house. Guy saw them in the farmyard disputing. The men seemed to think Mme Kanyi had mishandled the affair. Then Bakic hustled them out. Guy saw the crowd close round them and then move off down the lane in a babel of explanation and reproach.

Brian Hall
From *The Impossible Country: A Journey Through the Last Days of Yugoslavia (1994)*

All the stores in the centre of Zagreb had GOD PROTECT CROATIA in their windows, in identical white stick-on letters.

'I didn't notice it when it started,' Nino shrugged at my question, dodging people of the packed sidewalk. 'One store probably did it, and then the rest had to do it or they wouldn't look patriotic.'

We were hurrying to a VE Day demonstration in the Square of the Great Croats, but when we arrived the crowd was dispersing. Posters on the columns of the circular building in the middle of the square invited us to light candles and lay flowers on its marble steps, which were already sloppy with melted wax and crushed petals. The police directing traffic wore the same grey uniforms I had remembered, but the old red star on their caps had been replaced by the *Šahovnica*, and armorial shield bearing a red-and-white chess pattern. This had been the medieval coat of arms of Croatia, but it also happened to have been the symbol used by the Ustashas. Displaying the *Šahovnica* had been forbidden for forty-five years on pain of long imprisonment, and its appearance on posters in last year's election campaign had titillated my acquaintances. Now the *Šahovnicas* were everywhere, including on the republican flag, but unlike the sex magazines, which were also everywhere, they still evoked a hormonal response.

Croats could agree on the *Šahovnica*. It had been the symbol of Croatian statehood centuries before the Ustashas used it, and surely everyone, even the thin-skinned Serbs, could understand its legitimate role in current events. Even Nino, who was wary Croat nationalism, considered the Serbs' outrage over the reappearance of the *Šahovnica* wilful and perverse.

Some other actions taken by the Croatian Democratic Union, or HDZ, the party that won the elections in the spring of 1990, did not enjoy such consensus. Today's demonstration had been a protest against one of them, the square's new name, this awkward reference to 'Great Croats'. It used to be called 'Square of the Victims of Fascism', and during the election Croat intellectuals, who used to look down on the HDZ as a party of primitive nationalists, had joked that the HDZ never held its rallies in this square because the name made its leaders uncomfortable.

As indeed it did. Belgrade did not have a Square of the Victims of Fascism. The leader of the HDZ, Franjo Tuđman, had considered the name a provocation thought up by federal (ie Serb) Communists, an implication that all Croats had Fascistic tendencies. Tudman and his cronies lacked nothing if not imagination, and they could not see that changing the name only made them look more like Fascists.

The intellectuals were appalled – and old Partisans were insulted. 'There was no referendum about the change,' said Marin Geršković, the head of the League of Social Democrats, whom Nino buttonholed for me in the dissolving crowd. 'The HDZ was drunk with victory. They forgot they only got forty-two percent of the vote. Croats were also victims of Fascism! More Croats were Partisans than they were Ustashas.'

'Really?' I said. 'How many?'

'That I don't know. You should ask an expert. But I know for a fact there were more Partisans.'

Nino meant something different by 'victim'. 'I consider that my grandfather was also a victim of Fascism,' he said. Nino's grandfather had been a Fascist – an Ustasha judge in the Croatian city of Karlovac. 'He was a victim of that ideology.'

We came away from the square. The controversy over the name was only the latest in a colourful history. The circular colonnaded building had originally been an art pavilion, designed by the Dalmatian sculptor Ivan Meštrović in the abstract classical style of the '30s which now looked, indeed, Fascist, or Social Realist, depending on the context. During the war, Ante Pavelic, the *Poglavnik* (Head Man) of the Independent State of Croatia, turned it into a mosque as part of his strategy of rapprochement with the Bosnian Muslims, in the hope they would help him kill Serbs. Today, the building was flanked by the fountain Islam requires for ablutions before prayer, and the people living nearby still called it 'the mosque', although – and perhaps because – since the war it had been called the Museum of the Revolution. And now, enthroned amid this grandiose new name, it was nothing. The exhibition had been closed by the new government, because it was Communist history. Ex-history.

Last year, Nino had voted for one of the intellectuals' parties. A dozen of them had come together in a grand coalition occupying an office that always bustled with bright young people, where the party leaders wandered in and out, talking a blue streak, their interview schedules in disarray. Foreign reporters needing background information were invariably steered toward historians, legal experts and economists working for the coalition. They had all the famous dissidents of Croatia's last twenty years, and the statesman-like leaders of the abortive nationalist movement of 1971. All the HDZ had was Tuđman, who with his heavy dark glasses and florid face looked like a mafia don, and bunch of *émigré* footsoldiers speaking Croatian with wide Australian accents.

The Coalition's rallies had well-known comedians to warm-up the audiences and eloquent, tart speeches by Vlado Gotovac, a playwright-cum-politician who was always introduced with poignant longing as 'the Croatian Havel'. The HDZ rallies were notable mainly for the phalanx of bodyguards surrounding a visibly frightened Tuđman – there had been a murky episode with a Serb and a gun a few months before – and speeches by a frisky gnomish monk in habit who screamed invective against the Serbs and wondered aloud what the Croats had done to deserve God's having blessed them with Dr Franjo Tuđman.

To his footsoldiers, too, he was always 'Doctor'. You had to know that he was a university professor, a historian. He had been kicked out of the Communist Party in 1968 for signing a declaration on Croatian language rights. In one of his books, he had set out to prove that not nearly as many Serbs had died in Croatian concentration camps during the Second World War as was usually claimed.

Supporters of the Coalition sniffed. He was not a good writer, they said. And 'Doctor'? Surely you'd heard that he got his degree by stealing someone else's work. They did, however, credit him for having told the truth about the concentration camps.

Come election day, the HDZ bulldozed the Coalition, which collapsed like a house of cards and vanished overnight. Tuđman spent the evening watching the returns on television and laughing incredulously. The Communists, who had shamelessly renamed themselves the Party of Democratic Change, came in a distant second. True, the HDZ had only won forty-two percent of the vote, but it took over sixty percent of the seats in parliament. That was the Communists' fault. They had rigged the election rules to assure parliamentary dominance to the largest party, since, in a field of over thirty parties with themselves controlling the media, it had never occurred to them that they would not be the largest.

Tuđman had won by keeping the message simple, wrapping himself in red and white, making promises without worrying about whether or not he could keep them, and calling into question the patriotism of his opponents. (When he was at untelevised rallies he simply called them traitors and claimed later that he had been misquoted.) He had also organized in Australia before he did so at home, because he knew that if he had the *émigré* community on his side, the Croats still living in Croatia – that is, the voters – would tend to follow the *émigrés* lead, because they were western and therefore understood democracy better.

This insecurity in the face of all things western ran deep. When I was watching the pre-election debates on Zagreb TV, people kept turning to me and saying ruefully, 'To you, this must seem like the playing of little children.' I did not have the heart to tell them that precisely what made it so touchingly innocent was the fact that the participants actually discussed the issues, forgetting the camera, turning in their seats to argue directly with their opponents.

Nino and I had reached the attic apartment he shared with his girlfriend Nataša and their mutual friend Silvija. 'Nice,' I murmured, opening the rattly steel-framed doors on the two bedrooms and the long room under the eaves that must have been the kitchen, judging from the quartet of gas eyes and the metal sink at one end. The herring-bone parquet floors in the bedrooms had been badly glued to the concrete slab, and clattered xylophonically as you walked across them. There was a terrace with a view of the hills to the north; and a clothes line placed so that if you dropped anything it would fall three storeys.

I could understand how proud Nino was of it. Last year he, Nataša and Silvija had been living with their respective parents, even though all three had had decent jobs for years. Privately owned apartments were scarce and exorbitant, while 'social' apartments (ones owned by companies and leased to their employees) had waiting lists of years, sometimes decades – and in any case were being phased out.

Nino told me the rent was six hundred and fifty dollars (a common labourer in Zagreb made two hundred dollars a month, a lawyer perhaps six hundred dollars) and it had to be paid in hard currency, which meant he had to trade on the black market and risk getting ripped off by the itchy hustlers who hung out below the cathedral. Requiring payment in hard currency was illegal, but virtually universal for private apartments. There were no leases. The rent could go up by any amount, any month.

When the two young women got home from work the four of us went out and caught up over a pizza. Silvija was the News Director at Zagreb's *Radio 101*, which until the previous year had been officially a 'youth' station. A small woman, she dressed entirely in black, and the thick bars of her jet-black eyelashes contrasted with her short hair of vivid plum. Tonight she looked tired and sad, as she often did in the couple of days preceding her Saturday news programme.

Nataša was a researcher and reporter at the same radio station. Also small, she tended towards rumpled sweatshirts and wore no make-up, which was unusual for a Yugoslav woman. She spoke with a slight rasp that fell pleasantly on the ear.

Nino wore his usual tweedy sports jacket and trousers ending above the ankle. Sandy-haired, with ice-grey eyes and a strong nose, he was good-looking except for his bad teeth, which he covered with his upper lip as he talked, giving a slight whiffling intonation to his speech.

Our conversation turned inevitably to Borovo Selo. Before May 1st no one had ever heard of this small village on the Danube near Vukovar, but the name by now had acquired the punch of Lockerbie for Americans, of Munich for Israelis. Maps accompanying news reports on Zagreb television about fighting in Slavonia now always marked Borovo Selo prominently, even if the fighting was elsewhere, as if the village were the area's root of conflict, of evil. It was a Serb village.

But in Croatia. And therefore it was legitimately under the jurisdiction of the Croat police, the Croats argued, despite the Serb militias and 'defence committees', all illegal, that had sprung up in Serb-populated regions of Croatia since the previous summer.

According to the official version in Zagreb, on the night of May 1st two patrol cars had driven in to the centre of Borovo Selo. When two policemen climbed out of one of the cars villagers immediately opened fire, wounding both. The second car fled. Not daring to go in again that night, the police the next morning called the head of the defence committee in Borovo Selo, a man named Vukašin Šoškočanin, to demand an explanation. He said he had no personal knowledge of an incident, but he would investigate. He called back a short while later saying the villagers had the two policemen, and someone should come and pick them up. A second car was sent, this time backed up by a bus full of policemen, and when the two vehicles reached the centre of Borovo Selo, the villagers again opened fire. In the mêlée, twelve policemen and three villagers were killed. Three of the dead policemen were mutilated.

But my interlocutors were sceptical. Were the numbers right? Why did the police go into Borovo Selo in the first place? Why did this little village have so many Serb gunmen?

Across the Danube from Borovo Selo lay Serbia. Nataša said 'people were saying' that specially trained Serb irregulars had been ferried across the river. None of the three dead Serbs were from Borovo Selo. Perhaps more Serbs had died – the shooting had gone on for two or three hours – but their bodies had been spirited away.

The mutilations were the first atrocity of this new war. I sensed everyone had been waiting for this. People had frequently told me the year before that, if fighting broke out, I, Europe, westerners – all civilised people – would be astounded at how brutal it would be. Yugoslavs said things like this with a strange, grim satisfaction. Perhaps it was the satisfaction of having your worst doubts about yourself confirmed. This was the Balkans, Yugoslavs liked to say, shrugging. The single word explained: corruption, chaos, cruelty, genocide.

Yet much about this atrocity was confused. The first reports had said the two policemen wounded in the night had had their eyes gouged out and their throats cut. Now it was said they had been sent, alive, with gunshot wounds but no other indignities, to a hospital in Novi Sad – presumably by the Serb villagers, although I suspected few Croats would be interested in specifying that. Instead, they concentrated on the mutilations, which now they claimed happened to *other* policemen, the next day.

During the shoot-out? I asked. Would there be an opportunity in the middle of a firefight?

Perhaps afterwards, Silvija said. The Serbs won the battle, taking hostages. They were in control of the situation for several hours before they handed over the twelve bodies.

'Perhaps more than twelve,' Nino said. 'They might be under-reporting the dead.'

'Who?'

'The authorities.'

'Why?'

'Maybe it looks bad.'

Silvija was sure of one thing. There had been atrocities. As News Director at the radio she had been invited to a press conference given by the Croatian Interior Ministry and shown photographs that had not been released to the public. 'I couldn't recognize these bloody bits and pieces as parts of people. Heads, arms...' she trailed off.

'You're sure the pictures were accurate?'

'They were photographs! And the Serbs are capable of it. A friend of mine was trapped for ten days behind the blockade near Vukovar. She saw a policeman wounded. The Serbs pulled off his helmet and beat his head with their rifles, destroying his face. He is alive, but brain-damaged. She saw this with her own eyes.'

I thought of the old adage that you can tell something about a nation by its vocabulary, Inuit having a dozen words for snow, Bedouin for sand, Meso-Americans for tubers, and so on. Serbo-Croatian had a disturbingly large number of words for butchering. One of them was *kundačiti*, which meant 'to beat with the butt end of a rifle'.

'I think Borovo Selo was a Croatian game,' Nino said. 'Those police boys were set up. Why would they be sent right into the middle of a Serb village without reinforcements? The Croatian government wanted to show what the Serbs are capable of.'

'Then why under-report the dead?'

He shrugged. 'Maybe they didn't.'

I asked Nino, Nataša and Silvija if they thought the Serbs living in Croatia had any legitimate concerns.

'Of course,' Nino said. 'Tuđman did some very stupid things at the beginning. You know I don't like the HDZ.'

'I know.'

'They changed the constitution to say that Croatia was the nation-state of the Croats. That offended the Serbs. As it should have! They are citizens of Croatia. If we don't make them feel like citizens of Croatia, how can we ask them to support us?'

'We thought the Constitution should just say, "Croatia is the country of its citizens",' Silvija said, Nataša nodding. 'It's wrong to even talk about nations in the constitution.'

One hears this frequently from Yugoslav intellectuals, this plaintive call for a 'country of its citizens'. They had their fingers exactly on the problem. Yugoslavia, like other countries that had staggered out from the rubble of the Ottoman and Habsburg Empires waving the bullet-riddled standard of national self-determination, had never developed a legal concept of the citizen. Individuals were granted rights on the basis of their nationality, not because of any notion that every human being possessed inherent rights. Politicians might promise 'equal rights' to a minority, but the fact remained that those people were constitutionally *defined* as a minority, as guests in someone else's nation-state. This made it extremely difficult to allay their fears, for the simple reason that their fears were well founded.

'But the HDZ insisted on this new wording,' Nataša said, 'and the Serb delegates walked out of the Parliament. That was it. They never came back.'

'Other things?' I asked.

'Oh, the new flag, with the *Šahovnica*, sure. I wouldn't have picked it. And Tuđman made a big mistake by never going to the Serb areas after he was elected.'

'Why would he?' Silvija expostulated. 'They tried to shoot him!'

'Because it is part of Croatia,' Nino said. 'Tuđman is the President of Croatia.'

'How about the policy of replacing Serbs on the police force with Croats?' I asked.

'That merely makes sense,' Nino said. 'Under the Communists the Croatian police force was more than fifty percent Serb, even though they make up only fifteen percent of the population. And almost all the senior officers were Serb. OK, that was somewhat natural. It's a cultural thing. Serbs love to order other people around. But we have to make the police force reflect the population.'

'And the oaths?' The new government had demanded that Serb policemen and other state employees sign an oath declaring loyalty to Croatia, and renouncing the 'bandits and terrorists', that is, the Serbs who were blockading the roads and demanding autonomy in the Krajina.

'Bad idea,' Nino conceded. 'But the point I wanted to make is, sure, HDZ did some stupid things. They are primitive people, I know that. I agree completely. You remember I said that last year.'

'I remember.'

'But the Serbs kill us for this! That's all I'm saying. Do you kill people just because you don't like this oath, because you don't like the new flag?'

'Serbs aren't normal,' Nataša said, screwing an index finger into her temple. 'They were right to be angry, but not like this. You bump into a Serb and he pulls a gun out and shoots you.'

Back at the apartment, we watched the news on television. Vojislav Šešelj was on again. Zagreb TV devoted a lot of air time to him, because he was a scary Serb. He led an opposition party in Serbia that was really a private army. His followers called themselves Chetniks.

To appreciate the horror this word evoked in Croats, one had to remember that the Chetniks had occupied the loser's place alongside the Ustashas in the post-war textbooks of Yugoslavia, which had pictured them both as having been slavering lunatics, baby-killers, drinkers of blood. The Chetniks and the Ustashas had been the twin national demons – one Serb and one Croat – that had been haunting Yugoslavia's national past, ready to rise ghoulishly from the grave and unleash racism and genocide the moment the Communist Party ceased its internationalist vigilance, its ritual chanting of 'Brotherhood and Unity!' Anyone under fifty years of age had grown up with those teachings, and though the Party might now have been discredited, you never forget what you learned in first grade.

And here they were, night after night, on television. They wore the familiar brimless olive wool Chetnik cap, which had been standard issue in the old Royalist Army before it acquired horns. They sported the trademark Chetnik coiffure of long, unkempt hair and beard. They waved Bowie knives in the air and held them in their teeth. The demon was loose. Šešelj had a bullet head, an academic's soft body, the bland unshakeable gaze of the deepest sort of fanatic. He was saying that he sent his men to

Borovo Selo, and he would send more. He had five thousand men now under arms, and would have ten thousand by June. Like Tuđman, he had a PhD, but no one said he stole it. Even Croats admitted he was intelligent. But in the '80s he had been imprisoned in Bosnia, which had always been known for its particularly harsh police methods. Something had happened to him in prison. He had come out a different man.

Had Borovo Selo been the beachhead of a Serb invasion? There it blinked on the map on the screen. Reports were coming in of scattered shooting in Slavonia. Nataša said Šoškočanin, of the Borovo Selo defence committee, had boasted on Novi Sad TV that he had personally killed six Ustashas, and would kill six hundred more to defend his village.

'They always call us Ustashas,' Silvija said. 'They call *themselves* Chetniks, but no Croat today would call himself Ustasha. That was madness, and we know it. The Serbs don't.'

Misha Glenny
From *The Fall of Yugoslavia (1992)*

The Twilight Zone

On the straight road from Ojisek to Vukovar, the contours of a distant dreamy mirage soon reveal themselves to be those of your worst nightmare. Four figures dressed in jeans stand with two Kalashnikovs apiece jutting from their hips, while their T-shirts are patterned with grenades. Trpinja is just past Bobota, the centre of Serb extremist operations in this strategic cluster of villages. The perversity of this war is demonstrated by the fact that Bobota is one of the five richest villages in Yugoslavia, thanks to the exceptional fertility of the land tilled by its inhabitants. Most of the houses have swimming pools, while Mercedes are dotted around the main road. It is no longer possible to travel to Bobota as all unidentified vehicles are fired on without warning. If Bobota is in an advanced state of war readiness, then Trpinja is well on its way. Jeans and designer shades complement the T-shirts of the keepers of Trpinja's gate who would strike terror into the hearts of mafiosi gunmen.

I and my two passengers are pulled from my Austrian-registered car. Our passports are taken from us and I am pushed against the wall where I answer questions with a gun to my stomach and one to my head. I explain I am travelling to Belgrade. One particularly unpleasant man, who is short of three front teeth, interrogates me while his larger comrades start examining the contents of the car in minute detail. For some reason, the villagers decide that a single cassette will provide proof as to our sympathies. Fortune has rarely looked down on me with greater kindness as the tape they chance upon is dominated by an interview in Serbo-Croat with Žarko from Tenja – they could equally have chosen an interview with Glavaš! After fifteen nerve-racking minutes, the toothless boss returns and pointing to the tape says: 'It's okay, he's one of us.' The biggest, meanest goon of all sits in the passenger seat of my car. Without looking at me, he says: 'Drive. Anyone takes pictures, I'll kill them.' After a minute, he starts to talk in an unexpectedly conciliatory manner. 'I must apologize that we have to put you through all that,' he began, 'but you must understand that we no longer trust anyone here any more. We know that we will all probably die fighting to defend our village but we will never let the Ustashas take it.' I had no reason to disbelieve him. 'By the way, if you had been German or Austrian, it would have been a very different story.'

By early July, a division in the European Community over its response to the Yugoslav crisis was already evident. Germany, supported most vocally by a broad political spectrum in Austria, had made little secret of its sympathy for Croatia and Slovenia. This was shared neither by the British Foreign Office, whose diplomats opposed Hans-Dietrich Genscher's efforts to recognize

Croatia and Slovenia, nor by the State Department in Washington. The German and Austrian positions reflected both countries' economic, cultural and historic interests in the region, but in Serbia they were perceived to represent the imperialist expansion of a unified German state into Eastern Europe. Colloquially, Germany was now referred to within Serbia as 'The Fourth Reich', while many Serbs believed Tudman to be a German puppet whose ideology reflected a natural German inclination towards fascism. This was utter nonsense but it was nonsense which a large number of men with heavy weaponry believed, and so German citizens were taking a big risk travelling around Serb areas. There was a parallel anti-British sentiment in Croatia, especially in the crisis areas, but it was slower to develop and never assumed the conspiratorial proportions that the Serb perception of the German position did.

Notwithstanding Serbia's exaggerated response, the German insistence on recognition was critically flawed. Eventually, Germany applied enormous pressure on the British and the French to accept European Community (EC) recognition of Slovenia and Croatia. Recognition did not stop the fighting between Croat forces, on the one hand, and the *Jugoslavenska narodna armija* (JNA*) and Serb irregulars, on the other. The fighting was stopped in accordance with a ceasefire agreement negotiated by Cyrus Vance, the UN Special Envoy to Yugoslavia, contained in a broader framework which included the dispatch of UN peace troops to the disputed territories in Croatia. Not only did recognition fail to stop the fighting, it had no significant impact on the core problem in Croatia – the Serbian question. The issue which provoked war in the first place remains a matter of seemingly irreconcilable dispute. The Vance plan at least meant that the conflict in the crisis areas would be frozen until a proper political solution could be found. It places on UN troops an unenviable burden of administering territories where there are

---

* The JNA to whom Glenny refers were the Yugoslav People's Army, controlled from Belgrade

mixed populations and two central authorities demanding the setting-up of administrations which are mutually exclusive.

By the time such arguments reached the fighters in Trpinja, they boiled down to the fact that I was not German and as a result, I am still alive. I was allowed through the barricade at the other end of Trpinja with grace because I was accompanied by Mr Big who shook my hand and wished me and my passengers well.

On the outskirts of Vukovar, we stopped at a café – here were the same monsters with the same murderous intent as our inquisitors in Trpinja. The difference was, of course, that these were Croats who launched into flavoursome attacks on the Chetniks. The arguments were the same, the anger was the same, the irrational beliefs were the same – Serbs and Croats in the eastern Slavonian region were trapped in the logic of mutually assured destruction, although this still prepared none of us psychologically for Vukovar.

After the unnerving experience of Trpinja, Vukovar was a welcome sight. This was the prettiest of the small Danubian towns characterized by a variety of rural and urban architecture with many attractive neoclassical pillars holding up the buildings in the centre. The townspeople were visibly nervous. Borovo Selo, the centre for Serb extremist operations, was but two and a half miles from Vukovar's centre, while the military could target the city from various directions with ease. Heavy artillery was positioned across the river in Vojvodina, to the south, to the north and to the south-west. Already Croatian access to Vukovar was limited to a tortuous route from the neighbouring town of Vinkovci nine miles away. Similarly, the Serbs in Vukovar felt under pressure from the aggressive representatives of the HDZ controlling the town, especially from the local Interior Minister, Tomislav Merčep, whose reputation for brutality grew as did the struggle, such that President Tuđman eventually decided to pull him out of eastern Slavonia because he gave the Croats such a bad reputation. Tuđman tried to do the same with Glavaš later on but failed because of Glavaš influence.

After our brief visit to Vukovar, we headed toward Vojvodina, passing through Šarengrad and Ilok. Three months hence, the Croat inhabitants of Ilok would be given an ultimatum by the JNA to evacuate their town, which is well known for the large number of wooden buildings. If they did not voluntarily join the hundreds of thousands of distraught Serb and Croat refugees who had already been chased from their homes, the JNA would bomb it from the air, from the Danube and from the eastern bank in Vojvodina. They left. After them, so did Ilok's Hungarians. As late as March 1992, the Slovak inhabitants of Ilok (Vojvodina and eastern Slavonia boast one of the densest mixes of Central European peoples) contacted the Czechoslovak ambassador in Belgrade in desperation as they were being threatened and cajoled by JNA officers to abandon their homes as the officers were planning to move Serb refugees into them.

Just outside Ilok on the Croat side of the 25. Maj bridge which spans the Danube and separates Slavonia from Vojvodina, a Croat policeman sat in his squad car, observing the APCs and one tank which squatted on the Vojvodina side of the bridge. When I arrived in Belgrade, I turned on the radio to hear that a JNA tank had flattened the Croat police squad car on the Western end of the 25. Maj bridge. The policeman was killed instantly.

There is a secret history to Vukovar before the seige of the town began in early August – there were considerable tensions in the town between Serbs and Croats but the details remain mysteriously vague. I only visited the town one more time. That was on the second day of the siege in early August. I travelled by Vinkovci in convoy with Marc Champion from the *Independent*. We arrived in Vinkovci which had itself taken a steady battering from the army and Serb irregulars stationed in a village suburb, Mirkovci. The air was clouded with the dull thud of regular artillery and tank fire, some of it landing on Vinkovci, most on Vukovar. At the press centre we were told that the news from Vukovar was encouraging: two hundred soldiers had lost their lives in the first thirty-six hours of fighting. JNA losses throughout eastern Slavonia were exceptionally high during the fighting, but such a figure was a fine example of wishful thinking. Marc and I were told we could travel to the tiny village of Bogdanovci, which is within one and a half miles of Vukovar, at our own risk. Here we could discuss entry to Vukovar with the local National Guard.

We arrived at this tiny village which was buzzing with National Guard activity. Enormous blasts from JNA tanks a few fields away accompanied our discussion with the local commander who said we could travel across the cornfields at our own risk. He would take us as far as the outskirts and then we would be on our own. At this point, a red Opel coming from Vukovar screeched to a halt. The driver said that the bombardments and the fighting around the barracks and the police station had intensified and that the situation had become exceptionally dangerous. Marc and I discussed the matter and decided against going to Vukovar – later on we admitted to each other how often and how deeply we regretted that decision. We had travelled to the edge of a crime without parallel in post-war Europe. It was our duty to report the precise details about Vukovar but we were too scared. Regardless of the complex causes of the Yugoslav crisis, the JNA and Serb irregulars must be condemned for the wholesale destruction of this town for no apparent purpose. The exhilaration of Serb fighters and many civilians at the news of Vukovar's liberation can be to an extent explained by ignorance. But anybody who believes that you can liberate a pile of useless rubble which you yourself have created needs remedial education in semantics.

I returned to Ojisek many times in the next few months. In late August I travelled to Sarvaš, the last village to the north-east of Ojisek which was still being contested by the JNA and the National Guard. As I drove out of Ojisek, a light rain accentuated the cold, blustery afternoon. On the edge of the village was a Croat gun nest. They said I could go and look at my own risk. Slowly I drove through the village, seeing the now familiar patterns of destruction. One old woman wandered out into the front garden of her house, which was riddled with bullet holes. I reached the point of no return. This was the Catholic church whose spire had become famous after it was filmed being blown away by a mortar and cannon attack. Opposite the church was a shop and café, bombed and burnt to the ground. I got out and looked around. Dead pigs. In the distance, I could just make out a Serb-manned barricade at the other end of the village. A MiG jet swooped down low, crushing the silence and bursting my eardrums. Terrified, I ducked and for a few seconds remained immobile with fear before leaping into my car. Gunfire burst out around me while grenades began falling. I revved the car and pulled out the clutch suddenly so that the vehicle would shoot forward unexpectedly. One spray of automatic fire caught the left-hand side of the car, whose fuel tank was mercifully on the right-hand side. I reached the Croat gun nest, where one soldier leapt out and asked if I was injured. I told him I was just shaken, upon which he screamed: 'Then just get out!'

A couple of months later after Sarvaš had been the last of these villages on the Vukovar road to fall to Serbs, I visited Ojisek airport which was curiously still under Croat control despite being surrounded by dozens of JNA tanks. The commander of the small National Guard platoon took me to the roof of the control tower building. From here, the strategic value of the villages became clear: Sarvaš, Bijelo Brdo, Vera, Trpinja, Bobota, Silaš, Celje (the one Croat village that had been thoroughly plundered by Serbs) and, finally, Tenja formed a huge circle round the airport. Through his binoculars, the commander showed me where the JNA tanks were hiding behind the cornfields and the trees which lined the villages. 'I've told the JNA that if they attack the airport, then we'll blow up all the jet fuel,' he said. Thereupon he brought out a map of the airport showing the extent of the underground fuel reservoir – this lay in channels under Bijelo Brdo, Bobota, Silaš, Celje and part of Tenja. 'If they attack, the fuel goes up and takes their villages with it,' he concluded. He then showed me the bombs which he had planted on the pump system. I was never able to establish whether this was a Croatian fantasy tactic or whether the jet fuel represented a real threat.

Within a month of the war's outbreak, Croats had become completely committed to the defence of their republic's borders as defined by Tito's Yugoslavia. The greatest political threat to Tuđman came not from the opposition, all of whom joined a new coalition government of Franjo Gregurić, formed in August. It was the right wing of the HDZ which seemed concerned to undermine the President, who they believed was prepared to concede territory within the framework of EC negotiations. Tens of thousands of Croat men had responded to the call-up which in some areas was compulsory. In contrast to the mobilization of reservists which was ordered in Serbia and Montenegro, the Croatian government found little if any resistance to its mobilization orders except, of course, among the Serb minority who were ordered to join the National Guard in parts of the republic. Not only were the Croats willing to fight, they fought exceptionally bravely and for the most part effectively, destroying a myth rooted in the Second World War that Croats are cowards who cannot recognize one end of a gun from the other. Where Croatia suffered serious defeats, it was not usually the fault of the fighters but of the military command structure which for a long time was notoriously poorly organized. Even after various Croat forces had been placed under the unified command of the former JNA officer, General Anton Tus, serious logistical and tactical errors continued to be made.

The intense commitment felt by most Croats was best demonstrated to me by a surreal encounter during one of Zagreb's most vaunted air raids. Much evidence suggests that the air-raid warnings were given in order to promote a war psychosis among Zagreb's population. If this was the aim, it was successful. One night, I was walking through the city in search of a drink with Hermann Tersch, the brilliant East European correspondent of El Pais. The sirens began wailing and within thirty seconds all the lights in Zagreb had been extinguished. The sky was overclouded, leaving Hermann and me completely blind – we could see literally nothing. After a long day, we were determined to find a drink. During the air raids, all restaurants and drinking establishments were closed down. However, Hermann has a robotic ability, enabling him to detect functioning watering holes in the most adverse conditions. Using his uncanny sixth sense, we felt our way to a small square just below Ilica Street which leads onto Ban Jelačić Square. Through an open gate and across a courtyard we crept along until we reached a narrow lane where stood an oasis of light in the black desert. In we strode to order our whiskies. Slowly scanning the bar, it became clear that this was the local frequented by the junkies of Croatia's capital. Every guest was drugged to the eye-balls. We saw one member of the National Guard slumped across his automatic weapon in a catatonic state. The guests may have heard the air-raid warning but they had no intention, or were not capable, of taking any notice of it. Hermann and I struck up a conversation with a junkie, one of whose eyes appeared to have detached itself from the socket – it floated this way and that without any apparent coordination. Talking half in Serbo-Croat and half in English, this young man, who could not have been more than a few weeks away from a sad, self-inflicted death, just managed to get his message across to us. 'If they get the chance, the Serb Chetniks will kills us all. We must all fight the Chetniks to save our homeland. Our homeland is being attacked – you must tell the world so that Croatia can survive.'

I was in Zagreb on another gloomy August day when a shooting incident took place involving Serb paramilitaries and the Bosnian police from Velika Kladuša, which is just across the Croatian-Bosnian border south of Zagreb on the edge of Petrova Gora, a range of hills which was among the most impenetrable Partisan strongholds during the Second World War. I decided to visit Velika Kladuša and the larger town of Bihać in Bosnia where there was a military airport and a large JNA barracks to gauge the situation there. This involved crossing Serb-Croat lines just south of Karlovac. This proud military city had suffered some damage when shooting between the JNA headquarters and local Croat militia broke out, but it was generally still untainted by the fighting in August – Karlovac would be devastated later.

At the Karlovac town hall we were informed that the situation a mile or so out of town was unpredictable. Croat forces were in control of the road until just beyond the Kupa river which forms Karlovac's southern boundary. As we approached the Croat barricade, we joined a small queue of cars, filled with desperate people who, for some unfortunate reason, were destined to commute between the Serb-controlled areas and Karlovac. We were all waved through without difficulty. A mile further on, the straight road sinks steeply as it skirts the northern tip of Petrova Gora. The Serb front line was positioned by a lay-by next to an isolated house just beyond the dip as the road rises gently.

The Serb side of the border was a hive of operational activity as a crucial logistical process was under way. The JNA had decided to cut its losses and leave Karlovac where its men and equipment were under threat from the remarkably effective blockades which the National Guard had thrown up around them. In Varaždin, the JNA commander had surrendered the entire barracks and its contents to the National Guard which was able to begin the formation of its first tank and heavy artillery brigades. Two JNA barracks immediately south of Zagreb were threatened by the National Guard tactics: Jastrebasko and Karlovac. The latter was evacuated first, while the former went in accord with a later agreement brokered by the European Community.

On the Karlovac front line, there were some large stationary JNA vehicles whose function appeared to be merely to intimidate rather than anything more sinister. The JNA took but a cursory glance at our papers but members of the Martićevci waved us into the lay-by where they were checking every vehicle and its passengers. With the usual swing of the automatic gun, we were ushered out of the car which was by then being thoroughly searched as we stood under the watchful eye of the barrel. 'Where are you going?' said the militia captain whose cap was adorned with the four Cyrillic Cs. 'We are travelling to see the Prime Minister of the Krajina Government, Mr Babić,' I lied, suspecting that there was little way they could have checked whether Babić was expecting us a hundred miles away. At that point communications among Serbs throughout Krajina and Lika were still poor. Babić was still the idol of all Serb fighters, such that if invoked with sufficient authority, his name alone could open doors. After staring at our passports for a minute, he returned them and with a nonchalant flick of his head muttered: '*Hajde!*' (Get going).

Although not especially fertile, the region is covered by rich grassland and deciduous trees. The hills look luscious but they also provide ideal hiding places for guerrillas – Partisans swarmed throughout Kordun during the Second World War harrying the Ustashas. The Serb villages of Petrova Gora provided them with shelter and food. Dotted around the Partisan strongholds were some Ustasha centres from where the Croats launched what were often futile forays against the Partisans. As we passed through the villages of northern Kordun, the Croat villages were easily identifiable. They were empty, a few windows smashed here and there, with only a single dead pig on this occasion. Most of the inhabitants had just run and left since the Martićevci and the JNA had secured their positions along this main road south. Every single road sign had the Serbian cross scrawled on it or simply the words *Ovo je Srbija* (This is Serbia), written in Cyrillic. The Serb villages were easy to recognize because life carried on in them as normal. This was an eerie pattern, indeed.

There were no other vehicles on the road except for a regular stream of empty tank transporters coming towards us while we overtook large numbers of personnel carriers and transporters loaded with tanks travelling south. Just below Slunj, thirty miles south of Karlovac, before one reaches the tourist attraction, the

Plitvice lakes, the JNA has one of its largest installations in Yugoslavia. The army was shifting all its hardware from Karlovac to this base. How they were able to pass through Slunj, I do not know as this was one of the best defended Croat towns of all. Their passage may have been negotiated as part of the agreement regulating the evacuation of Karlovac.

Halfway between Karlovac and Slunj, we were stopped by a Krajina patrol. We were directed to a lay-by. The two policemen behaved like traffic police. They were correct and thorough. But there were five Serb reservists from the JNA with them who had evidently been brutalized by the war. After we had gone through the initial interrogation, the first policeman walked off to radio something from his vehicle. One of the reservists with long, straggly hair was lying on a mound of sand. He stood up and, noticing Kirsty, he shouted: 'Leave the girl here.' I pretended not to hear but he approached the car with another vile-looking colleague. As an unpleasant smile began to crack the line of his face, he repeated: 'I said, leave the girl here, motherfucker.' At this point the policeman returned from his car, handed back our passports and said: 'Get going,' before turning to the reservists and saying: 'Leave it out.' A woman was taking a big risk by crossing into occupied Krajina, peopled by war-mad, rapacious Serbian reservists.

We turned off just before Slunj on to the road towards Velika Kladuša which is in the north-western wedge of Bosnia. A few empty villages were sprinkled along this road until, to my great surprise, we came to one where a Croat flag blew defiantly from the top of the church. Below this sat a very old man but other than that the village appeared deserted. This was Cetingrad, a Croat nationalist stronghold. I asked the man if anything had happened in the village. He looked as if he had been brainwashed and he repeated a single phrase over and over, '*Ništa neznam*' (I know nothing). Before and after Cetingrad, I saw ten manned machine-gun nests – I no longer cared who they belonged to and whether they had seen any action. I simply smiled at all the gunners, hoping that they would not act hastily. It worked and with a great sigh of relief, Kirsty and I arrived in Velika Kladuša.

The return journey to Karlovac was similar but we succeeded in reaching Zagreb unharmed. A week later, two Polish journalists visited the mayor of Vrginmost, a village on the Kordun-Banija border. Although guests of the local Serb leader, they were picked up by a group of terrifying Chetniks in the village who took them prisoner, confiscated all their belongings including their car and threatened to kill them, before the Polish ambassador was able to intercede and save their lives. They were finally dumped at the army headquarters in Banja Luka, almost paralysed with fear. Kirsty and I were not only stupid, we were fortunate. Twenty-two journalists were killed during the first nine months of fighting in Yugoslavia, while four went missing presumed dead. From the beginning of the conflict, journalists were even prized targets. Some were killed by the JNA, some were killed by the Chetniks, some were killed by the Croats, some were killed accidentally by driving over mines. Journalists were fodder like the villagers and other innocents.

Epilogue

by Peter Frankopan

M Y FAVOURITE PLACE in the Mediterranean is on the island of Hvar, the sparkling jewel of the Adriatic Sea. Up above the citadel which sits above the harbour, protecting the town, you look down on to the old town of Hvar, dominated by the Cathedral of St Stephen, its magnificent sixteenth-century bell tower; you see the vast old arsenal, built to service war galleys of the Venetian fleet, and where the famous theatre was built in 1612 for the cultural stimulation of the townsfolk. *Palazzi* of the old noble families of the island fan out round the bay anti-clockwise from the Governor's Palace, with their orange roofs seeming to trap the bright sunshine spilling on to them. And then, straight ahead, protecting the harbour and breaking the horizon, the Pakleni islands, forested rings astride thin stone rims, hovering over the sea.

I like to sit and stare out over the town, out to sea, letting my eyes follow salutations in the town square, or track the gentle, white wash of a boat sashaying into the bay as it makes its way to put in. I like the silence from up above. You hear the chirping of birds, of course, the restless singing of the cicada and the gentle noise of the wind which laps across the hillside, bringing much needed relief from the afternoon sun. But otherwise, serenity.

I take a book, climb up and then find a place to read. It doesn't matter what the book is about, or whether I even flick the pages open. The tranquillity up there; the heat and the soothing wind; the splendour and pomp of the buildings decorating what is after

247

all a very small town; the scattering of islands a throwing distance away; and the majesty of the sea. It is a magical place.

As you slip away from Hvar to the north, south, east or west, to other islands or to the mainland, you soon realise that the vision from up above the town is one which finds countless parallels, equals even, all over the coast of Dalmatia and Croatia. As this book shows, visitors to the region have experienced a very particular enchantment from the combination of the towns, the sea and the past, a juxtaposition of the physical setting of the land with the people who have lived and breathed within it. Croatia and Dalmatia emerge as outstanding and fascinating cradles of civilisation as well as places where the values of civilisation have been bitterly contested. And yet they emerge too as something of an enigma – especially to the Anglo-Saxon eye – somehow difficult to place, hard to make sense of.

This important collection of travel writing throws together a selection of views, impressions and experiences spread across many centuries and indeed across many languages. What is striking is that what emerges from this rich and varied material on the culture, people and geography of the region, is a picture which is coherent. The physical beauty, the architectural splendour, and the political, social and economic heritage of the region intertwine in differing measures to leave a wider view not unlike that from above the town of Hvar: a glorious, unexpected gem.

Bibliography

Anonymous. *Camp Life and Sport in Dalmatia and the Herzegovina* (Kegan Paul 2003)

Bridge, Ann. *Illyrian Spring* (Bernhard Tauchnitz 1936)

Contemporary Sources for the Fourth Crusade. Ed Alfred J Andrea (Brill, Leiden 2000)

Čurčija Prodanović, Nada. *Yugoslav Folk-Tales* (Oxford University Press, London 1957)

Dedijer, Vladimir. *Tito Speaks: his self portrait and struggle with Stalin* (Weidenfeld & Nicolson, London 1953)

Dedijer, Vladimir. *The War Diaries of Vladimir Dedijer* (University of Michigan Press 1990)

Evans, Arthur John, Sir. *Through Bosnia and the Herzogovina on Foot During the Insurrection 1875* (Longmans 1876)

Fortis, Alberto. *Travels in Dalmatia* (London 1778)

Gibbon, Edward. *The History of Decline and Fall of the Roman Empire* (Chatto and Windus 1875)

Glenny, Misha. *The Fall of Yugoslavia: the Third Balkan War* (Penguin, London 1992)

Green, Leonard. *A Memory of Ragusa* (London 1929)

Hall, Brian. *The Impossible Country: a journey through the last days of Yugoslavia* (Secker & Warburg, London 1994)

Hichens, Robert Smythe. *The Near East: Dalmatia, Greece and Constantinople* (Century, New York 1913)

Koljević, Svétozar. *Yugoslav Short Stories* (Oxford University Press, London 1966)

Maclean, Fitzroy. *Eastern Approaches* (Penguin, London 1991)

Morris, Jan. *Trieste and the Meaning of Nowhere* (Faber and Faber, London 2001)

Rhodes, Anthony. *Where the Turk Trod: a journey to Sarajevo with a Slavonic Mussulman* (Weidenfeld & Nicolson, London 1956)

Sitwell, Osbert, Sir. *Noble Essences: a book of characters* (Little, Brown & Co, Boston 1950)

Strutton, Bill. *Island of Terrible Friends* (Hodder & Stoughton, London 1961)

Thompson, Mark. *A Paper House: the ending of Yugoslavia* (Hutchinson 1992)

Waugh, Evelyn. *Sword of Honour* (Penguin, London 1999)

West, Rebecca. *Black Lamb and Grey Falcon: the record of a journey through Yugoslavia in 1937* (Macmillan 1941)

Wilkinson, John Gardner, Sir. *Dalmatia and Montenegro* (Murray 1848)

ELAND

61 Exmouth Market, London EC1R 4QL
Tel: 020 7833 0762   Fax: 020 7833 4434
Email: info@travelbooks.co.uk

Eland was started in 1982 to revive great travel books that had
fallen out of print. Although the list has diversified into biography
and fiction, it is united by a quest to define the spirit of place. These
are books for travellers, and for readers who aspire to explore the world
but who are also content to travel in their own minds. Eland books open out
our understanding of other cultures, interpret the unknown and
reveal different environments as well as celebrating the
humour and occasional horrors of travel.

All our books are printed on fine, pliable, cream-coloured paper.
Most are still gathered in sections by our printer and sewn as well
as glued, almost unheard of for a paperback book these days.
This gives larger margins in the gutter, as well as
making the books stronger.

We take immense trouble to select only the most readable books
and therefore many readers collect the entire series. If you
haven't liked an Eland title, please send it back to us saying
why you disliked it and we will refund the purchase price.

You will find a very brief description of all our books on the
following pages. Extracts from each and every one of them can be
read on our website, at www.travelbooks.co.uk. If you would
like a free copy of our detailed catalogue, please contact
us at the above address.

ELAND

'*One of the very best travel lists*' WILLIAM DALRYMPLE

Memoirs of a Bengal Civilian
JOHN BEAMES
*Sketches of nineteenth-century India
painted with the richness of Dickens*

Jigsaw
SYBILLE BEDFORD
*An intensely remembered autobiographical
novel about an inter-war childhood*

A Visit to Don Otavio
SYBILLE BEDFORD
*The hell of travel and the Eden of arrival
in post-war Mexico*

Journey into the Mind's Eye
LESLEY BLANCH
*An obsessive love affair with Russia and
one particular Russian*

The Devil Drives
FAWN BRODIE
*Biography of Sir Richard Burton,
explorer, linguist and pornographer*

Turkish Letters
OGIER DE BUSBECQ
*Eyewitness history at its best: Istanbul
during the reign of Suleyman the
Magnificent*

My Early Life
WINSTON CHURCHILL
*From North-West Frontier to Boer War
by the age of twenty-five*

A Square of Sky
JANINA DAVID
*A Jewish childhood in the Warsaw
ghetto and hiding from the Nazis*

Chantemesle
ROBIN FEDDEN
*A lyrical evocation of childhood in
Normandy*

Viva Mexico!
CHARLES FLANDRAU
A journey among the Mexican people

Travels with Myself and Another
MARTHA GELLHORN
*Five journeys from hell by a great
war correspondent*

The Weather in Africa
MARTHA GELLHORN
*Three novellas set amongst the
white settlers of East Africa*

Walled Gardens
ANNABEL GOFF
An Anglo-Irish childhood

Africa Dances
GEOFFREY GORER
*The magic of indigenous culture
and the banality of colonisation*

Cinema Eden
JUAN GOYTISOLO
*Essays from the Muslim
Mediterranean*

A State of Fear
ANDREW GRAHAM-YOOLL
*A journalist witnesses Argentina's
nightmare in the 1970s*

Warriors
GERALD HANLEY
Life and death among the Somalis

Morocco That Was
WALTER HARRIS
*All the cruelty, fascination and
humour of a pre-modern kingdom*

Far Away and Long Ago
W H HUDSON
A childhood in Argentina